The Complete Discord Guide

From Setup to Advanced Features

Kiet Huynh – A Discord user

Table of Contents

CHAPTER I
Getting Started with Discord

1.1 What is Discord?

1.1.1 The History and Purpose of Discord

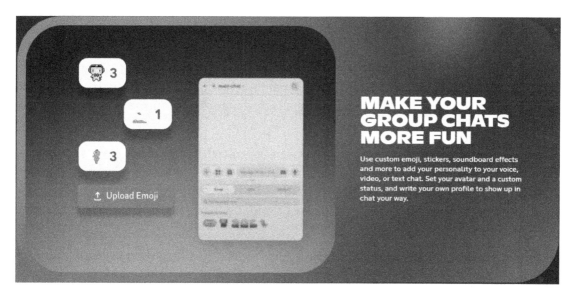

Discord is a free communication platform that has gained immense popularity since its launch in 2015. Originally designed for gamers, Discord has evolved into a versatile tool used by a wide variety of communities, including businesses, educators, hobbyists, and content creators. To understand the significance of Discord, we need to explore its history, how it emerged, and why it has become one of the most widely used platforms for online communication.

The Origins of Discord

The Problem with Online Communication Before Discord

Before Discord, online communication tools were fragmented. Gamers and online communities primarily relied on software like Skype, TeamSpeak, and Ventrilo for voice and text communication. While these platforms were functional, they had major drawbacks, such as high latency, poor audio quality, and complex setup processes.

- **Skype** was widely used for voice and video calls but had a reputation for being resource-intensive, causing lag in games and reducing overall performance.

- **TeamSpeak and Ventrilo** provided voice communication but required users to rent servers, manually configure settings, and endure outdated interfaces.

- **IRC (Internet Relay Chat)** was popular for text communication but lacked modern features like voice chat, video, and user-friendly interfaces.

With no single platform providing an optimal mix of voice, video, and text communication with a seamless user experience, the need for a better alternative became apparent.

The Birth of Discord

Discord was created by **Jason Citron**, an entrepreneur with a background in gaming. Citron had previously founded **OpenFeint**, a social gaming network for mobile games, which he later sold for $104 million. Following this success, he founded **Hammer & Chisel**, a game development studio.

While working on a multiplayer online battle arena (MOBA) game called **Fates Forever**, Citron and his team struggled with poor communication tools, which hindered their ability to coordinate effectively. Realizing that existing platforms were not meeting the needs of modern gamers, he pivoted away from game development and focused entirely on building a new communication platform—**Discord**.

Launched on **May 13, 2015**, Discord aimed to provide:

- Low-latency, high-quality voice chat for gamers.

- A free and easy-to-use interface that didn't require server rentals or complex setups.

- Text chat with modern features like rich embeds, emojis, and role-based permissions.

With these improvements, Discord quickly gained traction, especially within gaming communities on Reddit and Twitch.

How Discord Gained Popularity

Early Adoption by Gamers

At first, Discord was primarily adopted by gamers who needed a lightweight, efficient voice communication tool for multiplayer games. Thanks to its free server hosting, easy setup, and clear audio quality, it rapidly gained users. Many streamers and esports teams switched from TeamSpeak and Skype to Discord, further accelerating its popularity.

One of the key moments in Discord's early success was its marketing approach—developers actively engaged with Reddit gaming communities, offering real-time support and feedback. This grassroots strategy led to word-of-mouth promotion, which was instrumental in its viral growth.

Expansion Beyond Gaming

As Discord evolved, it introduced features that appealed to a broader audience, such as:

- Customizable servers with roles and permissions.
- Video calling and screen sharing, making it a competitor to Zoom and Skype.
- Integration with third-party services, such as YouTube, Spotify, and Twitch.

By 2018, Discord had become more than just a gaming platform—it was being used by:

- Hobbyist communities (e.g., book clubs, coding groups, music enthusiasts).
- Businesses and remote teams (as an alternative to Slack and Microsoft Teams).
- Educators and students (for study groups, virtual classes, and tutoring).

During the COVID-19 pandemic in 2020, Discord saw an explosion in users as more people sought virtual spaces for communication. The company responded by rebranding its tagline from "Chat for Gamers" to "Your Place to Talk", officially positioning itself as a universal community platform.

The Purpose of Discord Today

A Versatile Communication Platform

Today, Discord is used by millions of people for a variety of purposes, including:

1. **Gaming Communities**
   - Provides in-game communication with low latency voice chat.
   - Enables clan, guild, and esports team management.

  - Integrates with Twitch and YouTube for content sharing.

2. **Professional and Educational Use**

  - Businesses use Discord for team collaboration, project management, and customer support.

  - Educators create study groups and virtual classrooms.

  - Developers and tech communities share coding resources and tutorials.

3. **Social and Hobbyist Communities**

  - Fans of TV shows, music, and books create discussion groups.

  - Artists, musicians, and writers collaborate and showcase their work.

  - Cryptocurrency and stock trading groups use Discord for real-time updates.

4. **Content Creation and Streaming**

  - Streamers use Discord to engage with their audience.

  - YouTubers and influencers build subscriber-exclusive communities.

  - Creators use Discord to host Q&A sessions, workshops, and networking events.

Why Discord Stands Out

Discord continues to dominate the online communication space due to:

- User-Friendly Interface – Simple and intuitive navigation.

- Customization – Extensive server settings, role permissions, and integrations.

- Reliability – Low-latency voice chat with minimal lag.

- Free and Affordable Premium Features – While the core platform is free, users can opt for Discord Nitro to unlock enhanced perks like higher-quality streaming and server boosts.

The Future of Discord

Ongoing Development and Innovations

Discord is constantly evolving, with frequent updates introducing new features and enhanced security measures. Some recent and upcoming developments include:

- AI-powered moderation tools to combat spam and toxicity.

- Improved video and voice quality for professional use.

- Expanded monetization options for content creators and community managers.

With its flexibility and commitment to user experience, Discord is expected to continue growing as one of the leading platforms for online communities, collaboration, and communication.

Conclusion

Discord began as a solution to a simple problem: providing gamers with a better way to communicate. However, its innovative features, user-friendly interface, and adaptability have allowed it to grow far beyond gaming. Today, Discord is a powerful communication hub used by people across various industries and interests.

As we move forward in this guide, you will learn how to set up your own Discord account, join and manage servers, customize your experience, and leverage advanced features to make the most out of this incredible platform.

Next Section: 1.1.2 How Discord Compares to Other Communication Platforms

In the next section, we'll compare Discord to other platforms like Slack, Zoom, and Microsoft Teams, and explore what makes it unique.

1.1.2 How Discord Compares to Other Communication Platforms

Discord is a versatile communication platform that has gained immense popularity among gamers, professionals, educators, and social groups. While Discord offers a wide range of features, many users wonder how it compares to other communication platforms such as Slack, Zoom, Microsoft Teams, Skype, and WhatsApp.

This section will explore the key differences, strengths, and weaknesses of Discord compared to these other platforms, helping you understand where it excels and where it may not be the best choice.

1. Key Communication Platforms and Their Purposes

Before diving into the comparisons, it's essential to understand the primary purpose of each platform:

- **Discord** – Initially designed for gamers, now widely used by various communities for real-time voice, video, and text communication.

- **Slack** – Primarily a business collaboration tool with a strong focus on organized messaging, integrations, and workplace productivity.

- **Zoom** – A video conferencing tool used mostly for professional meetings, webinars, and virtual events.

- **Microsoft Teams** – A corporate collaboration platform integrating messaging, video conferencing, and file sharing within the Microsoft ecosystem.

- **Skype** – One of the earliest video and voice calling apps, mainly used for personal and professional communication.

- **WhatsApp** – A mobile-first messaging app offering text, voice, and video communication, commonly used for personal interactions.

Now, let's compare Discord against these platforms based on key features.

2. Comparing Discord with Other Communication Platforms

2.1 User Interface and Usability

Platform	User-Friendliness	Customization	Best For
Discord	Easy to use, modern UI	Highly customizable	Gamers, communities, hobbyists, small businesses
Slack	Business-oriented, structured	Limited customization	Workplaces, professional teams
Zoom	Simple UI for meetings	Minimal customization	Video conferencing, online classes
Microsoft Teams	Complex, integrated with Microsoft 365	Limited customization	Large organizations, corporate teams

| Skype | Outdated UI, simple | Basic customization | Personal and business calls |
| WhatsApp | Simple, mobile-friendly | Very limited | Personal messaging |

- **Discord's UI** is modern, sleek, and designed for ease of use, allowing quick access to servers, voice channels, and text chats.

- **Slack** and **Microsoft Teams** are more structured and tailored for corporate environments, which may feel restrictive compared to Discord's flexibility.

- **Zoom and Skype** have simpler interfaces but are primarily focused on voice and video calls rather than community interaction.

Winner: Discord – It offers a balance between simplicity and deep customization, making it ideal for casual and professional users alike.

2.2 Voice and Video Communication

Platform	Voice Channels	Video Calling	Screen Sharing	Noise Suppression
Discord	Yes (always open)	Yes (up to 25 users per call)	Yes	Yes (Krisp AI)
Slack	Limited (paid plans only)	Yes (up to 15 users)	Yes	No
Zoom	No (one-time meetings)	Yes (up to 1,000 participants)	Yes	Yes
Microsoft Teams	No (one-time meetings)	Yes (up to 1,000 participants)	Yes	Yes
Skype	No	Yes (up to 50 participants)	Yes	No
WhatsApp	No	Yes (mobile only)	No	No

- **Discord's voice channels** allow users to join and leave voice chats freely, unlike Zoom or Teams, where you must start a meeting.

- **Zoom and Teams** excel in large-scale video conferencing but require scheduled meetings.

- **Skype and WhatsApp** offer basic calling features but lack advanced community features.

Winner: Discord for casual conversations and communities; Zoom for professional meetings.

2.3 Messaging and Community Features

Platform	Text Messaging	Organized Channels	File Sharing	Bots & Automation	Community Features
Discord	Yes	Yes (text, voice)	Up to 25MB free, 500MB Nitro	Yes	Yes (roles, permissions)
Slack	Yes	Yes (channels)	5GB free, paid plans for more	Yes	Limited
Zoom	Basic chat	No	Limited	No	No
Microsoft Teams	Yes	Yes (Teams and Channels)	Large file sharing with OneDrive	Limited	Enterprise focus
Skype	Yes	No	Basic	No	No
WhatsApp	Yes	No	Limited	No	No

- **Discord's community features** (roles, permissions, bots) make it stand out.

- **Slack and Teams** are better for corporate communication, with a stronger focus on work collaboration.

- **Skype and WhatsApp** are more limited in group management.

Winner: Discord for casual and community-driven use; Slack/Teams for work collaboration.

2.4 Integrations and Automation

Platform	Integrations	Bots	Customization
Discord	Many (Spotify, Twitch, YouTube)	Yes	High
Slack	Business tools (Google Drive, Trello)	Yes	Medium
Zoom	Limited (Calendars, webinar tools)	No	Low
Microsoft Teams	Microsoft 365 suite	Limited	Medium
Skype	Basic (Outlook)	No	Low

WhatsApp	Very limited	No	Low

- **Discord** has a massive bot ecosystem that enables automated moderation, music playback, and custom commands.

- **Slack and Microsoft Teams** offer great business integrations but are not as flexible.

- **Zoom, Skype, and WhatsApp** have very limited customization options.

Winner: Discord for customization and automation; Slack for professional integrations.

3. When to Use Discord vs. Other Platforms

- **Use Discord if**:

  - You need a **free, flexible communication platform** for gaming, social groups, or small businesses.

  - You want **always-open voice channels** rather than scheduled meetings.

  - You require **community management tools** like roles, permissions, and bots.

- **Use Slack if**:

  - You are in a **corporate environment** that requires structured team communication.

  - You need **third-party business tool integrations** (Google Drive, Trello).

- **Use Zoom if**:

  - You primarily need **video conferencing** for large meetings and webinars.

  - You need a **reliable tool for virtual meetings** rather than long-term communities.

- **Use Microsoft Teams if**:

  - Your organization is already using **Microsoft 365** for document collaboration.

  - You require **corporate security and compliance features**.

- **Use Skype or WhatsApp if:**
  - You only need **basic calling and messaging** for personal use.
  - You prefer **mobile-first communication**.

Conclusion

While Discord originated as a gaming communication tool, it has grown into a powerful, community-driven platform with voice, video, and messaging features that compete with top business and social platforms. Compared to Slack, Zoom, Microsoft Teams, Skype, and WhatsApp, Discord excels in flexibility, customization, and community management.

However, for professional environments requiring structured communication, Slack and Teams may be better options. For video conferencing, Zoom remains the industry leader.

Ultimately, choosing the right platform depends on your needs. If you're looking for a free, feature-rich platform for communities and social interactions, Discord is hard to beat.

1.2 Creating and Setting Up Your Discord Account

1.2.1 How to Sign Up for Discord

Discord is a widely used communication platform that offers voice, video, and text chat for individuals and communities. To start using Discord, the first step is to create an account. This process is simple and only requires a few minutes. In this section, we will cover the step-by-step process of signing up for Discord, choosing a username, and configuring basic settings to get started smoothly.

1. The Requirements for Creating a Discord Account

Before signing up for Discord, ensure you meet the following basic requirements:

- **A valid email address or a mobile phone number** – This is required for verification purposes.

- **A device with internet access** – You can sign up via a web browser, a desktop app (Windows or macOS), or a mobile app (iOS or Android).

- **You must be at least 13 years old** – Discord has an age restriction in place to comply with online safety regulations.

2. Step-by-Step Guide to Creating a Discord Account

2.1 Signing Up on the Discord Website

One of the easiest ways to sign up for Discord is through its official website. Follow these steps:

Step 1: Visit the Discord Website

- Open your preferred web browser (Google Chrome, Firefox, Microsoft Edge, etc.).

- Go to https://discord.com.

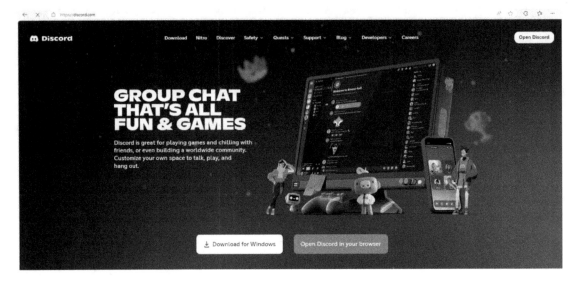

Step 2: Click on "Sign Up"

- On the homepage, locate the **"Login"** button in the top right corner.

- Click it, and on the login page, you'll find the **"Register"** option at the bottom.

- Click **"Register"** to begin creating a new account.

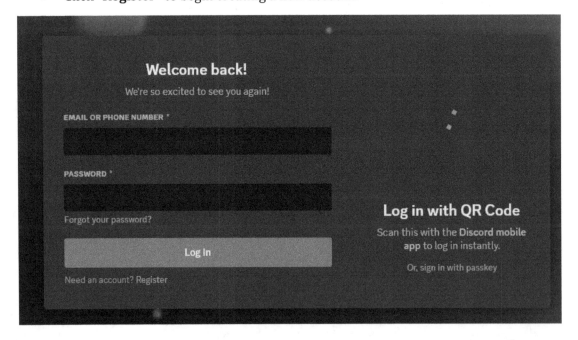

Step 3: Fill in Your Account Information

You will be asked to enter the following details:

- **Email address** – This must be a valid email that you have access to.

- **Username** – Your unique Discord identity. You can change this later.

- **Password** – Choose a strong password with a mix of uppercase letters, lowercase letters, numbers, and symbols.

- **Date of birth** – Discord requires this to enforce its age policy.

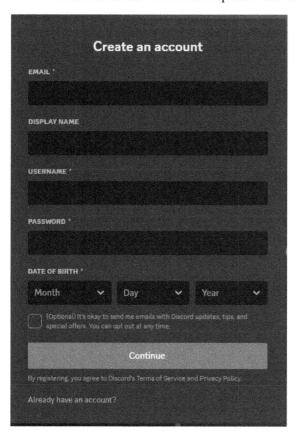

Step 4: Complete the CAPTCHA Verification

- Discord will ask you to verify that you are not a bot by completing a CAPTCHA challenge.

Step 5: Click "Continue"

- After entering all required information and passing the CAPTCHA, click **"Continue"** to proceed.

Step 6: Email Verification

- Discord will send a verification email to the address you provided.

- Open your email inbox, find the verification email, and click the **"Verify Email"** button.

- If you do not receive the email, check your spam folder or request a new verification email.

2.2 Signing Up via the Mobile App

If you prefer to sign up using your smartphone or tablet, follow these steps:

Step 1: Download the Discord App

- For **Android** users, go to the **Google Play Store** and search for "Discord."

- For **iOS** users, go to the **App Store** and search for "Discord."

- Download and install the app.

Step 2: Open the App and Click "Register"

- Once the app is installed, open it.

- Tap the **"Register"** button to begin creating an account.

Step 3: Enter Your Account Information

Similar to the web signup process, you will need to enter:

- A valid email address or phone number

- A username of your choice

- A secure password

- Your date of birth

Step 4: Verify Your Account

- If you signed up using an email, check your inbox and verify your email.

- If you signed up using a phone number, you will receive an SMS verification code. Enter the code to confirm your phone number.

3. Choosing a Username and Discriminator

Your username on Discord consists of two parts:

- **Your chosen name** – This can be anything (e.g., "GamerX," "MusicLover," or "JohnDoe").

- **A four-digit discriminator** – Discord automatically assigns this (e.g., JohnDoe#1234).

Unlike most platforms that require unique usernames, Discord allows multiple users to have the same username because of the **discriminator system**. However, if you subscribe to **Discord Nitro**, you can customize your discriminator.

Tips for Choosing a Good Username

- Keep it simple and easy to remember.

- Avoid using personal information like your full name.

- If you plan to use Discord for professional purposes, choose a more formal username.

4. Setting Up Two-Factor Authentication (2FA) for Security

To protect your account, it is highly recommended that you **enable two-factor authentication (2FA)**. This adds an extra layer of security by requiring a verification code when logging in.

Steps to Enable 2FA

1. Go to **User Settings** by clicking on the gear icon.

2. Select **"My Account"** from the menu.

3. Click on **"Enable Two-Factor Authentication"**.

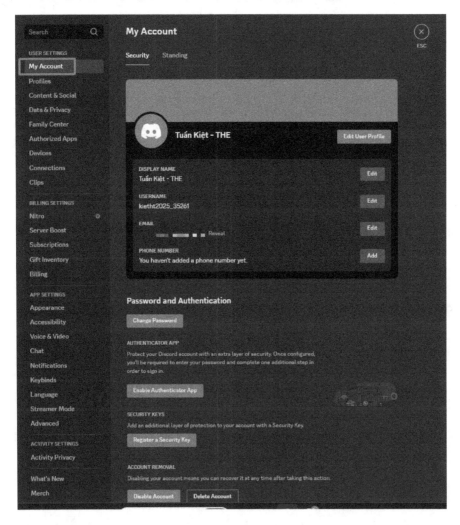

4. Download an authenticator app (e.g., **Google Authenticator** or **Authy**).

5. Scan the QR code provided by Discord.

6. Enter the 6-digit code from the authenticator app.

7. Save the backup codes in case you lose access to your authentication app.

By enabling 2FA, your account will be much more secure against hacking attempts.

5. Logging into Your Account on Different Devices

Once your account is created, you can log in on various devices, including:

- **Web Browser:** Visit https://discord.com/login and enter your credentials.
- **Desktop App:** Download and install the Discord app on your computer, then log in.
- **Mobile App:** Open the Discord mobile app and enter your credentials.

If you have **2FA enabled**, you will need to enter a verification code when logging in from a new device.

6. Troubleshooting Common Signup Issues

Here are some common problems users face during the signup process and how to resolve them:

Issue	Solution
Didn't receive the verification email	Check spam/junk folder or resend the email from Discord.
Username already in use	Try a variation of your username or add numbers.
Weak password error	Make sure your password includes uppercase, lowercase, numbers, and symbols.
CAPTCHA not working	Refresh the page and try again. If the issue persists, try a different browser.

Issue	Solution
Age restriction warning	Ensure your birthdate meets Discord's requirements (13+ years old in most regions).

Conclusion

Creating a Discord account is a straightforward process, but taking the time to set up your account properly—choosing a good username, enabling 2FA, and verifying your email—will help you make the most of the platform securely.

Now that you have successfully created an account, it's time to explore the Discord interface and understand how to navigate through its various features.

Next Section: 1.2.2 Understanding the Discord Interface

In the next section, we'll take a closer look at the Discord interface, explaining the dashboard, servers, chat features, and settings.

1.2.2 Understanding the Discord Interface

Once you've created a Discord account and logged in, you'll be introduced to the **Discord interface**, which serves as the control center for all your communication, server management, and community interactions. Understanding this interface is crucial for navigating Discord efficiently and making the most of its features.

This section will break down the key elements of the Discord interface, explain their functions, and provide tips on how to use them effectively.

1. The Main Discord Interface: A First Look

When you first open Discord (either via the desktop app, web browser, or mobile app), you'll see a well-organized layout divided into several sections. Each section has a distinct function, helping you navigate through servers, chat with friends, and manage your settings.

Here's an overview of the key components:

1. **Server List (Left Sidebar)** – Displays all the servers you've joined.

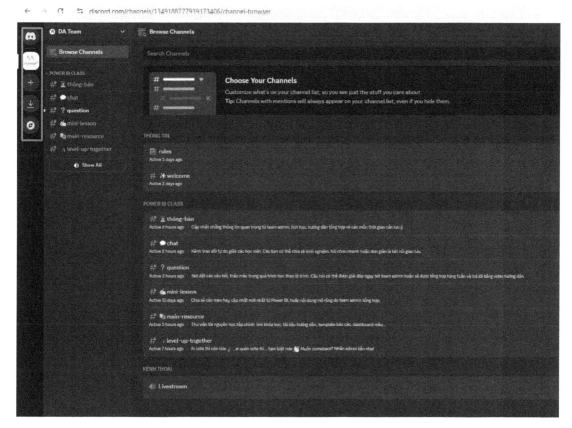

2. **Direct Messages (DMs) and Friends Tab** – Your private chats and friend list.

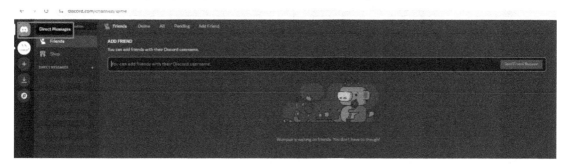

3. **Channel List (Inside a Server)** – Shows text and voice channels within a server.

4. **Chat Window** – The main area where you see and send messages.

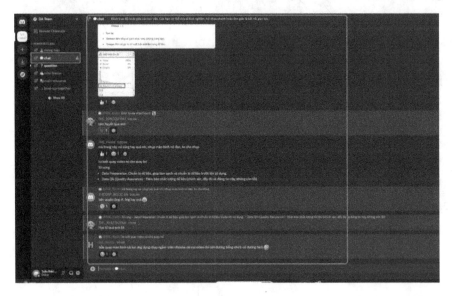

5. **Member List (Right Sidebar)** – Displays online and offline members in a server.

6. **User Controls (Bottom Bar)** – Your profile settings, mute options, and more.

Now, let's explore each section in detail.

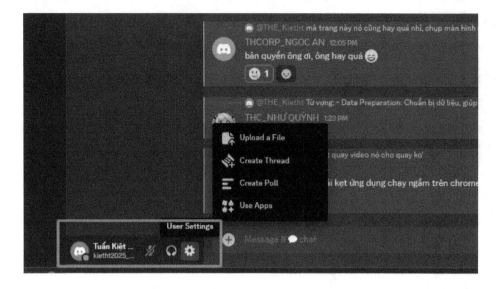

2. The Server List (Left Sidebar)

The **server list** is the leftmost column of Discord and contains all the servers you have joined. If you're new to Discord and haven't joined any servers yet, this section will be mostly empty.

Features of the Server List:

- **Server Icons** – Each server you join has a unique icon. Clicking on an icon will take you to that server's channels.

- **Home Button (Discord Logo)** – At the top, clicking this button brings you to the "Home" screen where you can access direct messages and your friends list.

- **Explore Public Servers** – A magnifying glass icon allows you to discover and join public Discord servers.

- **Add a Server (+ Button)** – Lets you create a new server or join an existing one with an invite link.

Pro Tips:

✅ Right-click on a server icon to quickly access server settings, mute notifications, or leave the server.

✅ Drag and reorder server icons to prioritize frequently used servers.

3. Direct Messages (DMs) and Friends Tab

Discord isn't just about servers—it also allows **private messaging** between users. You can access your friends list and direct messages from the **Home button** (Discord logo) at the top left.

Key Features in Direct Messages:

- **Friends List:** Shows your online and offline friends. You can add, remove, or block users here.

- **Active Now:** Displays friends who are currently online and what they are doing.

- **Private Messages:** Chat one-on-one with friends or create **group DMs** with up to 10 people.

How to Start a DM:

1. Click the **Home Button** (Discord logo).

2. Go to the **Friends** tab.

3. Click on a friend's name and start chatting.

4. The Channel List (Inside a Server)

When you click on a server icon, the left sidebar changes to show the channels and categories within that server. Channels are divided into text channels (for messaging) and voice channels (for audio communication).

Understanding Channels:

- **Text Channels (◆#general, #announcements, #memes, etc.)**
    - Used for typed conversations, sharing links, and posting updates.

- o Can have specific permissions (e.g., only admins can post in #announcements).

- **Voice Channels (🔊 General, Gaming Room, Music Room, etc.)**

  - o Allows users to join and speak with others using voice chat.

  - o Some servers have **stage channels**, designed for large audiences where only certain people can speak.

- **Categories** – Channels are often grouped under categories (e.g., "Gaming," "Support," "Events") for better organization.

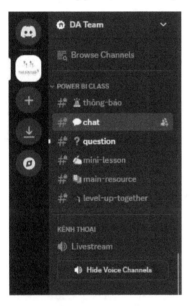

Pro Tips:

✅ Click the **pushpin** icon in a text channel to view pinned messages.
✅ Use **slash commands** (e.g., /help, /giphy dance) to quickly interact with bots and features.

5. The Chat Window (Main Messaging Area)

The **chat window** is where all messages appear when you open a text channel or private DM. It's the central space for conversations, updates, and media sharing.

Key Features of the Chat Window:

- Message Input Box – Type messages, attach files, or send GIFs.

- Pinned Messages – Important messages saved by server admins or users.

- Mentions and Replies – Tag users using @username or reply to messages.

- Message Reactions – React to messages with emojis.

- Threaded Conversations – Allows focused discussions within a channel.

Pro Tips:

✓ Use **Markdown formatting** to style messages (e.g., **bold**, *italic*, ~~strikethrough~~).

✓ Press Shift + Enter to create a line break without sending a message.

6. Member List (Right Sidebar)

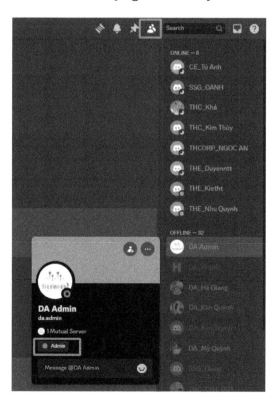

On the far right of the screen (inside a server), you'll find the **member list**, which displays all users currently in the server.

Features of the Member List:

- **Roles & Colors** – Users may have **roles** (e.g., Admin, Moderator, VIP), which can affect their name color.

- **Online Status** – Indicates if users are online, idle, or in a voice channel.

- **Bots** – Some servers use bots for automation, moderation, or fun commands.

Pro Tips:

✓ Right-click on a user to **send a DM, mute, or report** them.

✓ Hover over a user's name to see their

activity status (e.g., playing a game, listening to Spotify).

7. User Controls (Bottom Bar)

At the very bottom of the Discord window, you'll see **your profile area**, which includes your **avatar, username, microphone, and other settings**.

Main Controls:

- **Microphone & Headset Icons** – Quickly mute/unmute yourself or deafen all sound.

- **User Settings (⚙️☐ Icon)** – Access account settings, appearance, notifications, and security settings.

- **Custom Status** – Set your own status message (e.g., "Studying," "Streaming," "AFK").

Pro Tips:

✅ Use Ctrl + Shift + M to **toggle mute** without clicking.
✅ Click your profile to **change your status** (Online, Idle, Do Not Disturb, Invisible).

Conclusion

Understanding Discord's interface is the first step in using the platform effectively. Whether you're navigating servers, chatting with friends, or managing notifications, knowing where everything is located will make your experience **smoother and more enjoyable**.

In the next section, **1.2.3 Configuring Account Settings and Privacy Options**, we'll dive into how to customize your Discord experience, enhance security, and manage notifications. Stay tuned!

1.2.3 Configuring Account Settings and Privacy Options

Once you have created your Discord account and familiarized yourself with the interface, it is essential to configure your account settings and privacy options to enhance security, customize your experience, and control how others interact with you. Discord offers a wide range of settings that allow you to adjust everything from profile customization and notifications to privacy and security controls.

This section will guide you through accessing your account settings, adjusting privacy and security options, and customizing your overall experience on Discord to suit your personal preferences.

1. Understanding the Discord Settings Menu

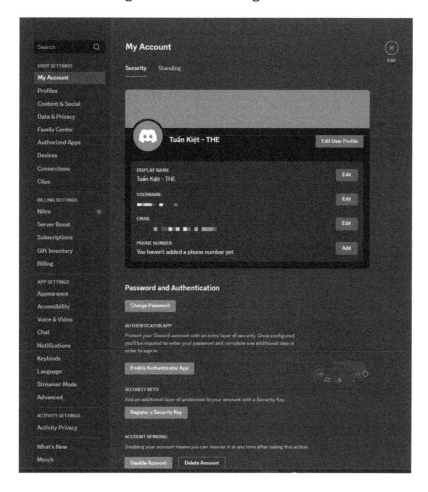

To configure your account settings, you first need to access the **User Settings** menu. Here's how:

1. **Open Discord** on your desktop or mobile device.

2. Click on the **gear icon** ⚙☐ at the bottom-left corner next to your username.

3. This will open the **User Settings** menu, where you can navigate different sections such as **Account, Privacy & Safety, Notifications, Voice & Video, Appearance, and more**.

Each section contains various settings that help you **optimize security, privacy, and usability**. Let's go through them one by one.

---

2. Configuring Account Settings

2.1 Changing Your Username and Profile Picture

Your username is how people recognize you on Discord. To change your username:

1. Go to **User Settings → My Account**.

2. Click the **Edit** button next to your username.

3. Enter a new **Username** and **Discriminator (#0000-#9999, if applicable)**.

4. Click **Save Changes**.

To change your profile picture:

1. Click on your current profile picture.

2. Upload a new image (JPEG or PNG, under 8MB).

3. Adjust and save your new profile picture.

2.2 Setting Up Two-Factor Authentication (2FA) for Security

Two-Factor Authentication (2FA) enhances the security of your Discord account by requiring a second verification step (usually from an authentication app like Google Authenticator or Authy).

To enable 2FA:

1. Navigate to User Settings → My Account.

2. Click Enable Two-Factor Authentication.

3. Scan the QR code with an authentication app and enter the generated code.

4. Save the backup codes in case you lose access to your authentication app.

Enabling 2FA helps protect your account from unauthorized access and is highly recommended.

2.3 Changing Your Email and Password

To update your email:

1. Go to **User Settings → My Account**.

2. Click **Edit** next to your email address.

3. Enter a new email and confirm the change through the verification email sent by Discord.

To change your password:

1. Click **Change Password** in the **My Account** section.

2. Enter your current password and new password.

3. Click **Save Changes**.

Changing your password periodically is a good security practice.

3. Adjusting Privacy & Safety Settings

Privacy and security settings control who can contact you, see your activity, and send friend requests. You can adjust these settings in the Privacy & Safety tab under User Settings.

3.1 Safe Direct Messaging Options

Discord provides **automatic filtering** to prevent **unwanted or inappropriate messages** in your Direct Messages (DMs). You can choose between:

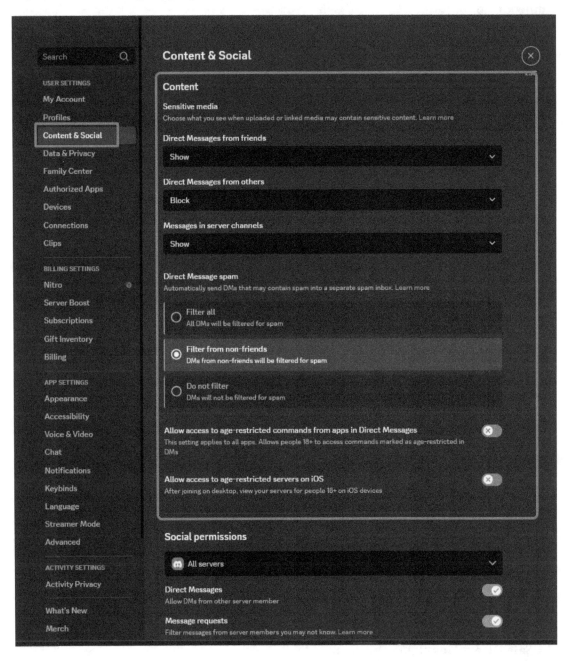

3.2 Controlling Who Can Send You Friend Requests

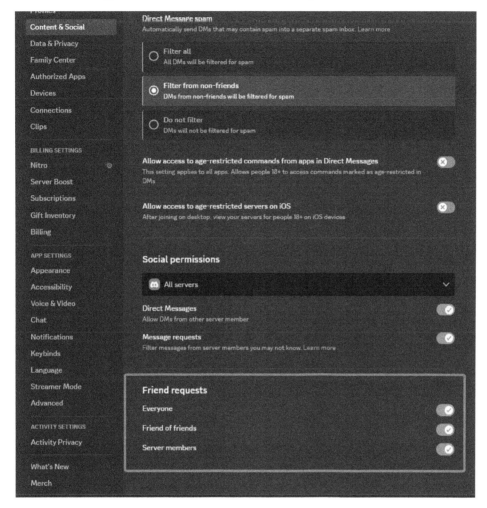

To limit **friend requests**:

1. Go to **Privacy & Safety** under **User Settings**.

2. Scroll to **Friend Request**.

3. Choose:

    o **Everyone** – Anyone can send you friend requests.

    o **Friends of Friends** – Only people who share mutual friends can send requests.

- o **Server Members** – Only people in the same servers as you can send requests.

For better security, it is advisable to disable friend requests from everyone except Friends of Friends.

3.3 Managing Server Privacy and DMs

Some Discord servers allow members to send direct messages (DMs) to anyone in the server. If you want to restrict this:

1. Go to Privacy & Safety → Server Privacy Settings.

2. Toggle off Allow Direct Messages from Server Members.

This setting prevents strangers from sending you messages when you join a new server.

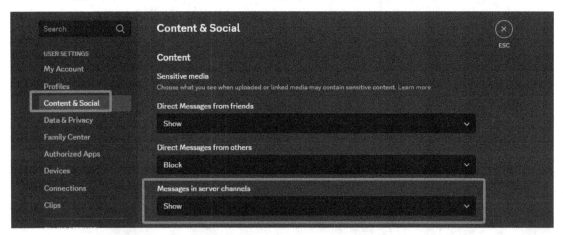

4. Customizing Notifications and Activity Status

4.1 Managing Notifications

If you are in multiple servers, **notifications** can become overwhelming. To manage them:

1. Go to **User Settings** → **Notifications**.

2. Adjust notification preferences, including:

   - o Enable/Disable Desktop Notifications.

   - o Mute specific servers (Right-click on a server → Mute Server).

- Set notification preferences for mentions only (@username, @everyone, @here).

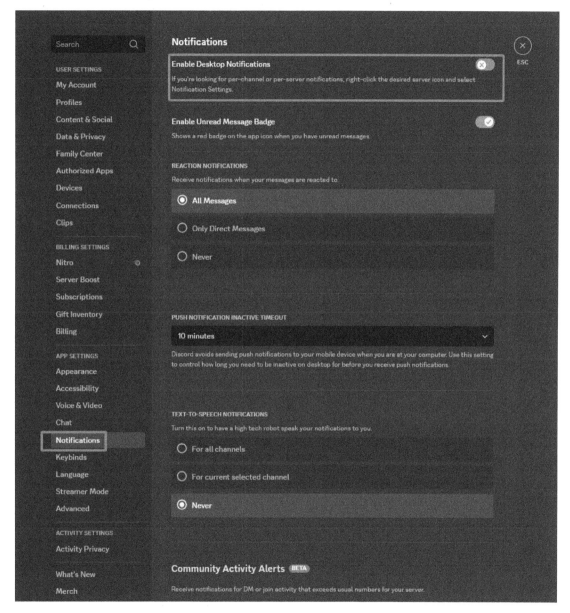

4.2 Setting Your Online Status

Discord provides different status options to let others know your availability:

- Online (Green) – Active and available.

- Idle (Yellow) – Away or inactive for a while.

- Do Not Disturb (Red) – Mutes notifications.

- Invisible (Gray) – Appears offline but still online.

To change your status:

1. Click your **profile picture** at the bottom left.

2. Select a **status option**.

You can also set a **custom status** (e.g., "Working, back in 30 mins").

5. Managing Connected Apps and Integrations

Discord allows you to connect third-party apps like **Spotify, Twitch, YouTube, and Steam**. To manage integrations:

1. Go to **User Settings → Connections**.

2. Click the **app you want to connect** (e.g., Twitch).

3. Log in and authorize Discord to access your account.

This allows Discord to display your **gaming activity, streaming status, and social media links**.

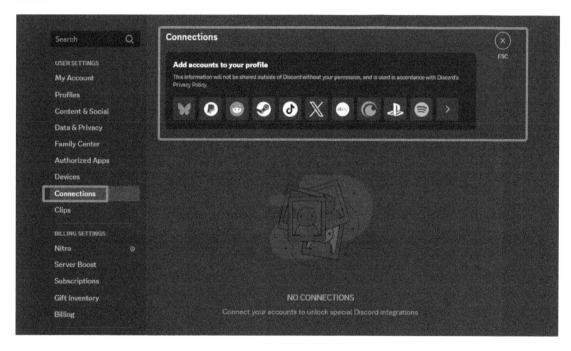

6. Blocking and Reporting Users

If you encounter **spam, harassment, or inappropriate behavior**, you can block or report users.

6.1 Blocking Users

1. Right-click on a user's name.

2. Click **Block** – This prevents them from messaging you or tagging you.

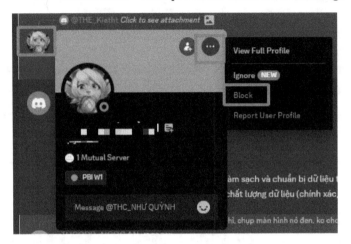

6.2 Reporting Users for Violations

If someone violates **Discord's Terms of Service** (e.g., harassment, threats), you can report them:

1. Right-click their **username**.

2. Click **Copy ID** (Developer Mode must be enabled).

3. Go to **Discord's Trust & Safety Page** (https://dis.gd/request).

4. Submit a **detailed report** with screenshots and message links.

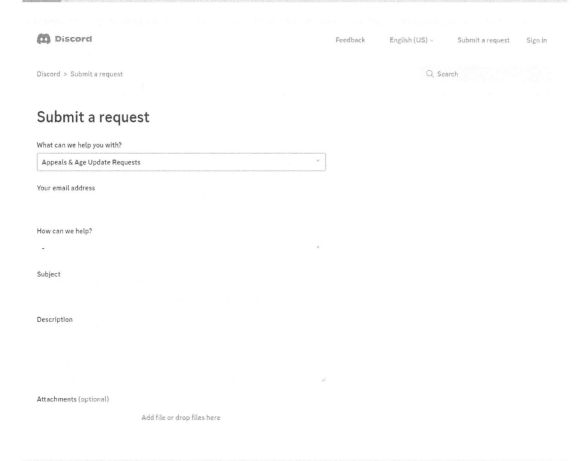

Conclusion

Configuring your account settings and privacy options is crucial for security, customization, and user experience on Discord. By adjusting security settings, notifications, friend requests, and privacy controls, you can create a safe and enjoyable environment while using the platform.

Next Section: 1.3 Navigating the Discord Interface

In the next section, we'll explore **how to navigate Discord's interface**, including **servers, channels, and direct messages**.

1.3 Navigating the Discord Interface

1.3.1 Home, Servers, and Direct Messages

Discord's interface is designed to be intuitive and easy to navigate, providing users with a streamlined experience whether they are chatting with friends, participating in server discussions, or managing their own communities. To effectively use Discord, it's essential to understand the three primary areas of its interface:

- **Home** – The central hub where users access their friends list, direct messages (DMs), and Nitro subscriptions.

- **Servers** – Community spaces where users can engage in group discussions through text and voice channels.

- **Direct Messages (DMs)** – Private one-on-one or group conversations outside of servers.

In this section, we will explore each of these areas in detail, breaking down their features and functionalities to help you navigate Discord like a pro.

Understanding the Home Tab

What is the Home Tab?

When you first open Discord, the **Home tab** is the default screen you'll see. This is where you can:

- View and manage your **friends list**.

- Send and receive **direct messages** (DMs).

- Access **Nitro perks** (if you're subscribed).

- See **pending friend requests**.

The Home tab is particularly useful if you use Discord for one-on-one conversations rather than participating in servers.

Navigating the Home Tab

The **Home tab** is located at the top-left corner of Discord, represented by the **Discord logo**. Clicking on it will bring you back to your direct messages and friends list, regardless of where you are in the app.

Below are the key sections within the Home tab:

Friends List

The **Friends** section is where you can view your existing friends, add new ones, and check their online status. The friends list is divided into four tabs:

- **All** – Displays your full friends list.
- **Online** – Shows only friends who are currently online.
- **Pending** – Lists friend requests you have sent or received.
- **Blocked** – Displays users you have blocked.

Each friend's **status indicator** (Online, Idle, Do Not Disturb, Invisible) helps you see whether they are available to chat.

Direct Messages (DMs) Section

Underneath your friends list, you will find a **list of recent DMs**. Clicking on any conversation will open a private chat with that user or group. We'll discuss DMs in more detail later in this section.

Nitro and Activities

If you subscribe to **Discord Nitro**, you'll see a section highlighting your **Nitro benefits**, such as custom emojis, animated avatars, and enhanced streaming quality. The **Activity Feed** also shows what your friends are playing or listening to (if they have connected accounts like Spotify or Steam).

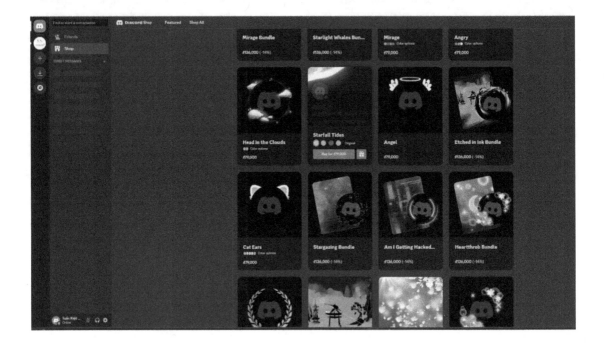

Understanding Discord Servers

What Are Servers in Discord?

Servers are the backbone of Discord. They act as community hubs where users can join discussions, share content, and collaborate with others. Each server consists of text channels, voice channels, and categories that help organize conversations.

Think of a Discord server like a forum or a virtual meeting space, where users can gather based on shared interests, work-related discussions, or social interactions.

Finding the Server List

The server list is located on the left-hand side of the Discord interface. Here, you will see:

- A plus (+) icon to create or join a server.

- A list of all servers you have joined, displayed as circular icons.

- Server folders, which allow you to organize multiple servers.

Navigating a Discord Server

Once you click on a server, you will enter its **main interface**, which consists of several key sections:

1. Server Name and Settings

At the top-left corner, you'll see the server name. Clicking on it opens a dropdown menu with options like:

- Server Settings (for admins and owners).

- Notification Settings (to mute specific servers).

- Privacy Settings (to manage user interactions).

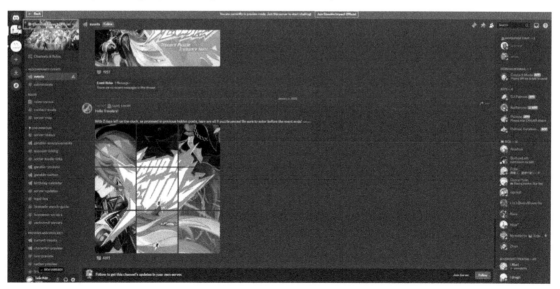

2. Channel List

The channel list is located on the left-hand side of the server window. It includes:

- Text Channels – For written conversations.

- Voice Channels – For audio and video communication.

- Categories – Groups of related channels.

Each channel may have different **permissions**, meaning some users can read but not send messages, while others have full access.

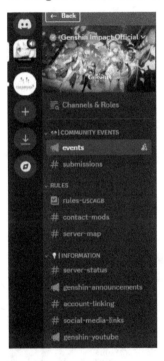

3. Member List

On the right-hand side of the server interface, you'll see the **member list**, which displays all users currently in the server, along with their roles and statuses.

4. Message Window

The main panel of the interface is where you read and send messages. It includes features like:

- Pinned messages (important server announcements).

- Embedded links, images, and videos.

- Reactions and emojis to interact with messages.

Understanding Direct Messages (DMs)

What Are Direct Messages?

Direct messages (DMs) allow you to have private conversations outside of servers. You can send a DM to a single person or create a group chat with multiple users.

Accessing DMs

You can access DMs in three ways:

1. Clicking on the Home tab and selecting a conversation from the Direct Messages list.

2. Clicking on a username from your friends list or a server's member list and selecting "Message".

3. Using the search bar at the top of Discord to find a specific user.

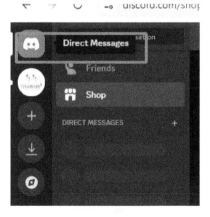

Sending Messages in DMs

DMs function similarly to text channels in a server. You can:

- Send text, images, and files.

- Use emojis and GIFs.

- React to messages.

- Use Markdown formatting (bold, italic, strikethrough).

Creating a Group DM

If you want to **chat with multiple people**, you can create a **Group DM** by:

1. Clicking on the **New Message** icon.

2. Selecting multiple friends from your list.

3. Naming the group and starting a conversation.

Unlike servers, Group DMs **do not** have channels, roles, or permissions—they function as a single ongoing chat.

Voice and Video Calls in DMs

You can start a voice or video call in a DM by clicking the phone or camera icon in the chat window. Calls support:

- Screen sharing (great for collaboration or gaming).

- Camera and microphone controls.

- Push-to-talk functionality.

Conclusion

Mastering the Discord interface is essential for seamless navigation and communication. By understanding the **Home tab, Servers, and Direct Messages**, you can effortlessly interact with friends, join communities, and organize your conversations efficiently.

In the next section (**1.3.2 Using the Friends List and Adding Friends**), we'll dive deeper into how to connect with people on Discord and build your social network.

1.3.2 Using the Friends List and Adding Friends

One of the core features of Discord is its Friends List, which allows users to connect with people directly without needing to be part of a server. While Discord is widely used for community-based interactions, having a well-organized Friends List makes it easy to communicate with close contacts, whether for gaming, casual chats, or collaboration.

This section will provide an in-depth guide on how to use Discord's Friends List, including adding, managing, and organizing friends for an optimal experience.

1. Understanding the Friends List

The **Friends List** in Discord serves as a centralized hub where you can view and manage all your direct connections. Unlike servers, which are public or semi-private spaces, the Friends List is for **one-on-one and small group interactions**.

To access the Friends List:

1. Open **Discord** and look at the **left sidebar** of the main interface.

2. Click on the **Friends** tab (icon of two people).

3. You will see a categorized list of all your friends, along with their **status indicators** (Online, Idle, Do Not Disturb, or Offline).

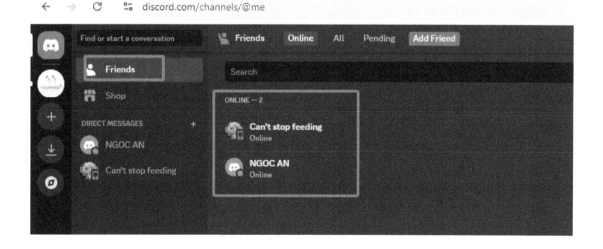

Categories in the Friends List

When you open the Friends List, you'll notice several tabs that help you navigate and organize your contacts:

1. **All** – Displays all friends you've added on Discord.

2. **Online** – Shows only friends who are currently online.

3. **Pending** – Displays friend requests that you have sent or received but have not yet been accepted.

4. **Blocked** – Lists all users you have blocked, preventing them from messaging you or seeing your activity.

By using these categories effectively, you can quickly locate friends based on their availability and manage your pending requests or blocked users.

2. How to Add Friends on Discord

To interact with someone on Discord directly, you first need to add them as a friend. There are multiple ways to do this, depending on whether you know their Discord username, are in the same server, or have an invitation link.

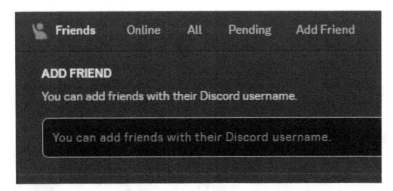

2.1 Adding a Friend by Discord Username (Discord Tag)

Each Discord user has a unique **Discord Tag** consisting of:

- **Username** (e.g., "GamerPro")

- **A four-digit number** (e.g., "#1234")

A complete Discord Tag looks like: **GamerPro#1234**.

Steps to Add a Friend by Discord Tag:

1. Open Discord and go to the **Friends** tab.

2. Click on **"Add Friend"** (Green button at the top).

3. Type the full **Discord Tag** of the person you want to add.

4. Click **"Send Friend Request"**.

If the username and tag are correct, the request will be sent. The person will need to **accept** your request before you can start chatting.

Important Notes:

- If the user has **friend requests disabled**, they won't receive your request unless you share a mutual server.

- The username is **case-sensitive**, meaning "gamerpro#1234" and "GamerPro#1234" are **not** the same.

2.2 Adding a Friend from a Shared Server

If you're in the **same Discord server** as the person you want to add, you can send a friend request directly from their profile.

Steps to Add a Friend from a Server:

1. Open a **server** where the person is a member.

2. Click on their **username** in the server chat or member list.

3. A small pop-up will appear with their profile.

4. Click **"Send Friend Request"**.

This method is convenient because it allows you to add someone without needing their **Discord Tag**.

Tip: If you're unsure about a user's exact username, clicking on their profile in a server is a reliable way to find and add them.

2.3 Adding a Friend via QR Code (Mobile Only)

For mobile users, Discord offers a unique way to add friends using **QR codes**.

Steps to Add a Friend via QR Code:

1. The friend you want to add must go to **Settings > Scan QR Code** on their Discord mobile app.

2. They will be given a QR code to share with you.

3. Open your **Discord mobile app** and scan the QR code to send a friend request instantly.

This is one of the quickest methods to **add friends in person**, especially during gaming events or meetups.

3. Managing and Organizing Your Friends List

Once you've added friends, you may want to **organize, remove, or block** certain contacts based on your preferences.

3.1 Assigning Nicknames to Friends

Although you can't change a friend's actual username, you can **set a custom nickname** for them on your Friends List.

Steps to Set a Nickname:

1. Click on the **Friends** tab.

2. Right-click the friend's name.

3. Select **"Edit Note"** and type a nickname or note.

This is useful if a friend has a complicated username or you want to add **reminders** (e.g., "John - Fortnite Teammate").

3.2 Removing or Blocking Friends

If you no longer want to stay connected with someone, you can either **remove** or **block** them.

Steps to Remove a Friend:

1. Open the Friends tab.

2. Right-click the friend's name.

3. Select "Remove Friend".

They will no longer appear on your list, but they can still message you unless you block them.

Steps to Block a User:

1. Open the Friends tab or find the user in a server.

2. Right-click their name and select "Block".

3. They will be moved to your Blocked list.

Blocking prevents them from:

*   Sending you messages.

*   Seeing your online status.

*   Interacting with you in shared servers.

Tip: Use blocking only when necessary, as it completely cuts off communication.

4. Understanding Friend Status and Activity

When viewing your Friends List, you'll notice different **status indicators** next to their names. These show their availability and activity on Discord.

4.1 Status Indicators

*   ☐ Online – The user is currently active.

*   ☐ Idle – The user is away from their device.

*   ● Do Not Disturb – The user has muted notifications.

*   ○ Offline / Invisible – The user is either offline or appearing offline.

Users can manually set their status by clicking on their profile picture.

4.2 Rich Presence and Game Activity

Discord allows users to share what they're doing, such as:

- Playing a game (e.g., "Playing League of Legends").

- Listening to Spotify.

- Streaming on Twitch.

To enable or disable this feature:

1. Go to Settings > Activity Status.

2. Toggle "Display currently running game as a status message".

This feature is great for finding friends who are playing the same game, but it can also be disabled for privacy.

Conclusion

The Friends List in Discord is a powerful tool that allows you to connect, organize, and manage your direct contacts efficiently. Whether you're adding friends via username, shared servers, or QR codes, Discord provides various ways to make the process seamless. Additionally, organizing your list through status indicators, nicknames, and blocking options helps you tailor your experience to fit your needs.

With a well-managed Friends List, you can enjoy faster communication, better collaboration, and a more personalized Discord experience.

Next Section: 1.3.3 Understanding Status Indicators and Notifications

In the next section, we will explore how Discord's status settings and notification system help you stay connected while managing distractions effectively.

1.3.3 Understanding Status Indicators and Notifications

Discord provides a comprehensive status system and notification settings to help users manage their availability and stay updated on important messages. Understanding how status indicators work and how to customize notifications can significantly improve your Discord experience, allowing you to balance engagement with privacy and focus.

This section will cover:

- What status indicators are and how they function.

- The meaning of each status type.

- How notifications work and how to customize them.

- Strategies to reduce distractions while staying connected.

What Are Status Indicators in Discord?

Status indicators in Discord provide a quick and easy way for users to show their current activity or availability. They appear as small colored dots next to your profile picture, making it easy for friends and server members to see whether you're online, away, or unavailable.

Status indicators are automatically updated based on your activity but can also be manually adjusted. There are five main status types:

1. **Online (Green)** – You're active and available to chat.

2. **Idle (Yellow)** – You're away or inactive for some time.

3. **Do Not Disturb (Red)** – You're online but don't want to be disturbed by notifications.

4. **Invisible (Gray)** – You appear offline but can still use Discord normally.

5. **Streaming (Purple)** – You're live-streaming on Twitch or another platform.

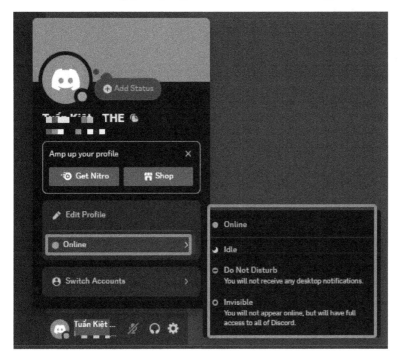

Understanding Each Status Type

1. Online (Green) – Available and Active

When your status is set to Online, it means you are currently active on Discord and available for conversations. Your friends and server members can see that you're online and may send you messages or mentions.

- If you're using Discord on your PC or phone, your status will automatically update to Online when you open the app.

- In voice channels, people can see your online status next to your profile.

- If someone sends you a message, you will receive notifications unless muted.

💡 *Tip:* If you don't want to be disturbed but still want to appear online, consider setting your status to **Do Not Disturb** instead.

2. Idle (Yellow) – Away or Inactive

The Idle status automatically activates if you have been inactive for a period of time. This means:

- You haven't interacted with Discord (e.g., typed a message, moved your mouse) for about 5-10 minutes.

- You may be away from your keyboard (AFK) or doing something else.

- People can still send you messages, but they'll know you may not respond immediately.

💡 *Tip:* You can manually set your status to **Idle** if you're stepping away but want others to know you're still around.

3. Do Not Disturb (Red) – No Notifications

Setting your status to Do Not Disturb (DND) signals that you don't want to be interrupted. When in this mode:

- You won't receive message notifications or sounds.

- Your profile displays a red status icon, indicating that you are online but prefer not to be contacted.

- This is useful when you need focus time for work, study, or gaming.

💡 *Tip:* If you're working on something important, use **DND mode** to minimize distractions while staying logged in.

4. Invisible (Gray) – Appear Offline but Stay Connected

The Invisible status allows you to use Discord while appearing offline to others. When set to Invisible:

- You can browse servers, chat in groups, and send messages without others knowing you're online.

- Other users will see a gray status indicator, making it look like you're offline.

- You will still receive messages and notifications, but others won't know you're active.

💡 *Tip:* Use **Invisible mode** when you want privacy while still being able to check messages and participate in conversations.

5. Streaming (Purple) – Live on Twitch or YouTube

If you stream games on Twitch or YouTube, Discord can automatically change your status to "Streaming" when you go live.

- This displays a purple status icon and a "LIVE" badge next to your name.

- It's a great way to let others know that you're streaming and encourage them to join your stream.

- You need to link your Twitch or YouTube account to enable this feature.

💡 *Tip:* If you don't want Discord to change your status while streaming, **disable this option in Settings > Connections**.

Managing Discord Notifications

While status indicators help show your availability, Discord notifications ensure you stay informed without being overwhelmed. Discord provides a highly customizable notification system, allowing you to:

- Receive alerts for important messages.

- Mute notifications from specific servers or users.

- Customize sound alerts based on different types of messages.

Types of Notifications in Discord

There are several types of notifications in Discord:

1. Direct Message (DM) Notifications – Alerts for private messages.

2. Server Notifications – Alerts from servers you've joined.

3. Mention Notifications (@yourname) – Alerts when someone tags you.

4. Role Notifications (@everyone, @here, @role) – Alerts for role mentions.

5. Voice Call and Video Notifications – Alerts for incoming calls and video chats.

💡 *Tip:* If you're in multiple servers, **customizing your notification settings** can help prevent information overload.

How to Customize Notifications

To manage notifications, follow these steps:

1. Go to User Settings (click the ⚙ icon in the bottom-left).

2. Select "Notifications" from the menu.

3. Customize your preferences:
   o Turn off sounds for specific events.
   o Enable/disable desktop notifications.
   o Adjust mobile push notifications.

4. Per-Server Notification Settings:
   o Right-click a server > Select "Notification Settings".
   o Choose between All Messages, Only Mentions, or Nothing.
   o Mute the server if you want zero notifications.

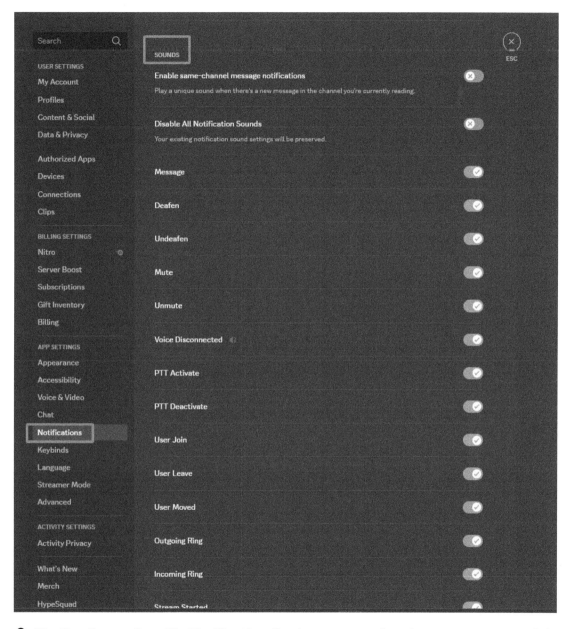

💡 *Tip:* Use **Server-Specific Notification Settings** to mute less important servers while keeping alerts from important ones.

Best Practices for Managing Status and Notifications

To get the best Discord experience, follow these best practices:

1. Use "Do Not Disturb" when focusing on work or studying.

2. Set "Invisible" when you want to browse Discord privately.

3. Mute large servers to avoid excessive notifications.

4. Customize notification settings per server to avoid distractions.

5. Enable "Push to Talk" in voice channels to reduce background noise.

Conclusion

Understanding status indicators and notifications allows you to control your availability, reduce distractions, and enhance communication on Discord. Whether you're actively chatting, away from your keyboard, or streaming, these tools help you stay connected on your own terms.

☞ *Next section: 2.1 Finding and Joining Servers* – Learn how to discover and join Discord communities!

CHAPTER II
Joining and Exploring Discord Servers

2.1 Finding and Joining Servers

2.1.1 Using Discord's Server Discovery

Discord is built around servers, which are virtual communities where users can communicate through text, voice, and video. Whether you're looking for a community centered around gaming, technology, study groups, hobbies, or professional networking, Discord's Server Discovery feature helps you find servers that match your interests. In this section, we'll explore what Server Discovery is, how to use it, and tips for finding the right server for you.

Understanding Server Discovery

What is Server Discovery?

Server Discovery is a feature in Discord that allows users to search for and explore public servers directly within the platform. It functions similarly to a search engine for Discord communities, helping users find servers based on keywords, topics, and interests.

Originally, users had to rely on third-party websites, invite links, or word of mouth to discover new servers. However, in 2020, Discord introduced Server Discovery to make it easier for users to find official, high-quality communities without needing external resources.

Who Can Use Server Discovery?

- Users with a verified email: To prevent spam and misuse, only users who have verified their email address can access Server Discovery.

- Users on the desktop and mobile apps: The feature is available on Windows, macOS, iOS, and Android, but it is not accessible in the web browser version of Discord.

- Users in regions where Server Discovery is supported: Some regions may have restrictions on Server Discovery due to local regulations.

What Types of Servers Appear in Discovery?

Not all servers are listed in Server Discovery. Only public servers that meet Discord's eligibility criteria appear in search results. These servers typically:

- Have at least 1,000 members.

- Follow Discord's community guidelines and terms of service.

- Are well-moderated and free from excessive spam, harassment, or inappropriate content.

- Have a clearly defined purpose or theme, making it easier for users to understand what the community is about.

How to Access and Use Server Discovery

Step 1: Opening Server Discovery

1. Launch Discord on your PC, Mac, or mobile device.

2. Look for the Compass Icon ($\mathbf{Q}$) on the left sidebar—this is the entry point for Server Discovery.

3. Click the icon to open the Server Discovery page, where you'll see a curated selection of popular public servers.

Step 2: Browsing Popular Servers

Once inside Server Discovery, you'll find:

- Trending Servers: Communities that are currently popular or growing rapidly.

- Category-Based Recommendations: Servers sorted by topics such as Gaming, Education, Music, Technology, Entertainment, Art, and more.

- Featured Servers: Communities that are hand-picked by Discord for their engagement, content quality, and community size.

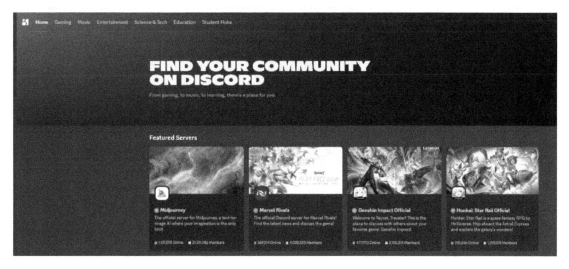

Step 3: Using the Search Bar

If you're looking for something specific, you can type keywords into the search bar at the top of the Server Discovery page.

For example, searching "Minecraft" will bring up public Minecraft-related servers, while searching "graphic design" will show communities focused on design, art, and creativity.

Pro Tip: Try using **multiple keywords** for more accurate results (e.g., "coding beginners" instead of just "coding").

Step 4: Previewing a Server

Before joining, you can preview a server by clicking on its name. This lets you:

- See the server description, rules, and main topics.

- View text channels and active conversations (if the server allows previews).

- Check the number of online members to gauge the server's activity level.

Step 5: Joining a Server

If you find a server you like:

1. Click the **"Join Server"** button.

2. The server will be added to your **left sidebar**, and you'll be automatically placed in the **welcome or rules channel**.

3. Read the **server rules**, introduce yourself (if required), and start exploring channels!

How to Find the Best Server for You

1. Define Your Purpose

Before joining a server, ask yourself:

- Are you looking for a social community or a learning environment?

- Do you want an active, fast-paced server or a smaller, more intimate one?

- Are you okay with strict moderation, or do you prefer relaxed communities?

Different servers have different cultures, so it's important to find one that matches your preferences.

2. Look at the Community Size and Activity

- Large servers (10,000+ members) tend to be very active, but conversations can move quickly, making it harder to keep up.

- Small to mid-sized servers (500-5,000 members) often have more engaging and meaningful interactions.

- Check if the server has active moderators—this ensures a well-maintained community.

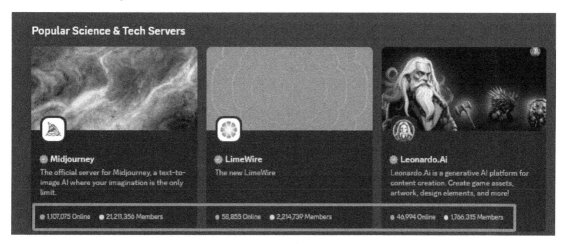

3. Read the Server Rules

Before joining, always read the **rules** to make sure the server aligns with your expectations. Some servers have:

- Age restrictions (e.g., 18+ only).

- Strict behavior guidelines (e.g., no swearing, no off-topic discussions).

- Content limitations (e.g., no NSFW or political debates).

4. Engage in the Community

Once you've joined a server:

- Introduce yourself in the designated channel.

- Read pinned messages to understand community guidelines.

- Start contributing to discussions rather than just lurking.

Active participation makes it easier to connect with other members and fully enjoy the experience.

Alternative Ways to Discover Servers

1. External Discord Server Listing Websites

If you can't find what you're looking for in Discord's built-in Server Discovery, consider using external platforms like:

- **Disboard (https://disboard.org/)** – One of the largest Discord server directories, allowing users to search by tags and categories.

- **Discord.me (https://discord.me/)** – A user-friendly directory with featured communities.

- **Top.gg (https://top.gg/)** – Primarily for Discord bots but also includes a server listing section.

2. Social Media and Forums

Many Discord communities promote their servers on platforms like:

- **Reddit** (e.g., r/discordservers, r/gaming).

- **Twitter/X and Instagram** (hashtags like #DiscordCommunity).

- **Facebook Groups and LinkedIn** for professional and niche communities.

3. Word of Mouth and Invite Links

Sometimes the best servers are **invite-only** or shared privately among members. If you're part of a niche interest group, **ask friends or online communities** for server recommendations.

Conclusion

Server Discovery is an incredibly powerful tool that helps users find public, high-quality Discord communities tailored to their interests. By using search functions, previewing servers, and engaging with communities, you can easily join discussions that align with your hobbies, professional goals, or educational interests.

In the next section (**2.1.2 Joining a Server with an Invite Link**), we'll cover how to join **private servers** using invite links and the best practices for navigating invitation-only communities.

2.1.2 Joining a Server with an Invite Link

Discord servers function as individual communities, each with its own set of channels, rules, and members. Unlike other social media platforms where users follow pages or groups, Discord servers require an invite link to join unless they are publicly discoverable. This section will guide you through everything you need to know about joining a Discord server using an invite link, including how invites work, different types of invite links, security considerations, and troubleshooting common issues.

What is a Discord Invite Link?

A Discord invite link is a unique URL or code that allows users to join a specific Discord server. These links are generated by server administrators or members with invite permissions and can be temporary or permanent.

Structure of an Invite Link

A standard Discord invite link looks like this:

https://discord.gg/abcd1234

- **https://discord.gg/** – The base URL that indicates it is a Discord invite link.

- **abcd1234** – A unique alphanumeric code assigned to the specific server.

https://discord.gg/nRQt⬛

Join the DA Team Discord Server!
Check out the DA Team community on Discord - hang out with 3 other members and enjoy free voice and text chat.
discord.gg
14:43

Some servers may use **custom invite links** if they have a boosted server (via **Discord Nitro Perks**), which makes the link more recognizable:

https://discord.gg/MyCoolServer

How to Join a Discord Server Using an Invite Link

Joining a server through an invite link is a simple process, but there are several ways to do it depending on whether you are using **Discord's desktop app, mobile app, or web browser**.

1. Using a Discord Invite Link on Desktop (Windows & macOS)

1. **Obtain the invite link** – A friend, community, or website must provide you with a valid invite link.

2. **Open Discord** – Launch the **Discord desktop app** or visit <u>discord.com</u> in your web browser.

3. **Click the '+' button** on the **left-hand sidebar**, next to your list of servers.

4. **Select "Join a Server"** – This option allows you to manually enter an invite link.

5. **Paste the invite link** in the provided field and click **"Join Server"**.

6. **Accept the server's rules (if applicable)** – Some servers require new members to **accept community guidelines** before accessing channels.

---

2. Using a Discord Invite Link on Mobile (iOS & Android)

1. **Copy the invite link** to your clipboard.

2. **Open the Discord app** on your mobile device.

3. Tap the **hamburger menu ☰** (three horizontal lines) in the top-left corner.

4. **Tap the '+' button** on the left-hand sidebar.

5. Select **"Join a Server"** and paste the invite link in the provided field.

6. Tap **"Join Server"** and accept any necessary rules.

3. Using a Discord Invite Link in a Web Browser (Without Installing Discord)

1. Click or paste the invite link in your browser's address bar.

2. If you have a Discord account, you can log in. If not, you'll be prompted to create an account.

3. After logging in, click **"Join Server"**.

4. If prompted, verify your email before gaining full access.

Different Types of Discord Invite Links

Not all invite links work the same way. Server administrators can customize invite settings, leading to different invite behaviors. Understanding these variations will help you avoid confusion when joining servers.

1. Permanent vs. Temporary Invite Links

- Permanent Invite Links – These never expire unless manually revoked by the server owner or admin.

- Temporary Invite Links – These expire after a certain time (e.g., 30 minutes, 1 hour, 1 day).

2. Limited-Use Invite Links

Some invite links have a set number of uses (e.g., only 5 people can use the link before it becomes invalid).

3. One-Time Use Links

Some servers generate invite links that work for only one person. Once used, they become invalid for others.

4. Vanity URL (Custom Invite Links)

Servers that reach Boost Level 3 can create custom invite links (e.g., discord.gg/GamingCommunity), making them easier to remember and share.

Security Considerations When Using Invite Links

While invite links are convenient, they can pose security risks if not handled properly. Here are some key precautions:

1. Avoid Clicking Suspicious Invite Links

Scammers sometimes send fake Discord invite links that redirect to phishing websites designed to steal your account credentials.

- Only accept invites from trusted sources.
- Check the URL before clicking—it should start with https://discord.gg/.

2. Be Cautious About Auto-Joining Servers

Some browser extensions or third-party bots automatically add users to servers without their knowledge.

- Review the servers you are a part of by clicking your **profile icon > Servers**.
- If you notice an unfamiliar server, **leave immediately**.

3. Enable Two-Factor Authentication (2FA)

Some malicious servers may try to trick you into sharing your login details.

- Enabling 2FA (Two-Factor Authentication) adds an extra layer of security.
- You can do this in User Settings > Security & Privacy > Enable Two-Factor Authentication.

4. Manage Your Server Privacy Settings

If you run a server, you can control how invite links are used by going to:

- Server Settings > Invites > Adjust expiration time, max uses, and permissions.

Troubleshooting Invite Link Issues

Sometimes, you may encounter problems when trying to join a server. Below are some common issues and their solutions:

Issue	Possible Cause	Solution
"Invalid Invite" Error	Expired or incorrect link	Request a new invite from the server admin.
"Invite Link Revoked"	The invite was deleted by the server owner	Ask the owner for a fresh invite.
"You Have Been Banned"	You were previously banned from the server	Contact the server admin if you believe it was a mistake.
"Invite Link Requires Verification"	Some servers require email or phone verification	Complete the verification process before joining.
"You've Reached the Maximum Server Limit"	Discord allows up to **100 servers** per user	Leave an unused server to make space for a new one.

Conclusion

Joining a Discord server using an invite link is the most common way to connect with communities. By understanding the different types of invite links, security precautions, and troubleshooting methods, you can ensure a seamless and safe experience when joining new servers.

In the next section, we will explore how to leave and manage your server list, ensuring that your Discord experience remains organized and enjoyable.

2.1.3 Leaving and Managing Your Server List

Discord provides a structured way for users to **join, manage, and leave servers**, ensuring that users can curate their experience based on their interests, communities, and social circles. Whether you're an active member of multiple servers or looking to streamline your

Discord experience by managing your server list, understanding how to leave and organize your servers is essential.

In this section, we will explore:

- How to leave a Discord server

- What happens when you leave a server

- Managing and organizing your server list

- Best practices for keeping your server list clutter-free

1. How to Leave a Discord Server

Leaving a Server on Desktop (Windows, macOS, Linux, and Web Browser)

If you no longer wish to be part of a Discord server, leaving it is simple. Follow these steps to leave a server on the desktop version of Discord:

1. **Open Discord**: Launch the Discord app or open it in your web browser.

2. **Navigate to the Server**: Look at the left sidebar where all your joined servers are listed. Click on the server you want to leave.

3. **Open the Server Options Menu**: Click on the server name at the **top left** of the screen to open the dropdown menu.

4. **Select "Leave Server"**: Scroll down in the dropdown menu and click on **Leave Server**.

5. **Confirm Your Action**: A confirmation popup will appear. Click **Leave** to exit the server permanently.

Once you leave a server, you will no longer have access to its channels, messages, or members, and it will be removed from your server list.

Leaving a Server on Mobile (iOS & Android)

If you are using Discord on a mobile device, follow these steps:

1. **Open the Discord App** and log in.

2. **Find the Server** in the left sidebar and tap on it.

3. **Tap the Three-Dot Menu**: In the top-right corner, tap the three dots next to the server name.

4. **Select "Leave Server"** from the menu.

5. **Confirm Your Decision** by tapping **Leave**.

After you leave, the server will disappear from your server list.

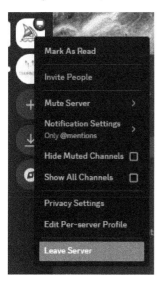

What Happens When You Leave a Server?

Leaving a Discord server has several consequences:

- You lose access to all messages, channels, and media shared within that server.

- Your name is removed from the server's member list, and others will no longer see you in the server.

- You will not receive any notifications or updates from the server.

- Your previous messages in the server remain unless they are manually deleted by a server admin.

- If you wish to rejoin, you must be invited again or find a public invite link.

Leaving a server does not notify other members, but if the server has role-based access, an admin may notice your absence.

2. Managing and Organizing Your Server List

Over time, you may find yourself joining too many servers, making it difficult to navigate Discord efficiently. Proper organization helps you prioritize important servers, reduce clutter, and improve your overall Discord experience.

Reordering Your Servers

You can rearrange servers in your server list for better organization. To do this:

- On Desktop: Click and drag a server up or down in the list.

- On Mobile: Press and hold a server icon, then drag it to the desired position.

This allows you to keep frequently used servers at the top and less important ones toward the bottom.

Creating Folders for Servers

If you are a member of multiple servers, **server folders** help organize them into categories.

How to Create a Server Folder (Desktop & Mobile)

1. Drag one server icon over another until a gray folder appears.

2. Release the mouse (or finger on mobile) to create the folder.

3. Right-click (or long-press on mobile) the folder to rename it or change its color.

4. Add more servers by dragging them into the folder.

Some users organize their servers based on:

- Purpose (e.g., Gaming, Work, Study, Friends)

- Activity Level (e.g., Active Servers, Occasional Use)

- Types of Servers (e.g., Public Communities, Private Groups)

Muting and Hiding Servers

If you want to remain in a server but reduce notifications and distractions, you can mute or hide it.

Muting a Server

- Right-click (desktop) or long-press (mobile) the server icon.

- Select "Mute Server" and choose a duration (e.g., 1 hour, 8 hours, Until I Turn It Back On).

- This prevents all notifications from that server.

Hiding Muted Servers

If you want to hide muted servers from your list, go to:

- User Settings > Notifications > Hide Muted Servers

- Toggle the setting ON to reduce clutter in your server list.

Leaving Inactive or Unused Servers

If your server list becomes too long, it's a good idea to leave inactive or unused servers. Ask yourself:

- Do I still participate in this server?
- Does this server provide useful content or discussions?
- Do I need notifications from this server?

If the answer is no, consider leaving to keep your Discord organized and efficient.

3. Best Practices for Managing Your Discord Servers

1. **Join Only Essential Servers**
   - Avoid joining every invite you receive. Stick to servers that align with your interests or needs.

2. **Use Server Folders**
   - Group servers into folders to categorize them efficiently.

3. **Prioritize Your Most Active Servers**
   - Keep frequently used servers at the top for easy access.

4. **Mute Unnecessary Notifications**
   - Reduce distractions by muting channels or entire servers.

5. **Regularly Review Your Server List**
   - Every few months, assess your servers and leave those you no longer use.

6. **Use Different Accounts for Different Purposes**
   - If you use Discord for both work and gaming, consider separate accounts for better organization.

Conclusion

Effectively managing your Discord servers improves organization, focus, and efficiency. By leaving unnecessary servers, organizing them into folders, and muting distractions, you can create a more enjoyable and streamlined Discord experience.

By following these best practices, you can ensure that your Discord server list remains clean and manageable, allowing you to quickly find and engage with the communities that matter most to you.

Next Section: 2.2 Understanding Channels and Categories

In the next section, we will explore text and voice channels, how they function, and how to manage them efficiently.

2.2 Understanding Channels and Categories

2.2.1 Text Channels vs. Voice Channels

Discord servers are structured using channels, which are organized into categories. Channels are where conversations and interactions take place, whether through text, voice, or video. Understanding the differences between text channels and voice channels is essential for navigating Discord efficiently and maximizing your experience.

1. What Are Text Channels?

A text channel is a space within a Discord server where members can communicate using written messages. These channels function similarly to group chats or forums, where users can send messages, share media, and use various interactive elements.

1.1 Key Features of Text Channels

1. **Message-Based Communication**

   o   Users can send plain text, formatted text, and multimedia messages.

   o   Messages persist, meaning users can scroll back to read previous conversations.

2. **Support for Media and Attachments**

   o   Users can share images, GIFs, videos, and links.

   o   Attachments such as PDFs, Word documents, and spreadsheets can be uploaded (subject to file size limits).

3. **Markdown Formatting for Text Customization**

   o   Users can format text using bold, italics, underlining, and strikethrough.

   o   Code blocks and lists can also be created for better readability.

4. **Reactions and Emojis**

   o   Users can react to messages using Discord's built-in emoji system.

o Custom emojis can be added to personalize server interactions.

5. **Mentions and Notifications**

o Users can mention others using **@username** to send notifications.

o Roles can be mentioned using **@role** to notify specific groups of users.

6. **Threaded Conversations**

o Discord allows threaded messages, enabling users to have side discussions within a channel without cluttering the main chat.

7. **Bots and Integrations**

o Many servers use bots to moderate text channels, play games, or automate tasks.

o Bots can be programmed to send automatic responses, alerts, or announcements.

1.2 Types of Text Channels

Discord servers can have different types of **text channels** based on their function:

1. **General Discussion Channels**

o A place for casual conversation among server members.

o Typically labeled as #general or #chat.

2. **Announcements Channels**

o Used for important server updates and news.

o Often restricted to administrators or moderators for posting.

3. **Help & Support Channels**

o Common in tech or community-based servers.

o Users can ask questions, request support, or troubleshoot issues.

4. **Media & Sharing Channels**

o Focused on sharing images, videos, memes, or artwork.

- o Common examples include #memes, #fanart, and #screenshots.

5. **Bot Commands Channels**

   - o Dedicated for interacting with bots, such as music bots or moderation bots.

   - o Keeps main discussion channels free from clutter.

6. **Role-Specific or Private Channels**

   - o Certain channels may be restricted to specific roles (e.g., admin-only or VIP chat).

   - o Helps organize discussions for different groups within a server.

2. What Are Voice Channels?

A voice channel is a channel where users can communicate via voice or video chat in real time. Unlike text channels, messages are not stored—conversations happen live.

2.1 Key Features of Voice Channels

1. **Real-Time Voice Communication**

   - o Users can join voice channels to talk without needing to start a call.

   - o Voice chat is low-latency, making it ideal for gaming and live discussions.

2. **Push-to-Talk and Voice Activity**

   - o Users can choose between push-to-talk (PTT) or voice-activated detection.

   - o PTT requires users to press a key to talk, preventing background noise.

3. **Screen Sharing and Video Chat**

   - o Users can share their screen for presentations, tutorials, or gaming.

   - o Video calls can be enabled within voice channels.

4. **User Limits and Permissions**

   - o Server admins can limit the number of users in a voice channel.

   - o Some voice channels may require special roles to join.

5. **Mute and Deafen Options**

   o Users can mute themselves or deafen (mute others) if needed.

   o Server admins and moderators can mute or disconnect users if necessary.

6. **Music and Entertainment Bots**

   o Many servers integrate music bots like Hydra or FredBoat to play music in voice channels.

   o Some bots provide ambient sounds, radio stations, or interactive voice commands.

2.2 Types of Voice Channels

Similar to text channels, voice channels can serve different purposes:

1. **General Voice Chat**

   o Used for casual voice conversations.

   o Typically named #voice-chat or #hangout.

2. **Gaming Voice Channels**

   o Dedicated to specific games or gaming sessions.

   o Often named after games (e.g., #csgo-lobby, #minecraft-chat).

3. **Private or VIP Channels**

   o Restricted to select users with special roles or permissions.

   o Common in paid or exclusive communities.

4. **Music and Radio Channels**

   o Designed for music bots to play songs.

   o Often used for background music in study or work servers.

5. **Event or Stage Channels**

   o Stage Channels are used for large-scale discussions, podcasts, or interviews.

o   Audience members can listen, while selected speakers can talk.

3. Comparing Text Channels vs. Voice Channels

Feature	Text Channels	Voice Channels
Communication Type	Messages (written chat)	Real-time voice and video
Persistence	Messages are saved and can be read later	Conversations disappear once ended
Multimedia Support	Supports text, images, GIFs, links, and files	Supports voice chat, video, and screen sharing
Best Used For	General discussions, announcements, sharing media	Live conversations, gaming, meetings, and music
Customization	Bots, emojis, reactions, threaded replies	User limits, permissions, push-to-talk

4. Best Practices for Using Channels Effectively

To ensure a smooth experience, consider the following best practices:

1. **Follow Server Rules** – Every server has guidelines on where and how to communicate.

2. **Use the Right Channel** – Keep conversations relevant to the channel's purpose.

3. **Avoid Spamming** – Excessive messages or unnecessary pings can annoy members.

4. **Respect User Preferences** – Not everyone wants to use voice chat; some prefer text.

5. **Optimize Audio Settings** – If using a voice channel, configure microphone sensitivity for clarity.

Conclusion

Both text channels and voice channels play vital roles in a Discord server's structure. Text channels are great for persistent communication, media sharing, and organized discussions, while voice channels offer real-time interaction, collaboration, and entertainment. Understanding how to use each effectively can significantly enhance your Discord experience.

In the next section, we'll explore **how to create and organize channels**, ensuring that your server is structured for maximum efficiency.

2.2.2 Creating and Organizing Channels

Discord servers are built around channels, which serve as the primary means of communication. Whether you're managing a small community, a gaming guild, or a professional workspace, properly structuring your channels is essential for organization and user engagement. This section will guide you through creating, customizing, and organizing Discord channels effectively.

1. Understanding the Role of Channels in Discord

Channels in Discord function similarly to chat rooms or meeting spaces within a server. They are categorized into two main types:

- Text Channels – For written conversations, sharing links, images, and files.
- Voice Channels – For real-time voice communication and video calls.

Each channel serves a unique purpose, and organizing them properly ensures a smooth user experience. A well-structured server reduces clutter, improves navigation, and enhances engagement among members.

2. How to Create a Channel in Discord

Creating a new channel in Discord is simple. Follow these steps:

Step 1: Open Your Server Settings

1. Click on your **Add a Server** name in the top-left corner.

2. Select **"Create Your Server"** from the dropdown menu.

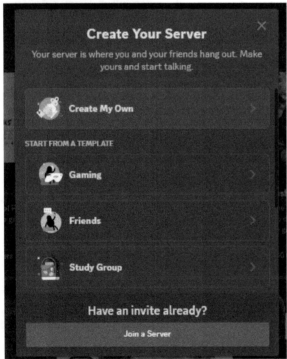

Step 2: Choose a Channel Type

You'll be given two main options:

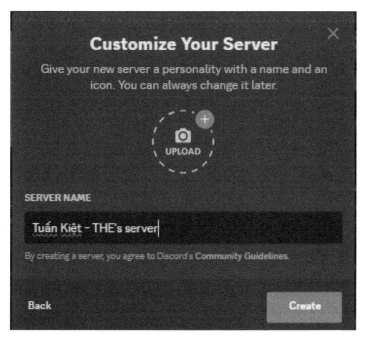

Step 3: Name Your Channel

- Keep it clear and concise (e.g., #general-chat, #announcements, #support).

- Use hyphens instead of spaces (e.g., #team-discussions, not #team discussions).

- Avoid overly long or vague names that might confuse users.

Step 4: Set Channel Permissions

Before clicking **"Create"**, you can **customize permissions**:

- **Private Channels** – Only accessible to specific roles.

- **Public Channels** – Open to all server members.

Once you're satisfied, click **"Create Channel"**, and your new channel will appear under its respective category.

3. Organizing Channels with Categories

As your server grows, having **too many channels** can become overwhelming. This is where **categories** come in handy. Categories help **group related channels together**, improving navigation and organization.

How to Create a Category

1. Right-click anywhere in the **channel list** on the left panel.

2. Select **"Create Category"** from the dropdown menu.

3. Enter a **descriptive name** (e.g., Gaming, Team Meetings, Help Desk).

4. Click **"Create"**, and a new category will appear.

How to Add Channels to a Category

1. **Drag and drop** channels into the category.

2. Click the **drop-down arrow** next to the category name to collapse or expand it.

3. Adjust **category permissions** if needed.

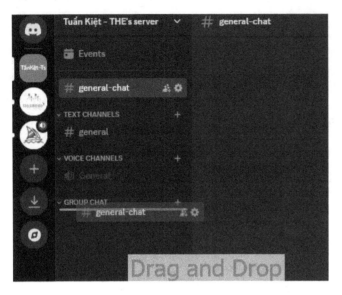

Example of a Well-Organized Server Structure

A gaming server might have:

Category: General

- #welcome (Introduce new members)
- #announcements (Important updates)
- #general-chat (Casual conversations)

Category: Game Discussions

- #fps-games (For first-person shooter discussions)
- #rpg-games (For role-playing game discussions)
- #strategy-games (For strategy game discussions)

Category: Voice Channels

- 🔊 General Voice
- 🔊 Gaming Squad 1
- 🔊 Gaming Squad 2

This structure keeps topics **separated and easy to navigate**, preventing clutter.

4. Managing Channel Permissions

Each channel can have **custom permissions** based on user roles. This is useful for:

- Restricting access to staff-only channels.

- Allowing moderators to mute or kick users in voice channels.

- Giving VIP members special perks.

How to Adjust Channel Permissions

1. Click the **gear icon** (⚙▢) next to the channel name.

2. Go to the **"Permissions"** tab.

3. Add roles/users and modify their permissions, such as:

   o Read Messages (View or hide channels).

   o Send Messages (Enable/disable chat).

   o Manage Messages (Allow mods to delete unwanted posts).

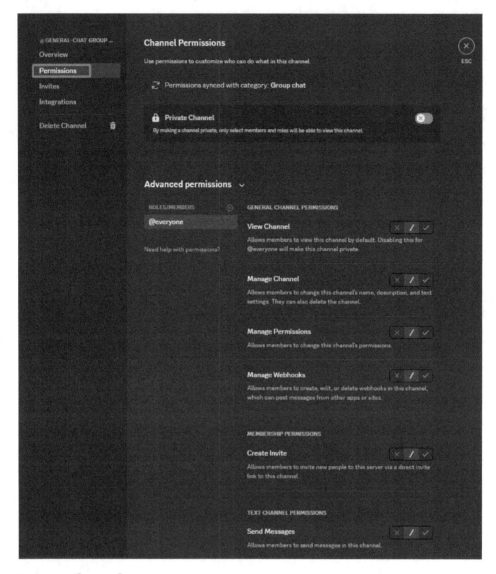

Private Channels

You can limit channel access by making it private:

- Enable "Private Channel" when creating a new channel.

- Only selected roles will have access.

This is perfect for staff discussions, VIP lounges, or confidential projects.

5. Advanced Channel Customization

Beyond the basics, you can further optimize your server with:

Slow Mode

- Prevents spam by setting a cooldown time between messages.

- Activate it under **"Edit Channel"** → **"Slow Mode"**.

- Set delays between **5 seconds to 6 hours**.

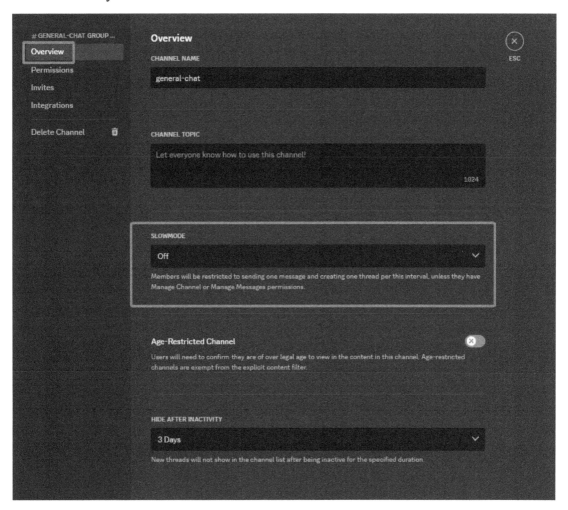

NSFW Channels

- For age-restricted discussions or mature content.

- Enable it by clicking **"Mark as NSFW"** in channel settings.

Threaded Conversations

- Helps keep discussions **organized within a single channel**.

- Click the **"+" icon** next to a message → **"Create Thread"**.

- Threads automatically **archive after 24 hours of inactivity**.

Auto-Archiving Channels

- Useful for temporary event channels.

- Can be **automatically deleted or hidden** after an event ends.

6. Best Practices for Organizing Channels

A well-structured server is engaging, easy to navigate, and enjoyable for members. Here are some best practices:

✅ Keep the number of channels reasonable – Too many can overwhelm users.
✅ Use clear naming conventions – Descriptive and easy to understand.
✅ Leverage categories – Group related channels for clarity.
✅ Utilize permissions wisely – Protect sensitive discussions.
✅ Regularly clean up inactive channels – Remove unnecessary clutter.

Conclusion

Creating and organizing channels in Discord is crucial for maintaining a structured and user-friendly server. With properly named channels, logical categories, and well-managed permissions, you can ensure a seamless experience for your community.

In the next section, we'll explore Managing Channel Permissions, where we'll dive deeper into how to customize user access and security settings for an optimized Discord server experience.

2.2.3 Managing Channel Permissions

Discord offers a powerful and flexible permission system that allows server administrators and moderators to control user access and activities within channels. Properly managing channel permissions is essential for maintaining security, organization, and user experience within a Discord server.

This section will cover:

- The role-based permission system in Discord.

- How to customize channel permissions for different user roles.

- Best practices for managing permissions efficiently.

Understanding Discord's Role-Based Permission System

Discord uses a hierarchical role-based permission system, meaning permissions are granted based on roles rather than individual users. Roles are assigned to users, and these roles determine what actions they can perform in the server and its channels.

Types of Permissions in Discord

There are **three levels of permissions** that can be configured in a Discord server:

1. **Server-Wide Permissions**

    o These permissions affect the entire server and apply to all channels within it.

    o Example: Admins might have "Manage Server" rights, while regular members do not.

2. **Category-Level Permissions**

    o These permissions apply to **all channels** within a specific **category**.

    o Example: A "Staff Only" category might restrict access to only moderators and admins.

3. **Channel-Specific Permissions**

- These permissions apply only to **individual channels** and can override category-wide settings.

- Example: A **text channel** may allow "Send Messages" for members but disable it in a read-only "Announcements" channel.

Types of Actions Controlled by Permissions

Discord provides over 30 different permissions, which can be categorized into:

1. General Permissions (e.g., Manage Server, Manage Roles)

2. Membership Permissions (e.g., Kick/Ban Members, Manage Nicknames)

3. Text Channel Permissions (e.g., Send Messages, Manage Messages, Use External Emojis)

4. Voice Channel Permissions (e.g., Speak, Mute Members, Use Voice Activity)

5. Advanced Permissions (e.g., Administrator, Manage Channels, View Audit Log)

Setting Up Channel Permissions in Discord

To manage channel permissions in Discord, follow these steps:

Step 1: Access Channel Settings

1. Open Discord and navigate to your server.

2. Right-click on the channel (text or voice) you want to modify.

3. Click Edit Channel to access the settings.

4. Go to the Permissions tab.

Step 2: Adding and Configuring Roles

1. In the Permissions tab, you will see a Roles/Members section.

2. Click + to add a new role or select an existing role.

3. Adjust the permissions for that role using the toggle switches (✓ Allow, ✗ Deny, or Default).

Step 3: Overriding Category Permissions

- If a channel is inside a category, it will initially inherit the category's permissions.

- You can override category settings by manually changing the permissions in an individual channel.

Step 4: Testing Permissions

1. Once permissions are set, you can test them by clicking View As Role (found in the Server Settings > Roles menu).

2. This lets you preview what different users will experience based on their assigned role.

Common Permission Configurations

1. Setting Up Read-Only Announcement Channels

- Use Case: A channel where only admins can post updates.

- Steps:

    o Set "Send Messages" to ✖ Deny for @everyone.

    o Allow "Send Messages" only for Admin/Moderator roles.

2. Private Staff-Only Channels

- Use Case: A secure channel for staff discussions.

- Steps:

    o Deny "View Channel" for @everyone.

    o Allow "View Channel" and "Send Messages" for the Staff role.

3. Temporary Voice Channels for Events

- Use Case: A voice chat that opens only during scheduled events.

- Steps:

    o Default "Connect" permission set to ✖ Deny.

    o During events, manually allow "Connect" for members.

Best Practices for Managing Channel Permissions

1. **Use Role-Based Permissions Instead of User-Specific Permissions**

   o Avoid setting permissions individually per user—instead, assign users to roles and manage permissions at the role level.

2. **Keep Role Hierarchies Simple**

   o Organize roles in a logical order (e.g., Admins > Mods > Verified Members > Guests).

   o Higher roles should have broader permissions, while lower roles have restricted access.

3. **Regularly Audit Permissions**

   o Periodically review permissions to ensure they align with server rules and security.

   o Check audit logs to see if unauthorized changes were made.

4. **Use Private Channels for Sensitive Information**

   o Ensure staff, VIP, or support channels are locked to only trusted users.

5. **Educate Server Moderators and Admins**

   o Train moderators on how to use permissions correctly to avoid accidental leaks or disruptions.

Conclusion

Properly managing channel permissions is critical for maintaining order, security, and a great user experience in a Discord server. By using role-based settings, customizing permissions at category and channel levels, and following best practices, you can ensure that your Discord server remains well-organized and efficiently moderated.

Next Section: 2.3 Participating in Server Conversations

Now that you understand channel permissions, the next section will cover how users interact within Discord servers—including sending messages, using emojis, and tagging other members effectively.

2.3 Participating in Server Conversations

2.3.1 Sending Messages and Formatting Text

Discord is a highly interactive platform that allows users to communicate via text, voice, and video. One of the most fundamental ways to engage in a server is by sending messages in text channels. Whether you are participating in a casual chat, sharing important updates, or engaging in structured discussions, understanding how to send and format text messages effectively is essential.

This section will cover everything you need to know about sending messages, using text formatting, employing special commands, and enhancing engagement with various built-in Discord features.

1. Sending Basic Messages in Discord

1.1 How to Send a Message

Sending a message in Discord is straightforward:

1. **Open a text channel** – Navigate to any server and click on a text channel where you have permission to chat.

2. **Locate the message input box** – At the bottom of the chat window, you'll find a text box where you can type your message.

3. **Type your message** – Enter your text as you would in any chat application.

4. **Press "Enter" to send** – Once you're satisfied with your message, press the "Enter" key to send it.

If you want to start a new line without sending the message, press **Shift + Enter** instead.

1.2 Editing and Deleting Messages

After sending a message, you may realize that you made a typo or need to delete it. Discord allows you to edit or remove your messages easily:

- **To edit a message:**

  1. Hover over the message you sent.

  2. Click on the **pencil (✏️) icon** that appears.

  3. Modify your text and press "Enter" to save the changes.

- **To delete a message:**

  1. Hover over the message you sent.

  2. Click on the **three-dot menu** (⋮) that appears.

  3. Select **Delete Message** and confirm the action.

Note: Server administrators and moderators may have permissions to delete messages sent by other users.

2. Formatting Text for Better Readability

Discord supports Markdown, a lightweight formatting syntax that lets users style their text easily. Below are various ways you can format your messages:

2.1 Bold, Italic, and Underline

- **Bold:** Use double asterisks **bold** → **bold**

- *Italic:* Use single asterisks or underscores *italic* or _italic_ → *italic*

- ***Bold & Italic:*** Use triple asterisks ***bold italic*** → ***bold italic***

- **Underline**: Use double underscores _underline_ → **underline**

2.2 Strikethrough and Spoilers

- ~~Strikethrough~~: Use double tildes ~~strikethrough~~ → ~~strikethrough~~

- ||Spoilers||: Use double vertical bars ||spoilers|| → Clicking the blacked-out section reveals the text

2.3 Quoting Messages

To quote a message in Discord, use the **>** symbol at the beginning of a line:

> This is a quoted message.

→

This is a quoted message.

For multi-line quotes, use **>>>** followed by your text:

>>> This is a

multi-line quote.

→

This is a
multi-line quote.

2.4 Using Code Blocks

Discord also allows users to format messages as code:

- **Inline code:** Use single backticks `code` → code

- **Multi-line code block:** Use triple backticks
- def hello():
-    print("Hello, world!")

2.5 Using Lists and Bullet Points

You can create lists in Discord for better message organization:

- **Bullet points:** Use hyphens or asterisks:
- - Item 1
- - Item 2

→

     o   Item 1

     o   Item 2

- **Numbered lists:**
- 1. First item
- 2. Second item

→

0.   First item

1.   Second item

3. Using Mentions and Tags

Mentions are useful for drawing someone's attention in a conversation.

- Mentioning a user: Type @username → @JohnDoe
- Mentioning a role: Type @role → @Moderators
- Mentioning everyone in a server: Type @everyone (notifies all members)
- Mentioning online members: Type @here (notifies only active members)

Server admins can restrict mentions to prevent spam.

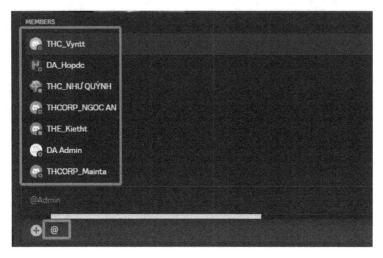

4. Sending Embedded Links and Attachments

4.1 Sharing Links

Simply paste a URL into the chat, and Discord will automatically generate a preview (if supported).

Example:

https://www.discord.com

→

Discord's official website

If you want to send a link without an embed preview, add < > around it:

<https://www.discord.com>

→ The link will be sent as plain text without a preview.

4.2 Uploading Files and Images

To share images, documents, or other files:

1. Click on the "**+**" icon next to the message input box.

2. Select **Upload a File** and choose a file from your computer.

3. Optionally, add a caption before sending.

Supported formats include .jpg, .png, .mp4, .pdf, .gif, and more.

5. Using Discord Slash Commands

Discord includes built-in **slash commands** that allow users to perform quick actions. Some common commands include:

- /nick [new name] → Changes your nickname on the server.
- /tts [message] → Sends a text-to-speech message.
- /me [message] → Displays a stylized third-person action.

Many bots also use **slash commands** to provide custom functionalities.

6. Best Practices for Server Conversations

Be Respectful and Follow Server Rules

Each Discord server has its own rules. Be sure to follow them and maintain a positive environment.

Avoid Spamming and Overusing Mentions

Excessive use of @everyone or sending too many messages in a short period can be considered spam.

Use Formatting for Clarity

Proper use of bold, italics, bullet points, and code blocks makes messages easier to read.

Keep Messages Concise

Avoid sending large blocks of text. Break information into smaller messages when necessary.

Conclusion

Text messaging is the foundation of Discord communication. By mastering basic messaging, text formatting, mentions, attachments, and best practices, you can communicate more effectively within any server.

In the next section, we will explore **using emojis, GIFs, and reactions** to enhance your Discord experience.

2.3.2 Using Emojis, GIFs, and Reactions

Engaging in conversations on Discord is more than just typing out messages. To create a lively and expressive chat experience, Discord offers several interactive elements, including **emojis, GIFs, and reactions**. These features allow users to express emotions, emphasize points, and interact with messages in a fun and engaging way. Whether you are chatting in a server, sending direct messages, or participating in a community discussion, mastering these tools can greatly enhance your communication experience.

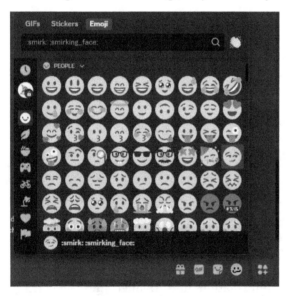

1. Using Emojis in Discord

1.1 What Are Emojis and Why Use Them?

Emojis are small digital images or icons used to express emotions, ideas, or objects. They help add personality to messages and make conversations more dynamic. In Discord, emojis can be used in multiple ways:

- Standard Unicode Emojis – These are the built-in emojis available on all devices, similar to the ones found on smartphones and social media platforms.

- Custom Emojis – Servers can upload their own unique emojis, which can be used exclusively within that server.

- Animated Emojis – Available through Discord Nitro, these are moving versions of custom emojis that add extra flair to conversations.

1.2 How to Use Emojis in Messages

There are three primary ways to use emojis in Discord messages:

Using the Emoji Picker

The easiest way to insert an emoji into a message is through the emoji picker:

1. Click on the smiley face icon in the message bar.

2. Browse through different categories or use the search bar to find a specific emoji.

3. Click on the emoji to insert it into your message.

Typing Emoji Shortcodes

You can also type emoji shortcodes manually. Discord supports **colon codes**, meaning you can type the emoji's name between colons to insert it.

- Example: Typing :smile: will insert ☺.

- Discord provides autocomplete suggestions when you start typing : followed by an emoji name.

Using Custom Server Emojis

If you are in a server that has uploaded custom emojis, you can use them by:

- Clicking on the emoji picker and selecting the server-specific emoji tab.

- Typing :customemojiname: to insert a specific custom emoji.

- Note: Custom emojis can only be used outside their original server if you have Discord Nitro.

2. Using GIFs in Discord

What Are GIFs?

GIFs (Graphics Interchange Format) are short, looping animations that add movement and humor to conversations. They are commonly used to react to messages, express emotions, or enhance storytelling in chat.

How to Send GIFs in Discord

There are two main ways to send GIFs in Discord:

Using the GIF Picker

Discord has a built-in GIF picker powered by Tenor and Giphy, allowing users to quickly find and send GIFs. To use it:

1. Click on the GIF icon next to the message bar.

2. Browse through categories or use the search bar to find a GIF.

3. Click on the GIF to send it instantly.

Uploading Your Own GIFs

If you have a custom GIF you'd like to share, you can manually upload it:

1. Click on the "+" (Attach File) button in the message bar.

2. Select the GIF from your computer or mobile device.

3. (Optional) Add a caption before sending the GIF.

Copy-Pasting GIF Links

You can also send GIFs by copying a direct link from a website like Giphy or Tenor and pasting it into the chat. Discord will automatically embed the GIF into the message.

3. Using Reactions in Discord

3.1 What Are Message Reactions?

Reactions allow users to respond to a message with an emoji without sending a separate reply. This feature is useful for polls, quick approvals, acknowledgments, and reactions to announcements.

For example:

- A user posts an announcement, and others react with 👍 (thumbs up) to show agreement.

- A server admin creates a poll, and members vote using different emojis.

3.2 How to Add a Reaction to a Message

To add a reaction:

1. Hover over a message (on desktop) or long-press the message (on mobile).

2. Click on the smiley face (+) reaction icon.

3. Choose an emoji from the reaction picker.

4. The reaction will now appear beneath the message.

3.3 Managing Reactions

Once an emoji reaction is added to a message, other users can click on the same emoji to "vote" for it, increasing its count.

- Adding multiple reactions: You can react to a message with more than one emoji.

- Removing your reaction: Click the emoji you reacted with to remove it.

- Viewing who reacted: Hover over an emoji reaction to see a list of users who reacted with that emoji.

3.4 Reaction Permissions and Restrictions

Server admins and moderators can control reactions using role permissions:

- Restricting certain users from adding reactions (useful in announcement channels).

- Limiting reactions to specific emojis for structured polls or voting systems.

- Removing inappropriate reactions by clicking on them and selecting "Remove Reaction".

4. Advanced Tips for Emojis, GIFs, and Reactions

Using Bots to Enhance Emoji and GIF Features

Discord bots can expand the functionality of emojis and GIFs. Some popular bots include:

- Emoji.gg Bot – Helps manage and search for custom emojis.

- GIF Bot – Provides random or trending GIFs.

- MEE6 and Dyno – Offer automatic reactions based on specific keywords.

Creating Custom Emoji Packs

Server owners can upload up to 50 custom emojis per server. To create an emoji pack:

1. Go to Server Settings → Emoji.

2. Click Upload Emoji and select an image (maximum 256 KB).

3. Assign a name to the emoji (e.g., :customemoji:).

4. Members can now use the custom emoji in chat.

Making the Most of Discord Nitro

If you subscribe to Discord Nitro, you unlock premium emoji features:

- Use custom emojis across all servers.

- Access animated emojis.

- Upload larger file-size emojis.

5. Conclusion

Emojis, GIFs, and reactions are essential tools for engagement on Discord. Whether you're chatting in a casual server, running a business community, or participating in an educational group, these features add personality, humor, and interaction to conversations.

By mastering custom emojis, GIF usage, and reactions, you can make your Discord experience more expressive and enjoyable.

Next Section: 2.3.3 Pinging Users and Using Mentions

In the next section, we'll explore how to effectively use **mentions and pinging** to notify users, grab attention, and manage server interactions.

2.3.3 Pinging Users and Using Mentions

In Discord servers, effective communication goes beyond simply sending messages. One of the most useful features of Discord's messaging system is the ability to **ping** users or **use mentions**. This feature helps you notify specific individuals or groups, ensuring that important messages don't go unnoticed. Whether you're alerting a friend, calling the attention of a moderator, or notifying an entire group, mentions are a powerful tool for enhancing server communication.

In this section, we will explore what **pinging and mentions** are, how they work, when to use them appropriately, and how to **manage mention notifications** to avoid excessive pings.

What is Pinging and Mentioning in Discord?

In Discord, "pinging" a user refers to the act of **mentioning their username** in a chat message. When a user is pinged, they receive a notification that highlights the message containing their mention.

Mentions can be used in text channels, direct messages (DMs), and server conversations, making them an essential tool for drawing attention to important messages.

There are three main types of mentions in Discord:

1. Individual User Mentions – Used to notify a specific user.

2. Role Mentions – Used to notify everyone with a certain role.

3. Channel Mentions – Used to refer users to a specific channel.

Each type of mention serves a different purpose, which we will discuss in detail below.

How to Mention Users in Discord

1. Mentioning an Individual User

The most common way to ping someone in Discord is by mentioning them directly in a message. This is done using the **"@"** symbol followed by the person's username.

Syntax:

@Username

For example, if you want to ping a user named *JohnDoe*, you would type:

@JohnDoe Hey, could you check this out?

What Happens When You Mention Someone?

- The mentioned user will receive a *notification* (unless they have muted the channel or disabled mentions).

- Their name will appear in a *highlighted color*, making it easy for them to find the message.

- If they are **offline**, they will see the mention when they next log in.

2. Mentioning a Role

In Discord, *server roles* allow users to be grouped based on responsibilities or permissions. If you want to notify multiple users at once, you can mention a specific role rather than individual users.

Syntax:

@RoleName

For example, if you have a role called *Moderators*, you can ping all users with that role by typing:

@Moderators We need assistance in the #general channel!

Who Can Mention Roles?

- *Only users with permission to mention roles* can do this. Server administrators can restrict role mentions in the settings.

- Some roles may be *protected from mentions*, meaning users without the proper permissions cannot ping them.

3. Mentioning Everyone or Here

Discord also provides two special mentions that allow users to notify *large groups*:

- *@everyone* – Notifies *all users* in the server, regardless of their online status.

- *@here* – Notifies *only online users* currently in the server.

Syntax:

@everyone

@here

For example, if you want to notify all users about an important announcement, you can type:

@everyone The server will undergo maintenance at 10 PM tonight.

Or, if you only want to notify active users:

@here Who's up for a gaming session right now?

When to Use These Mentions?

Since @everyone and @here can send notifications to hundreds or thousands of users, they should be used sparingly to avoid annoying server members. Many servers disable @everyone mentions except for administrators and moderators.

How to Mention a Specific Channel

If you want to refer users to a specific channel, you can mention the channel name in your message.

Syntax:

#channel-name

For example, if you want users to check out a rules channel named *#server-rules*, you would type:

Please read the rules in #server-rules before participating.

This creates a *clickable link* that takes users directly to the mentioned channel.

Best Practices for Using Mentions in Discord

✅ Use Mentions Responsibly

- Only ping users when necessary to avoid excessive notifications.
- Avoid spamming mentions, as it can be irritating for users.
- Use @everyone and @here only for important announcements.

✅ Respect Server Rules

- Many servers have strict rules against unnecessary pings, so always check the server guidelines before using mentions.
- Some roles may have mention restrictions, meaning you cannot ping them without permission.

✅ Use Role Mentions for Team Coordination

- If you're part of a team (e.g., moderators, event organizers), use role mentions to efficiently coordinate tasks.
- Example:
- @EventHosts Reminder: The live Q&A session starts in 30 minutes!

✅ Keep Notifications Manageable

- If you receive too many mentions, consider muting channels or adjusting mention settings in Discord.
- Administrators can control who can use mentions by modifying role settings.

Managing Mentions and Notifications

If you find mentions overwhelming, Discord provides several options to customize notifications and mute unnecessary pings.

1. Muting a Channel or Server

If you don't want to receive notifications from a specific channel or server, you can mute it:

- Right-click the channel or server name

- Select Mute Channel or Mute Server

- Choose how long you want to mute notifications (e.g., 1 hour, 8 hours, indefinitely)

2. Adjusting Mention Settings

To control which mentions notify you:

- Go to User Settings > Notifications

- Under Server Notification Settings, customize how you receive notifications.

- You can disable @everyone and @here mentions.

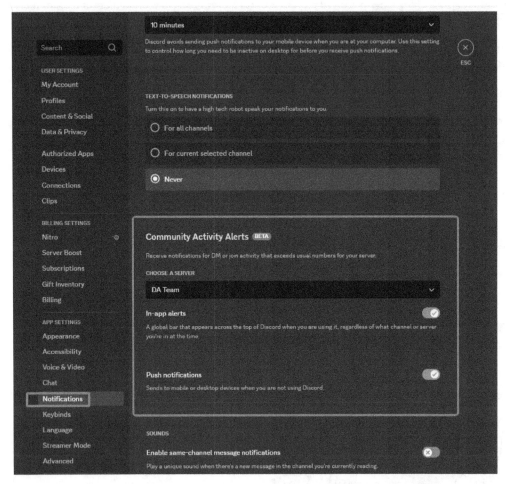

3. Using "Do Not Disturb" Mode

If you need a break from notifications, set your status to Do Not Disturb (DND). This will block all mention alerts until you change your status back.

Conclusion

Mentions and pings are essential for effective communication in Discord. They allow you to grab attention, notify groups, and direct users to important discussions. However, using them thoughtfully and responsibly ensures that they remain a helpful tool rather than an annoyance.

By following best practices and managing notifications wisely, you can maintain a healthy, productive Discord experience without being overwhelmed by excessive pings.

Next Section: Chapter 3 - Customizing Your Discord Experience

In the next chapter, we will explore how to **customize your Discord experience**, including themes, notification settings, and personalizing your profile.

CHAPTER III
Voice and Video Communication

3.1 Using Voice Channels

3.1.1 Joining and Leaving Voice Channels

Discord's voice channels provide a seamless way for users to communicate in real-time without the need for initiating calls. Unlike traditional voice chat applications, where users must manually call others, Discord's voice channels function more like virtual meeting rooms, where users can join and leave at any time. This feature is particularly useful for gaming, team collaboration, study groups, and social interactions.

This section will guide you through the process of joining and leaving voice channels, including understanding voice channel types, configuring microphone settings, troubleshooting common issues, and maximizing your audio experience.

1. Understanding Voice Channels in Discord

What Are Voice Channels?

Voice channels in Discord are persistent, open communication spaces within a server that allow users to join and talk instantly. Unlike text channels, where messages remain for later viewing, voice channels facilitate real-time voice communication.

Types of Voice Channels

There are several types of voice channels in Discord, each with unique features:

- **Standard Voice Channels:**

- o   These are the default voice channels in any Discord server.

- o   Users can freely join and leave without needing an invitation.

- o   Ideal for casual conversations, gaming, and discussions.

- **Stage Channels** (Available in Community Servers):

  - o   Designed for one-to-many communication, similar to a live podcast.

  - o   Only certain users (moderators or designated speakers) can speak, while others listen.

  - o   Perfect for Q&A sessions, live events, and large community discussions.

- **Private Voice Channels**:

  - o   Channels with restricted access based on user roles and permissions.

  - o   Useful for team meetings, friend groups, and exclusive discussions.

- **Temporary Voice Channels (Bots Required)**:

  - o   Some bots allow users to create temporary voice channels that disappear when everyone leaves.

  - o   Useful for on-the-fly meetings or private discussions.

2. How to Join a Voice Channel

Joining a voice channel is one of the most straightforward actions in Discord. You simply need to navigate to a server, locate a voice channel, and click to enter.

Step-by-Step Guide to Joining a Voice Channel

1. **Open Discord**

   - o   Launch the Discord app on Windows, macOS, Linux, iOS, Android, or open it in a web browser.

   - o   Ensure that you are logged into your account.

2. **Select a Server**

   - o   On the left-hand panel, you'll see a list of servers you have joined.

o   Click on the server that contains the voice channel you want to join.

3. **Locate the Voice Channels Section**

o   In the server's channel list, voice channels are indicated by a speaker icon 🎤.

o   If you don't see any voice channels, it may be due to:

▪   Role restrictions preventing you from seeing them.

▪   The server not having any voice channels configured.

4. **Click on a Voice Channel**

o   Simply click on the name of the voice channel to enter.

o   You should now see a voice connection indicator at the bottom left of the Discord interface.

o   If you are using Discord on mobile, tap on the channel name and then tap Join Voice.

5. **Confirm Your Microphone and Audio Settings**

o   Before speaking, ensure your **microphone and headset/speakers are working**.

o   You can adjust your input/output devices by clicking **User Settings (⚙️)** **> Voice & Video**.

6. **Start Speaking!**

o   If you are using **Push-to-Talk (PTT)**, press the assigned key to speak.

o   If using **Voice Activity Detection**, Discord will automatically transmit audio when it detects your voice.

---

3. How to Leave a Voice Channel

Leaving a voice channel is just as simple as joining one.

Methods to Leave a Voice Channel

1. **Click the Disconnect Button**

   o In the bottom-left corner, you'll see a small **phone icon with an "X"** (📞✕).

   o Click this icon to immediately disconnect from the voice channel.

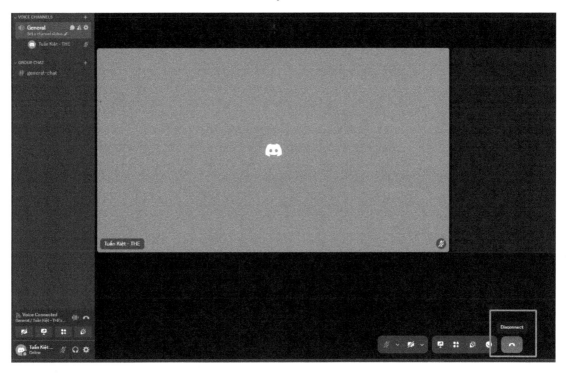

2. **Switch to Another Channel**

   o Clicking on a different **voice channel** will automatically switch you to that channel, leaving the previous one.

3. **Close Discord (Desktop & Mobile)**

   o If you **quit the Discord application**, you will be disconnected from the voice channel.

   o However, closing the window on desktop **without quitting Discord** will not disconnect you.

4. **On Mobile: Press "Leave Voice"**

○ If using the **Discord mobile app**, tap the **voice channel banner** at the bottom and press **"Leave Voice"**.

4. Troubleshooting Common Issues When Joining or Leaving a Voice Channel

Sometimes, you may encounter issues when attempting to join or leave a voice channel. Below are common problems and their solutions.

Issue #1: Can't Join a Voice Channel

Possible Causes & Solutions:

✓ You lack the necessary permissions.

- If the channel is restricted, contact a server admin to grant you access.

✓ Your microphone or headset is not connected properly.

- Ensure your devices are plugged in and correctly recognized in Voice & Video settings.

✓ Discord is blocked by your network or firewall.

- If you are on a school or work network, use a VPN or switch to mobile data.

Issue #2: No One Can Hear You

Possible Causes & Solutions:

✓ Your microphone is muted.

- Check if your mic icon is red with a line through it and unmute it.

✓ Your input device is incorrect.

- Go to User Settings > Voice & Video and ensure the correct mic is selected.

✓ Push-to-Talk mode is enabled but not configured.

- Assign a Push-to-Talk key in your settings and use it while speaking.

Issue #3: Can't Leave a Voice Channel

Possible Causes & Solutions:

✓ Discord is frozen or unresponsive.

- Restart the app or use Task Manager (Windows) / Force Quit (Mac).

✓ A bot or admin has locked you in the channel.

- Ask a server admin to check role permissions and ensure you have the ability to disconnect.

5. Tips for a Better Voice Channel Experience

Use a Good Microphone & Headset

- A dedicated microphone or headset improves sound quality.
- Avoid laptop built-in mics, as they often pick up background noise.

Adjust Your Discord Audio Settings

- Set a proper input sensitivity in Voice & Video settings.
- Enable Echo Cancellation and Noise Suppression for clearer audio.

Avoid Background Noise

- Use Push-to-Talk (PTT) if you're in a noisy environment.
- Adjust noise suppression settings to minimize unwanted sounds.

Mute Yourself When Not Speaking

- In large voice chats, muting yourself prevents unnecessary background noise.
- Use the mute button (microphone icon) in the bottom-left of Discord.

Test Your Voice Before Joining

- Go to **User Settings > Voice & Video** and use the **"Let's Check" test feature** to verify your mic.

Conclusion

Joining and leaving voice channels on Discord is a simple yet essential skill for effective communication. Whether you're using Discord for gaming, work, education, or socializing, understanding how to properly navigate voice channels ensures a seamless experience.

In the next section, we will cover **3.1.2 Adjusting Microphone and Audio Settings**, where you'll learn how to fine-tune your voice settings for the best sound quality.

3.1.2 Adjusting Microphone and Audio Settings

Voice communication is one of Discord's most powerful features, allowing users to talk in real time through voice channels. However, to ensure a smooth and high-quality experience, it's essential to configure microphone and audio settings properly. Poor audio settings can result in issues such as background noise, distorted sound, or microphone malfunctions. In this section, we will cover everything you need to know about adjusting your microphone and audio settings in Discord.

1. Accessing Voice and Audio Settings

To adjust microphone and audio settings in Discord, follow these steps:

1. **Open Discord and go to User Settings**

   o Click on the **gear icon** (⚙□) in the bottom-left corner next to your username.

   o This will open the **User Settings** menu.

2. **Navigate to the "Voice & Video" settings**

   o In the left-hand menu, under "App Settings," click on **"Voice & Video."**

   o This section contains all the settings related to microphone, speaker output, and audio quality.

3. **Select Your Input and Output Devices**

   o Under **Input Device**, choose the correct microphone from the drop-down menu.

    o Under **Output Device**, select the appropriate speakers or headset.

💡 *Tip:* If you're using an external microphone or headset, ensure it's plugged in before opening Discord, or restart Discord after connecting it to detect new audio devices.

2. Adjusting Microphone Sensitivity

A. Setting Input Volume

The **Input Volume** slider allows you to adjust how loud your voice is when speaking into the microphone.

- If people can't hear you, increase the input volume.
- If your voice sounds too loud or distorted, decrease the input volume.
- The goal is to find a balance where your voice is clear without background noise being picked up.

B. Enabling and Configuring Automatic Input Sensitivity

Automatic Input Sensitivity determines how much sound Discord should pick up from your microphone.

1. **Enable or disable automatic detection:**
   - By default, Discord automatically adjusts microphone sensitivity.
   - To fine-tune it manually, **toggle off** "Automatically determine input sensitivity."

2. **Manually adjust the sensitivity bar:**
   - Move the slider left or right to set the threshold for voice activation.
   - If set too high, Discord may not pick up your voice properly.
   - If set too low, it might pick up background noise like keyboard typing or fan noise.

💡 *Tip:* If your microphone is picking up too much background noise, consider **increasing the threshold** so that only louder sounds (like your voice) activate it.

3. Choosing Between Push-to-Talk and Voice Activity

A. Voice Activity Mode

- When enabled, Discord **automatically detects** when you're speaking.

- Works well for casual conversations and gaming when hands-free communication is needed.

- Best used with a properly configured microphone sensitivity to avoid picking up unwanted noise.

B. Push-to-Talk (PTT) Mode

- Requires pressing and holding a **designated key** to activate the microphone.

- Prevents background noise or accidental sounds from being transmitted.

- Ideal for noisy environments or professional settings.

How to Enable Push-to-Talk

1. Go to **Voice & Video settings** in Discord.

2. Under **Input Mode**, select **Push to Talk**.

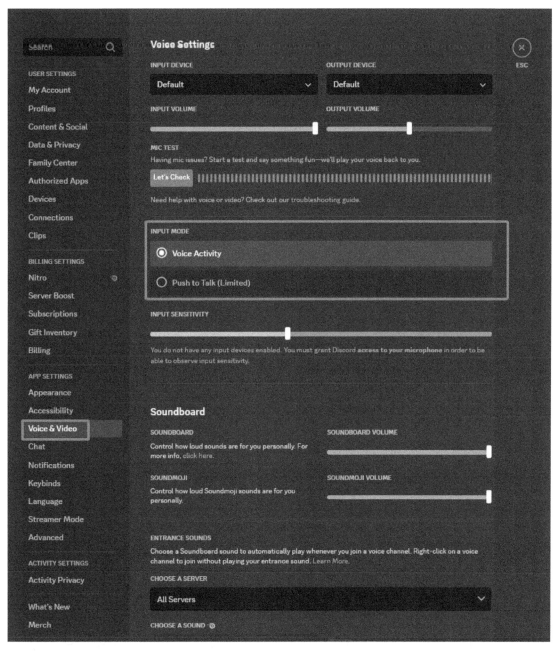

3. Assign a keybinding by clicking **"Shortcut"** and pressing a key (e.g., Left Control or Mouse Button 4).

💡 *Tip:* You can set a **release delay** to keep the microphone active for a brief moment after releasing the key, ensuring your voice isn't cut off too soon.

4. Managing Output Volume and Audio Balance

A. Adjusting Output Volume

If you have trouble hearing others, increase the **Output Volume** slider under "Voice & Video" settings.

- If other users sound too quiet, increase output volume.

- If they are too loud or distorted, decrease output volume.

B. Individual User Volume Control

If one person is too loud or quiet compared to others, you can adjust their volume individually.

1. Right-click their name in a voice channel.

2. Use the user volume slider to adjust their volume.

💡 *Tip:* This feature is useful in large voice channels where some users have louder microphones than others.

5. Enabling and Configuring Noise Suppression

A. Discord's Built-in Noise Suppression

Discord offers Krisp Noise Suppression, which filters out background noise like keyboard typing, fan noise, or dogs barking.

1. Go to Voice & Video settings.

2. Scroll down to Noise Suppression and enable "Krisp".

💡 *Tip:* If your microphone picks up a lot of background noise, enabling Krisp can significantly improve audio quality.

B. Echo Cancellation and Automatic Gain Control

These settings further improve microphone clarity:

- Echo Cancellation: Removes feedback if you're not using headphones.

- Automatic Gain Control: Adjusts your microphone's sensitivity dynamically based on your speaking volume.

6. Troubleshooting Common Microphone and Audio Issues

A. Microphone Not Working?

If your microphone isn't working in Discord, try the following steps:

1. Check if the microphone is muted (on the hardware or Discord).

2. Verify that the correct microphone is selected in "Voice & Video" settings.

3. Restart Discord after connecting a new microphone.

4. Check microphone permissions:

   o On Windows, go to Settings > Privacy > Microphone and ensure Discord has access.

   o On Mac, go to System Preferences > Security & Privacy > Microphone.

B. Other Users Can't Hear You Clearly?

If others say your voice is distorted, robotic, or too quiet:

- Lower Input Sensitivity if your voice cuts out.

- Increase Input Volume if your voice is too quiet.

- Enable Echo Cancellation and Noise Suppression if there is excessive background noise.

C. Audio Cutting In and Out?

- Disable "Automatically determine input sensitivity" and set a manual threshold.

- Use a wired connection instead of Wi-Fi to reduce network lag.

- Check for server issues in Discord's status page: status.discord.com.

Conclusion

Properly configuring your microphone and audio settings is crucial for clear communication on Discord. By adjusting **input sensitivity, volume levels, and noise suppression**, you can ensure high-quality voice chat with minimal background noise.

In the next section, we will explore **Push-to-Talk vs. Open Mic**, helping you decide which input mode is best for your needs.

3.1.3 Push-to-Talk vs. Open Mic

Voice communication is one of Discord's most powerful features, allowing users to seamlessly talk with friends, teammates, and communities in real-time. Within voice channels, Discord provides two primary methods of communication: **Push-to-Talk (PTT)** and **Open Mic (Voice Activity)**. Both options have distinct advantages and disadvantages, making them suitable for different scenarios. Understanding the differences and knowing how to configure them properly can significantly improve your experience on Discord.

1. What is Push-to-Talk (PTT)?

Push-to-Talk (PTT) is a mode in which your microphone remains muted by default, and you must press and hold a designated key to transmit your voice. Once you release the key, your microphone turns off again. This method is widely used in gaming, professional meetings, and public Discord servers where background noise management is crucial.

How Push-to-Talk Works in Discord

1. **Microphone Activation:** Your microphone remains **inactive** until you press and hold your assigned PTT key.

2. **Voice Transmission:** While holding the key, your voice is **transmitted in real-time** to the voice channel.

3. **Mute on Release:** Once you release the key, your microphone **automatically mutes** again.

Benefits of Using Push-to-Talk

- Eliminates Background Noise: Since your mic is only active when you press the button, background sounds like keyboard typing, fan noise, pets, or roommates won't be accidentally transmitted.

- Improves Audio Clarity: It ensures that only intentional speech is transmitted, reducing interruptions and unwanted sounds.

- Ideal for Group Communication: Many Discord servers, especially large ones, require PTT mode to keep conversations organized and free from constant open-mic noise.

- Reduces Echo Issues: If multiple people are in the same room, PTT helps prevent audio feedback from overlapping microphones.

Drawbacks of Push-to-Talk

- Requires Manual Activation: You must remember to hold the key while speaking, which may be inconvenient during intense gameplay or multitasking.

- May Cause Delays: If you forget to press the button before speaking, your words may be cut off.

- Not Ideal for Hands-Free Use: For activities that require both hands (e.g., using a controller), Push-to-Talk can be less convenient.

---

2. What is Open Mic (Voice Activity)?

Open Mic, also known as Voice Activity Detection (VAD), automatically activates your microphone when Discord detects your voice. You don't need to press a button—your microphone stays open, and Discord transmits your speech whenever you talk.

How Open Mic Works in Discord

1. Continuous Monitoring: Discord constantly listens to input from your microphone.

2. Voice Detection: When Discord detects speech, it transmits the audio.

3. Auto-Muting: If no speech is detected, Discord automatically stops transmission until it hears you again.

Benefits of Using Open Mic

- Hands-Free Communication: Perfect for situations where you need both hands free, such as using a controller, typing, or handling other tasks.

- Seamless and Natural Conversations: No need to remember to press a button—ideal for casual chats and long discussions.

- Better for Social and Casual Use: Great for talking with friends and family in relaxed settings where background noise isn't a concern.

Drawbacks of Open Mic

- Background Noise Issues: Discord may pick up unwanted sounds like keyboard clicks, breathing, background music, or environmental noise.

- Accidental Interruptions: If Discord misinterprets a sound as speech, it may activate the mic even when you're not talking.

- Echo and Feedback Problems: Open Mic can cause echoing, especially if multiple users are in the same room or using speakers instead of headphones.

3. How to Configure Push-to-Talk and Open Mic in Discord

Enabling Push-to-Talk

1. Open Discord and go to User Settings (⚙️ gear icon at the bottom left).

2. Navigate to Voice & Video under the App Settings section.

3. Under Input Mode, select Push to Talk.

4. Click on Record Keybind and press the key you want to use for PTT.

5. Adjust the Push-to-Talk Release Delay slider if needed. This controls how long Discord keeps transmitting after you release the button.

6. Close the settings and test it in a voice channel to ensure proper functionality.

Enabling Open Mic (Voice Activity)

1. Open Discord and go to User Settings (⚙️ gear icon).

2. Navigate to Voice & Video under App Settings.

3. Under Input Mode, select Voice Activity.

4. Adjust the Input Sensitivity slider. If set to Automatic, Discord will determine the best sensitivity. If using Manual mode, drag the slider to adjust when Discord should activate your mic.

5. Close settings and test in a voice channel to ensure your voice is detected properly.

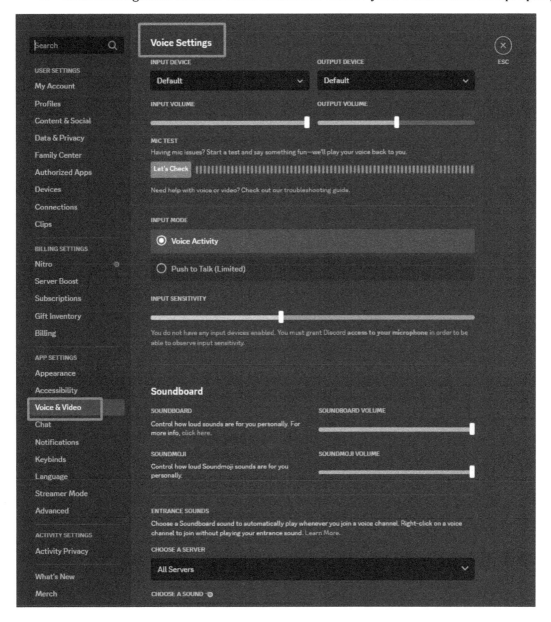

4. When to Use Push-to-Talk vs. Open Mic

Best Situations for Push-to-Talk

✓ In public servers where background noise must be minimized.
✓ In competitive gaming where clear communication is critical.
✓ In group meetings and professional settings to avoid disrupting others.
✓ When using a noisy microphone setup or gaming in a loud environment.

Best Situations for Open Mic

✓ In private voice chats with friends where background noise isn't an issue.
✓ When using headphones and a high-quality microphone to minimize unintended noise.
✓ In long conversations where pressing a key repeatedly is inconvenient.
✓ When engaged in casual gaming, social interactions, or podcasts.

5. Tips for Optimizing Your Voice Settings in Discord

Regardless of which mode you use, optimizing your settings ensures a better audio experience for you and others in your Discord community.

◆ Use a Quality Microphone – External USB microphones provide clearer audio than built-in laptop mics.
◆ Adjust Input Sensitivity – Fine-tune voice detection to avoid cut-off words or background noise activation.
◆ Use Headphones – Prevents audio feedback and echoing caused by open speakers.
◆ Test Before Joining Calls – Use the "Mic Test" feature in Discord settings to check if your audio is clear.
◆ Reduce Background Noise – Enable Noise Suppression (Krisp) in Discord to minimize unwanted sounds.

Conclusion

Push-to-Talk and Open Mic are two essential communication modes in Discord, each offering unique benefits depending on the situation. Push-to-Talk is perfect for minimizing background noise in professional or gaming environments, while Open Mic is ideal for casual conversations and hands-free communication.

By understanding how these modes work and configuring them correctly, you can enhance your Discord voice experience and communicate more effectively with your friends, teammates, and communities.

Next Section: 3.2 Video Calls and Screen Sharing

In the next section, we'll dive into **Discord's video calling and screen-sharing features**, covering how to start a call, optimize video quality, and share content efficiently.

3.2 Video Calls and Screen Sharing

3.2.1 Starting a Video Call on Discord

Discord offers a seamless way to communicate with others through **video calls**, making it a versatile platform for casual conversations, professional meetings, online classes, and gaming-related discussions. Whether you're connecting with friends, collaborating with teammates, or hosting an event, Discord's **video calling feature** provides high-quality video and audio, along with additional tools like screen sharing and virtual backgrounds.

In this section, we will cover everything you need to know about **starting a video call on Discord**, including how to initiate a call, adjust settings for better quality, and troubleshoot common issues.

---

1. How to Start a Video Call on Discord

Discord provides **three main ways** to start a video call:

1. **Direct Messages (DMs) and Group Chats** – You can start a one-on-one or small group video call directly from a private chat.

2. **Voice Channels in Servers** – You can join a voice channel in a server and enable video.

3. **Stage Channels (for larger audiences)** – While Stage Channels primarily focus on voice conversations, hosts can enable video sharing in certain settings.

Let's explore how to start a video call using each of these methods.

1.1 Starting a Video Call in Direct Messages (DMs)

If you want to start a video call with a friend or a small group, Discord allows you to do so directly from the **Direct Messages (DMs)** section.

Step-by-Step Guide for One-on-One Video Calls:

1. **Open Discord** and navigate to the **Direct Messages** tab.

2. Click on the **user's name** you want to call.

3. In the top-right corner of the chat window, click the **video camera icon**.

4. Your call will begin immediately, and the other person will receive a notification to join.

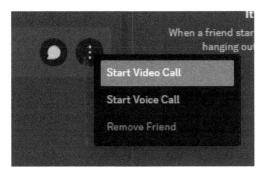

Starting a Video Call with a Group Chat:

If you have a **group DM** with multiple people, you can start a group video call by following these steps:

1. **Open the group chat** in the Direct Messages section.

2. Click on the **video camera icon** in the top-right corner.

3. The call will begin, and all members of the group will receive an invitation to join.

4. Each participant can **enable or disable their camera and microphone** as needed.

Note: Group DM video calls support up to **25 participants** at once.

1.2 Starting a Video Call in a Server Voice Channel

For larger discussions, Discord allows users to **enable video within a voice channel** in a server.

Step-by-Step Guide to Start a Video Call in a Server:

1. **Join a voice channel** in your Discord server.

2. Once inside, click the **video camera icon** at the bottom of the screen.

3. Your video feed will now be visible to other users in the channel.

4. Anyone else in the channel can also turn on their cameras to participate.

Managing Video Calls in a Server:

- Only users with the appropriate permissions can enable video in some channels. If you're unable to turn on your camera, check with the server admin.

- Some servers limit video calls to specific roles. If you can't start a video call, check the permissions settings.

- You can resize video windows by clicking and dragging the participant's video feed.

2. Adjusting Video Settings for Best Quality

Once you've started a video call, you may want to adjust certain settings to improve the video and audio quality.

2.1 Changing Video and Camera Settings

To access and modify your video settings:

1. Click on the User Settings (gear icon) in the bottom-left corner.
2. Navigate to Voice & Video settings.
3. Under the Video Settings section, select the camera you want to use.
4. Click the Test Video button to preview your camera feed.
5. Adjust video resolution (higher resolutions improve quality but require more bandwidth).

2.2 Adjusting Video Layouts in a Call

Discord provides multiple layout options for video calls:

- Grid View – Displays all participants in equal-sized windows.
- Focus View – Highlights the person currently speaking while keeping others minimized.
- Pop-Out View – Allows you to move the video feed outside the Discord window.

You can switch between these views by clicking the layout button in the top-right corner during a call.

3. Troubleshooting Common Issues

Sometimes, users may face issues when starting a video call on Discord. Here are some common problems and their solutions:

3.1 Camera Not Working?

- Check permissions: Make sure Discord has permission to access your camera.

- Restart Discord: Close the app and reopen it to reset any temporary issues.

- Test with another app: Check if your camera works in Zoom or Skype. If not, the issue may be with your device.

- Update drivers: Ensure your webcam drivers are up to date.

3.2 Poor Video Quality?

- Check internet speed: A slow connection can cause pixelation or lag.

- Lower resolution: Reduce video resolution in settings for a smoother experience.

- Close background apps: Other applications using bandwidth (e.g., downloads, streaming) can affect video quality.

3.3 Call Not Connecting?

- Check Discord server status: Visit Discord's status page to see if there are any ongoing issues.

- Restart your router: A quick reset can fix network problems.

- Use a wired connection: Ethernet provides a more stable connection than Wi-Fi.

---

4. Advanced Features in Discord Video Calls

Discord also offers advanced features to enhance your video calling experience:

Virtual Backgrounds

- Some Discord versions allow users to blur or change their background.

- You can enable this feature from the Video Settings menu.

Screen Sharing During a Video Call

- Click the "Share Your Screen" button to let others see your display.

- Choose specific applications or your entire screen to share.

Using Bots for Video Calls

- Some Discord bots offer extra functionalities like auto-recording or adding fun effects.

Conclusion

Starting a video call on Discord is easy and highly customizable, making it ideal for personal and professional use. Whether you're chatting with friends, collaborating on projects, or hosting virtual events, Discord's **video calling feature** provides a reliable and high-quality experience.

In the next section, we will explore **screen sharing on Discord**, including how to share your screen, adjust settings, and troubleshoot common issues.

3.2.2 Sharing Your Screen with Others

Screen sharing is one of Discord's most powerful features, enabling users to broadcast their screen to friends, colleagues, or community members in real time. Whether you're hosting a gaming session, conducting a virtual presentation, or collaborating on a project, Discord's screen-sharing functionality provides a smooth and efficient experience. This section will cover how to start screen sharing, configure settings for optimal quality, and troubleshoot common issues.

1. Introduction to Screen Sharing on Discord

Screen sharing on Discord allows you to stream your desktop, a specific application, or even a browser window directly into a voice or video call. Unlike traditional video conferencing tools, Discord offers **low-latency, high-quality** streaming, making it an ideal choice for gamers, educators, and professionals.

Key Benefits of Discord's Screen Sharing Feature:

- High-Quality Streaming – Supports up to 1080p at 60 FPS with Discord Nitro.

- Low Latency – Designed for smooth real-time interactions.

- Multiple Streaming Options – Share your entire screen or a specific window.

- Integrated Audio – Share system audio along with the video stream.

Whether you're streaming gameplay to friends, teaching someone how to use software, or collaborating remotely, Discord's screen-sharing tool is versatile and easy to use.

2. How to Share Your Screen on Discord

2.1 Prerequisites for Screen Sharing

Before you start screen sharing, ensure that:

- You have joined a voice or video channel in a server or started a private call.

- Your Discord app is up to date to avoid bugs or missing features.

- You have granted necessary permissions (on Windows or macOS) for Discord to capture your screen.

2.2 Steps to Share Your Screen

Method 1: Sharing Your Screen in a Private Call

1. **Open Discord** and navigate to your **Direct Messages (DMs)**.

2. Start a **voice or video call** by clicking the **phone or video icon**.

3. Once the call starts, click the **"Share Your Screen"** button at the bottom of the call window.

4. Choose what you want to share:

   o **Your Entire Screen** – Shares everything on your display.

   o **A Specific Application Window** – Only shares a single program.

   o **A Browser Tab** – Useful for presenting online content.

5. Click **"Go Live"** to start streaming.

Method 2: Sharing Your Screen in a Server Voice Channel

1. Join a **voice channel** in a Discord server.

2. Click the **"Share Your Screen"** button at the bottom-left of the app.

3. Select your **screen, application, or browser window**.

4. Adjust **quality settings** (resolution and frame rate).

5. Click **"Go Live"** to begin streaming to everyone in the channel.

3. Configuring Screen Share Settings for Best Quality

Adjusting Video Quality Settings

To improve the clarity and smoothness of your stream, Discord offers several quality settings:

- Resolution Options: 480p, 720p, 1080p (Higher resolutions require Discord Nitro).

- Frame Rate: 15, 30, or 60 FPS (Higher FPS is better for gaming and fast-moving visuals).

- Bitrate Control: Adjusts how much data is transmitted to improve stream stability.

Enabling System Audio Sharing

By default, screen sharing does not include system audio unless specifically enabled. To share audio:

- Ensure you select an application window (not the entire screen).

- On Windows, enable the "Share Audio" toggle before clicking "Go Live."

- On macOS, you may need to install an additional audio driver for Discord to capture system sound.

4. Advanced Features of Screen Sharing

Using Picture-in-Picture Mode

Discord allows users to watch a screen share while continuing to navigate through the app.

- Click the pop-out button to detach the screen share into a floating window.
- Resize and move the window anywhere on your screen.

Switching Between Applications While Streaming

You can change which application you're sharing without restarting the stream:

1. Click the "Screen" button again while streaming.
2. Choose a different application or browser tab.
3. Click "Go Live" again to switch seamlessly.

Streaming Multiple Screens

With Discord Nitro, users can share multiple screens at once, allowing for multi-tasking in team collaborations.

5. Troubleshooting Common Screen Sharing Issues

No Video or Black Screen Issue

If viewers see a black screen instead of your shared content:

- Disable Hardware Acceleration in Discord settings.
- Run Discord as an Administrator (Windows).
- Ensure your graphics drivers are up to date.
- Try sharing an application window instead of the full screen.

Audio Not Working While Screen Sharing

If your stream has no audio:

- Ensure "Share Audio" is enabled when selecting an application.
- Check Discord's Input/Output settings under "Voice & Video."
- On Mac, install the extra audio driver from Discord's support page.

Lagging or Low-Quality Stream

If your stream is buffering or pixelated:

- Lower the resolution and FPS settings.

- Close unnecessary background apps to free up bandwidth.

- Use a wired Ethernet connection for a stable internet connection.

6. Best Practices for Screen Sharing

- **Use Push-to-Talk** – Prevents accidental noise interference while sharing.

- **Optimize Your Screen Layout** – Keep only necessary windows open to avoid distractions.

- **Mute Notifications** – Turn off pop-ups that could interrupt the stream.

- **Engage with Viewers** – Use Discord chat to answer questions or clarify points while presenting.

7. Conclusion

Screen sharing on Discord is a powerful tool for collaboration, gaming, education, and entertainment. With high-quality streaming, low latency, and customizable settings, users can easily share their screens for various purposes. By following this guide, you can maximize the efficiency and clarity of your Discord screen-sharing sessions.

Next Section: 3.2.3 Managing Video Call Quality

In the next section, we will explore how to fine-tune video call settings to ensure the best possible communication experience on Discord.

3.2.3 Managing Video Call Quality

Video calls on Discord allow users to communicate face-to-face with high-quality audio and video, making it a powerful tool for both casual and professional use. However, ensuring a smooth and high-quality video call experience requires understanding and optimizing several key factors, including network settings, hardware performance, and Discord's built-in features.

In this section, we'll explore the factors affecting video call quality, how to optimize Discord's settings, troubleshoot common issues, and enhance the overall experience when using Discord for video calls.

1. Factors Affecting Video Call Quality

Several factors influence the quality of a video call on Discord. Understanding these elements will help you identify potential issues and improve the clarity, stability, and smoothness of your calls.

1.1 Internet Connection

Your network plays a crucial role in determining the quality of a video call. Here are the most important network-related factors:

- Bandwidth: Discord requires a stable internet connection with sufficient bandwidth. A minimum of 5 Mbps upload and download speed is recommended for smooth video calls.

- Latency (Ping): High ping can lead to delays and lag. Ideally, your ping should be below 50 ms for an optimal experience.

- Packet Loss: A high packet loss percentage can cause video freezing, choppiness, or disconnections.

- Wi-Fi vs. Wired Connection: A wired Ethernet connection is always more stable than Wi-Fi, reducing latency and improving video quality.

1.2 Hardware Performance

Your device's performance directly affects video call quality. The following hardware factors are important:

- CPU Usage: Video encoding and decoding are CPU-intensive tasks. If your CPU is under heavy load, your video may lag or freeze.

- RAM Availability: Insufficient RAM can cause stuttering. It is recommended to have at least 8GB of RAM for smooth performance.

- Graphics Processing Unit (GPU): Some high-quality video calls use GPU acceleration. A dedicated GPU can improve performance, especially for screen sharing.

- Webcam Quality: The resolution of your webcam affects the clarity of your video. A 1080p or higher webcam will provide the best results.

1.3 Discord Server Region and Call Settings

Discord automatically assigns a server region based on your location, but a poorly selected region can cause lag. Choosing the right server region can improve stability and reduce latency.

- Optimizing server region:

  - Open your Discord voice/video call and click the region selector (available in group calls and private servers).

  - Choose the region closest to all participants to reduce delay.

  - If a region is experiencing issues, try switching to another nearby region.

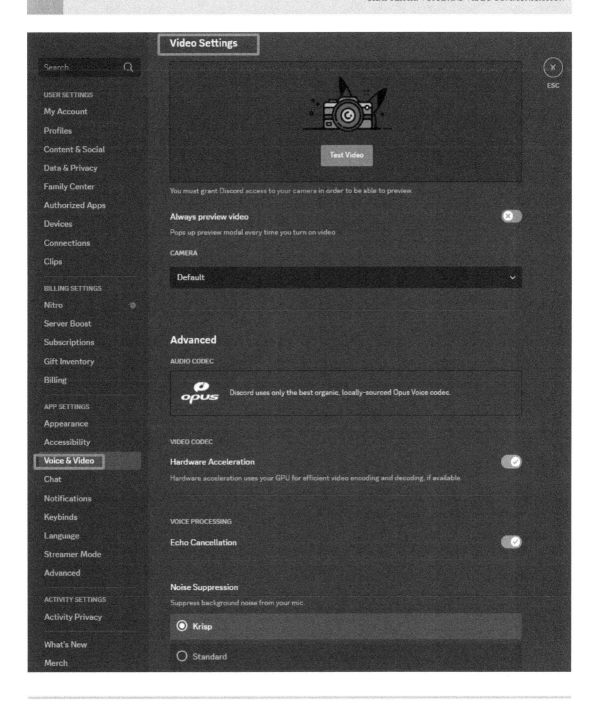

2. Optimizing Discord Video Call Settings

Discord provides several settings to enhance video call performance and quality. Adjusting these options can improve clarity, reduce lag, and ensure a smoother experience.

2.1 Adjusting Video Quality Settings

To customize video settings in Discord, follow these steps:

1. Open User Settings by clicking the ⚙☐ icon in the bottom-left corner.

2. Navigate to Voice & Video under the "App Settings" section.

3. Scroll down to the Video Settings section.

4. Adjust the following options:

    o Video Resolution: Set to 720p or 1080p for high-quality video (if supported by your webcam).

    o Frame Rate: Choose 30 FPS for standard quality or 60 FPS for smoother motion (useful for screen sharing gaming content).

    o Enable or Disable Hardware Acceleration: If you experience lag, try enabling or disabling this option based on your device's performance.

2.2 Managing Bitrate for Smoother Video Calls

Bitrate affects both audio and video quality in calls. Higher bitrates result in better quality but require more bandwidth and processing power.

To adjust bitrate:

- If you are on a Discord server, go to the Voice Channel Settings.

- Adjust the bitrate slider based on your network speed and hardware.

- Recommended bitrate settings:

    o Low quality: 64 kbps (for slow connections)

    o Standard quality: 96–128 kbps

    o High quality: 256 kbps or higher (for fast connections and Nitro users)

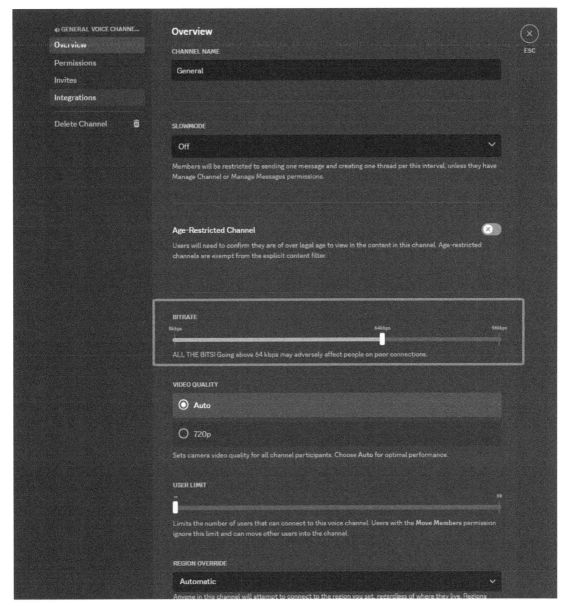

2.3 Using Noise Suppression and Echo Cancellation

Discord offers built-in noise suppression and echo cancellation features to improve voice and video clarity.

- **Krisp Noise Suppression** (AI-powered feature):

- o Helps reduce background noise (e.g., typing sounds, fan noise, barking dogs).

- o Can be enabled in Voice & Video settings under Noise Suppression.

- **Echo Cancellation and Automatic Gain Control (AGC):**

  - o Prevents audio feedback and distortion.

  - o Can be adjusted in Voice & Video settings.

3. Troubleshooting Common Video Call Issues

Even with optimized settings, you may still encounter issues with video calls. Here's how to identify and fix common problems:

3.1 Video Freezing or Lagging

Possible causes:

- Slow internet speed → Test your internet speed using Speedtest. https://www.speedtest.net/

- High CPU usage → Close unnecessary applications running in the background.

- Low RAM availability → Restart your computer or close memory-heavy programs.

Solutions:

- Lower the video resolution and frame rate in Discord Video Settings.

- Switch to a wired internet connection for better stability.

- Reduce the number of participants in the video call.

3.2 Poor Audio or Video Quality

Possible causes:

- Incorrect video settings in Discord.

- Weak network connection.

- Low-quality webcam or microphone.

Solutions:

- Ensure video resolution is set to 720p or higher in settings.

- Increase the bitrate for better clarity.

- Try using an external webcam or microphone for higher quality.

3.3 Screen Sharing is Blurry or Laggy

Possible causes:

- Low frame rate or resolution settings.

- High CPU or GPU usage.

Solutions:

- Increase the frame rate to 60 FPS in screen sharing settings.

- Enable "Use our latest technology to capture your screen" in Discord Voice & Video settings.

- Lower the number of background applications consuming CPU resources.

4. Enhancing the Video Call Experience

4.1 Upgrading to Discord Nitro

Discord Nitro offers higher video quality and additional features that enhance the overall experience:

- HD video streaming (1080p, 60 FPS).

- Better bitrate for improved audio quality.

- Increased file upload limit (from 8MB to 100MB).

4.2 Using External Software for Advanced Video Features

For users looking for professional-quality video calls, integrating Discord with external software can help:

- OBS Studio (for advanced screen sharing and streaming).

- NVIDIA Broadcast (for AI-powered background removal and noise cancellation).

Conclusion

Managing video call quality on Discord requires optimizing network settings, hardware performance, and Discord's built-in features. By following the best practices outlined in this chapter, you can ensure smooth, high-quality video calls for gaming, business meetings, education, or social hangouts.

3.3 Advanced Audio Settings

3.3.1 Noise Suppression and Echo Cancellation

Clear and high-quality audio is crucial for an enjoyable communication experience on Discord. Whether you're using Discord for gaming, business meetings, study groups, or social hangouts, background noise and echo can be distracting and frustrating for other participants. To address these issues, Discord provides **Noise Suppression** and **Echo Cancellation** features, which significantly improve voice clarity by filtering out unwanted sounds.

In this section, we'll explore how these features work, how to enable and configure them, and best practices for optimizing your audio experience on Discord.

1. Understanding Noise Suppression and Echo Cancellation

1.1 What is Noise Suppression?

Noise suppression is an audio enhancement technology that reduces unwanted background noise, such as:

- Keyboard typing sounds

- Fan noise or air conditioning

- Traffic or construction sounds

- Other ambient noises in your environment

Discord's **Noise Suppression** feature is powered by **Krisp**, a leading AI-based noise reduction technology. This feature uses machine learning algorithms to distinguish between your voice and unwanted background noise, filtering out non-speech sounds while preserving the clarity of your voice.

1.2 What is Echo Cancellation?

Echo cancellation is designed to **eliminate echo and feedback** caused by:

- Your microphone picking up the sound from your speakers

- Acoustic reflections from hard surfaces in a room

- Delayed audio feedback during calls

This feature prevents others from hearing their own voices echoed back to them, ensuring a smoother and more comfortable communication experience.

Both Noise Suppression and Echo Cancellation work together to create a clear and distraction-free voice chat environment on Discord.

2. Enabling Noise Suppression and Echo Cancellation on Discord

2.1 How to Enable Noise Suppression

Discord allows users to toggle Noise Suppression both globally (for all voice calls) and individually for each voice channel.

Enabling Noise Suppression for All Calls (Global Setting)

1. Open Discord and click on the User Settings (⚙️☐) icon at the bottom-left corner.

2. Scroll down and select Voice & Video under App Settings.

3. Locate the Noise Suppression section.

4. Toggle on "Noise Suppression (Krisp)" to activate the feature.

5. Speak into your microphone and check the Input Sensitivity bar to confirm that background noise is being filtered out.

Enabling Noise Suppression in a Specific Voice Channel

1. Join a voice channel in a Discord server.

2. Click on the Voice Settings (microphone icon) at the bottom of the screen.

3. Find the Noise Suppression option and toggle it on.

4. You may notice a Krisp logo indicating that the feature is active.

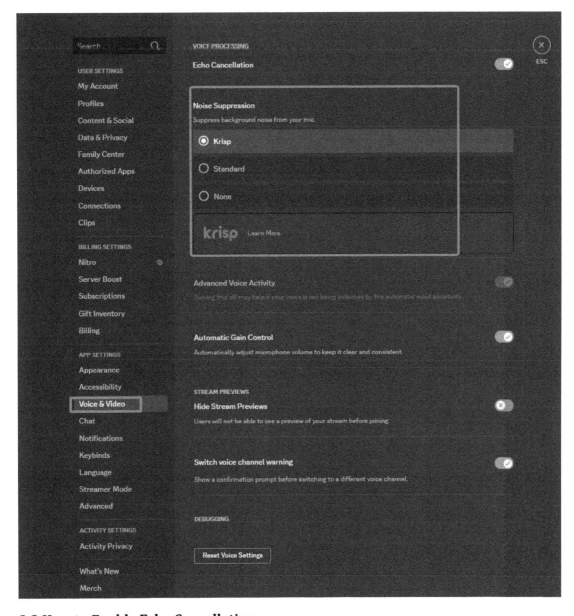

2.2 How to Enable Echo Cancellation

Echo Cancellation is also available within Discord's **Voice & Video settings** and can be activated in a few simple steps:

1. **Go to User Settings** by clicking on the ⚙️ icon in the bottom-left corner.

2. Navigate to **Voice & Video** under **App Settings**.

3. Scroll down to the **Advanced Voice Processing** section.

4. Toggle on **Echo Cancellation** to reduce audio feedback.

3. Testing and Adjusting Your Audio Settings

Testing Your Voice with Discord's Built-in Mic Test

Before using Noise Suppression and Echo Cancellation in a live call, you should test your settings using Discord's Mic Test feature:

1. Go to User Settings > Voice & Video.

2. Find the Mic Test section.

3. Click Let's Check and speak into your microphone.

4. Listen to the playback and adjust settings accordingly.

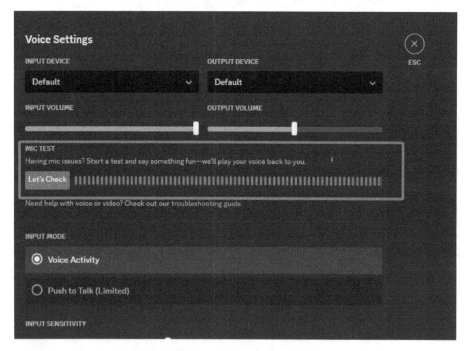

Adjusting Input Sensitivity for Best Performance

Noise Suppression and Echo Cancellation work best when paired with properly adjusted input sensitivity:

- **Automatic Input Sensitivity** (Recommended) – Discord automatically detects and filters background noise.

- **Manual Input Sensitivity** – Users can fine-tune the microphone's activation threshold.

- Adjust the **slider** to filter out unwanted background noise while keeping your voice clear.

---

4. Best Practices for Optimal Audio Quality

Using a Good Quality Microphone

While Noise Suppression and Echo Cancellation help improve audio quality, using a good microphone is essential for the best results. Consider:

- Using a USB or XLR microphone instead of a built-in laptop mic.

- Choosing a directional microphone that focuses on your voice.

- Using a pop filter or foam cover to minimize plosive sounds.

Wearing Headphones to Reduce Echo

One of the most effective ways to prevent echo is by wearing wired or wireless headphones instead of using speakers. This prevents your microphone from picking up output audio, reducing the need for excessive echo cancellation.

Adjusting Microphone Placement

- Position your microphone closer to your mouth for better voice capture.

- Avoid placing the mic too close to noisy devices such as fans or mechanical keyboards.

Using Push-to-Talk for Better Control

If you're in a noisy environment, enabling **Push-to-Talk (PTT)** can be a great alternative. This allows your microphone to transmit only when you press a specific key, preventing unwanted noise.

1. **Go to User Settings > Voice & Video**.

2. Select **Push to Talk** under Input Mode.

3. Assign a **keybind** for activating your mic.

5. Troubleshooting Common Issues with Noise Suppression and Echo Cancellation

Noise Suppression Not Working?

If you find that Noise Suppression isn't filtering background noise effectively, try these fixes:

✓ Restart Discord and ensure the feature is enabled.

✓ Update your audio drivers to the latest version.

✓ Disable conflicting software (e.g., third-party noise suppression programs).

✓ Adjust input sensitivity for better filtering.

Echo Still Present After Enabling Echo Cancellation?

If Echo Cancellation doesn't eliminate echo, try the following:

✓ Lower your speaker volume to reduce audio pickup by your microphone.

✓ Use headphones to eliminate feedback loops.

✓ Check your room acoustics—hard surfaces reflect sound and cause echo.

6. Future Improvements in Noise Suppression and Echo Cancellation

Discord continues to enhance its audio features, and in the future, we may see:

- More AI-driven noise suppression improvements with deeper learning models.

- Better integration with professional audio software for advanced users.

- Automatic room acoustics adjustments based on background noise levels.

Conclusion

Noise Suppression and Echo Cancellation are powerful tools that help create a clear and enjoyable communication experience on Discord. By enabling these features, adjusting settings, and following best practices, users can ensure high-quality voice communication in any environment.

By applying the tips and troubleshooting steps outlined in this chapter, you'll be able to optimize your audio settings and enjoy crystal-clear conversations on Discord.

Next Section: 3.3.2 Adjusting Individual User Volumes

In the next section, we'll cover how to fine-tune the volume of individual users in voice channels, ensuring a balanced listening experience for all participants.

3.3.2 Adjusting Individual User Volumes

Discord provides a variety of audio settings that allow users to enhance their communication experience. One of the most useful features is the ability to adjust the volume of individual users in a voice channel. This feature ensures that users can balance audio levels, making conversations clearer and more enjoyable.

In this section, we will explore:

- Why adjusting individual volumes is important
- How to adjust user volumes on desktop and mobile
- Troubleshooting common volume-related issues
- Advanced audio management for server administrators

Why Adjusting Individual Volumes is Important

1. Different Microphone Setups Lead to Different Volume Levels

Not all users have the same microphone setup. Some may use high-quality studio microphones, while others may rely on built-in laptop microphones or mobile headsets. As a result, volume levels vary significantly. Some users may sound too loud and distorted, while others may be too quiet and difficult to hear.

2. Background Noise Can Be Distracting

Certain users may have background noise from sources such as:

- Mechanical keyboards

- Loud fans or air conditioning

- People talking in the background

- Street noise from open windows

Instead of muting the user completely, adjusting their volume allows you to reduce the impact of these distractions.

3. Enhancing Team Communication in Gaming and Work Environments

In gaming, effective communication is crucial. If a teammate's microphone is too quiet, it can delay reactions and impact performance. Similarly, in a work meeting or online class, balancing volume levels ensures smooth discussions without interruptions.

How to Adjust Individual User Volumes on Desktop

Discord makes it easy to adjust user volumes in voice channels. Follow these steps:

Method 1: Adjusting User Volume in a Voice Channel

1. Join a voice channel in any server.

2. Locate the user's name in the voice chat list (on the right side of the screen).

3. Right-click on the user's name to open the user settings menu.

4. Find the "User Volume" slider in the menu.

5. Drag the slider left to decrease the volume or right to increase it.

6. Close the menu—your settings will be applied immediately.

This method allows you to individually control each user's volume without affecting others.

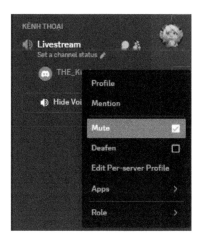

Method 2: Adjusting Volume from the Voice Chat Overlay

If you are gaming in full-screen mode, the Discord overlay provides a quick way to adjust user volumes.

1. Open the Discord overlay by pressing Shift + ~ (default hotkey, can be customized).

2. Hover over a user's name and avatar.

3. Click the volume slider icon.

4. Adjust the volume as needed.

This method is ideal for gamers and streamers who need to quickly balance audio levels during live sessions.

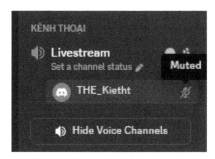

How to Adjust Individual User Volumes on Mobile (iOS & Android)

For mobile users, adjusting volume levels is just as simple:

1. Join a voice channel in a server.

2. Tap the user's name from the voice chat list at the bottom.

3. A pop-up menu will appear.

4. Use the volume slider to adjust their audio level.

5. Close the menu—changes take effect immediately.

Since mobile devices have built-in speakers with limited output, adjusting user volumes is helpful to avoid distorted or too-quiet audio.

Troubleshooting Volume-Related Issues

Sometimes, even after adjusting individual volumes, issues may persist. Below are some common problems and their solutions.

1. A User's Volume is Too Low Even at Maximum Setting

Possible Causes:

- The user's microphone is too far from their mouth.

- The user has low microphone input settings.

- Their Discord output volume is too low.

Solutions:

- Ask the user to increase their microphone input volume (Settings > Voice & Video > Input Volume).

- Suggest moving closer to their microphone.

- Check Windows or Mac sound settings to ensure their microphone is set to 100% input volume.

2. A User's Volume is Too Loud or Distorted Even at Minimum Setting

Possible Causes:

- The user has microphone boost enabled.

- Their microphone is too sensitive.

- Their hardware (headset/mic) has an issue.

Solutions:

- Ask them to reduce their microphone sensitivity (Settings > Voice & Video > Input Sensitivity).

- Suggest switching to a Push-to-Talk (PTT) mode to prevent background noise.

- If the issue persists, recommend using a different microphone.

3. Volume Settings Reset After Leaving and Rejoining a Channel

Possible Causes:

- Discord sometimes resets settings due to temporary bugs.

- User settings may not be saving correctly.

Solutions:

- Restart Discord and check if the issue persists.

- Log out and back in to refresh account settings.

- Update Discord to the latest version (Settings > Updates).

Advanced Volume Management for Server Administrators

For server owners and moderators, managing audio levels for an entire server is crucial, especially in large communities.

1. Setting Volume Limits with Discord Bots

Some Discord bots, such as Hydra, Dyno, or MEE6, allow admins to:

- Limit maximum user volume in voice channels.

- Auto-mute users with excessive noise.

- Balance audio levels across multiple users.

2. Enforcing Role-Based Audio Adjustments

Admins can create roles with different volume levels:

- VIP members or streamers may have higher volume priority.

- New users may have restricted volume levels until verified.

To set permissions:

1. Open Server Settings.

2. Navigate to Roles.

3. Customize voice permissions (such as Priority Speaker mode).

3. Using Third-Party Equalizers for Better Sound Management

If adjusting volume within Discord isn't enough, users can try:

- Windows Sound Mixer (Sound Settings > Advanced Sound Options).

- Third-party equalizers like Equalizer APO or Voicemeeter for fine-tuning.

Conclusion

Adjusting individual user volumes on Discord is a powerful feature that helps maintain clear, balanced communication in voice channels. Whether you're gaming, attending online meetings, or managing a community, fine-tuning audio levels enhances the overall experience.

Key Takeaways:

✅ You can adjust user volume on both desktop and mobile.
✅ Use the Discord overlay for quick volume changes while gaming.
✅ Troubleshoot common volume issues by checking user microphone settings.
✅ Admins can manage audio levels using bots, role-based permissions, and equalizers.

By mastering individual user volume controls, you can ensure a high-quality, distraction-free voice experience on Discord.

Next Section: 3.3.3 Streaming with High-Quality Audio

In the next section, we'll dive into how to optimize Discord for high-quality streaming, covering bitrate adjustments, audio settings, and integration with streaming tools.

3.3.3 Streaming with High-Quality Audio

Streaming high-quality audio on Discord is essential for various use cases, such as broadcasting music, podcasts, live performances, gaming audio, and professional discussions. Whether you're a content creator, musician, teacher, or simply want to share crisp audio with friends, Discord provides several tools and settings to enhance your streaming experience.

In this section, we will explore:

- Understanding Discord's Audio Streaming Capabilities

- Optimizing Audio Settings for High-Quality Streaming

- Using External Tools to Enhance Audio Quality

- Streaming High-Quality Music or Sound from Your Computer

- Common Issues and Troubleshooting High-Quality Audio Streaming

1. Understanding Discord's Audio Streaming Capabilities

What is Audio Streaming in Discord?

Audio streaming in Discord typically involves transmitting high-quality sound through voice channels or screen sharing with sound enabled. Unlike regular voice communication, where clarity is prioritized over fidelity, streaming audio often requires higher bitrate, better noise control, and stable connection settings.

Different Use Cases for Audio Streaming on Discord

- Streaming high-quality in-game audio while playing multiplayer games.

- Broadcasting music for group listening in Discord voice channels.

- Sharing sound effects or background audio for tabletop RPGs.

- Providing professional-grade audio for teaching, voice-over work, or podcasting.

Bitrate and Its Role in Audio Quality

Discord servers allow different bitrates, which determine the quality of transmitted sound. Bitrate is measured in kilobits per second (kbps), and the higher the bitrate, the better the audio quality.

By default, voice channels on Discord operate at 64 kbps, but with server boosting, you can unlock:

- 96 kbps (Standard Boosted Channel)

- 128 kbps (Tier 1 Boosted Server)

- 256 kbps (Tier 2 Boosted Server)

- 384 kbps (Tier 3 Boosted Server – Maximum Quality)

If you plan to stream high-quality music, podcasts, or professional audio, a higher bitrate is crucial.

2. Optimizing Audio Settings for High-Quality Streaming

Adjusting Voice Channel Bitrate

To improve streaming audio quality, you must adjust the bitrate of your Discord voice channel.

How to Adjust Bitrate in Discord

1. Open **Discord** and navigate to your server.

2. Click on the **voice channel** you want to modify.

3. Click the **gear icon** next to the channel name (**Edit Channel**).

4. Locate the **Bitrate slider** under the **Voice Channel Settings** section.

5. Increase the bitrate to **96 kbps or higher** for improved clarity.

6. Click **Save Changes**.

⚠ **Note**: Higher bitrates require **better internet connections**. If users in your channel have weak internet, they may experience lag.

Enabling High-Quality Voice Processing Features

Discord offers built-in voice processing features to improve audio transmission. You can adjust these settings in:

◆ User Settings → Voice & Video

Recommended Settings for High-Quality Audio Streaming

✅ **Noise Suppression: Disable** if you're streaming music or high-fidelity audio.

✅ **Echo Cancellation: Enable** to reduce feedback from your microphone.

✅ **Automatic Gain Control (AGC): Disable** for better consistency in volume.

✅ **Advanced Voice Activity: Disable** if using a professional microphone.

✅ **Opus Codec (Default):** Discord automatically uses Opus, which is optimized for voice.

---

3. Using External Tools to Enhance Audio Quality

While Discord's built-in audio settings are decent, external tools can further enhance quality.

Using a Virtual Audio Mixer (e.g., Voicemeeter Banana, VB-Audio)

A virtual audio mixer allows you to route high-quality audio through Discord with more control over volume, effects, and equalization.

How to Use Voicemeeter Banana for High-Quality Audio Streaming

1. Download and install Voicemeeter Banana.

   https://vb-audio.com/Voicemeeter/banana.htm

2. Open Voicemeeter Banana and set your hardware input to your microphone.

3. Set the virtual output (B1 or B2) as the default device in Windows Sound Settings.

4. In Discord, go to User Settings → Voice & Video and select Voicemeeter Output as your input device.

5. Adjust levels and effects within Voicemeeter for optimal sound.

This method is particularly useful for:

- Podcasters and musicians looking to stream professional audio.

- DJs or music streamers sharing lossless sound.

- Gamers who want separate audio controls for voice and game sounds.

4. Streaming High-Quality Music or Sound from Your Computer

If you want to stream music or sound effects in high quality through Discord, you can either:

1. Use a Bot (like Rythm or FredBoat) – However, many music bots were shut down due to copyright issues.

2. Use a Virtual Audio Cable (VAC) to route sound into Discord.

How to Stream Music Using a Virtual Audio Cable

1. Download and install VB-Audio Virtual Cable. https://vb-audio.com/Cable/

2. Open Windows Sound Settings → Set Virtual Cable as Output Device.

3. In Discord, go to User Settings → Voice & Video and set Virtual Cable as Input Device.

4. Play music on your computer, and it will be transmitted as crystal-clear audio in Discord.

Pro Tip: Combine Voicemeeter Banana + Virtual Audio Cable for full control over game, music, and microphone balance.

5. Common Issues and Troubleshooting High-Quality Audio Streaming

Despite setting up high-quality streaming, you may encounter issues such as choppy sound, distortion, or lag. Here's how to fix them:

Issue 1: Audio Sounds Robotic or Choppy

✓ Fix: Lower the bitrate to 96 kbps if your internet is unstable.
✓ Fix: Close background apps consuming bandwidth (e.g., downloads, streaming services).

Issue 2: Volume Levels Are Inconsistent

✓ Fix: Disable Automatic Gain Control (AGC) in Voice & Video settings.
✓ Fix: Manually adjust individual user volumes in Discord.

Issue 3: Background Noise is Too High

✓ Fix: Enable Krisp Noise Suppression for better clarity.
✓ Fix: Use a quality external microphone with a pop filter.

Issue 4: Music or Game Audio is Too Loud Compared to Voice

✓ Fix: Use a virtual mixer (Voicemeeter Banana) to balance volumes.
✓ Fix: Adjust per-user volume settings in the voice channel.

Conclusion

Streaming high-quality audio on Discord requires optimizing bitrate, tweaking advanced settings, and utilizing external tools for maximum clarity. Whether you're a content creator, educator, gamer, or musician, these settings will help you achieve studio-level sound during your streams.

In the next section, we'll explore how to optimize video quality for Discord screen sharing and video calls to further enhance your communication experience.

CHAPTER IV
Creating and Managing a Discord Server

4.1 Setting Up Your Own Server

4.1.1 Creating a New Server from Scratch

Creating your own Discord server is an exciting step that allows you to build a custom community around your interests, whether it's for gaming, business, study groups, hobbies, or professional collaboration. A Discord server acts as a virtual space where members can interact through text channels, voice channels, and video calls, while also providing customization options through roles, permissions, and integrations.

In this section, we will cover:

- What a Discord server is and why you might want to create one.

- A step-by-step guide to creating a server.

- Initial setup options, including naming, region selection, and server customization.

- Important settings to configure after creation to ensure security and usability.

What is a Discord Server?

A Discord server is essentially a dedicated space where users can communicate via text, voice, or video. Each server is independent and can be customized with channels, permissions, bots, and roles to fit its purpose. Unlike traditional group chats, servers offer structured communication, making them ideal for large and organized communities.

Some of the most common types of Discord servers include:

- Gaming Communities – Clans, guilds, or esports teams.

- Study Groups – For students and educational discussions.

- Business and Work Collaboration – Teams using Discord for internal communication.

- Content Creator Communities – For YouTubers, Twitch streamers, and podcasters.

- Fan Clubs and Hobby Groups – Book clubs, music lovers, tech enthusiasts, and more.

Regardless of your purpose, setting up a well-structured server ensures a smooth experience for members and encourages engagement.

Step-by-Step Guide to Creating a Discord Server

Step 1: Open Discord

Before you create a server, make sure you have **Discord installed** on your device or access it via a web browser. If you haven't signed up yet, create an account at <u>discord.com</u>.

You can create a server from:

- The Discord desktop app (Windows, macOS, Linux).

- The Discord mobile app (Android, iOS).

- The web version of Discord (accessed via a browser).

Step 2: Click the "+" Button to Create a New Server

1. Open Discord and log in to your account.

2. On the left sidebar, locate the server list. You will see a "+" button at the bottom of your server list.

3. Click the "+" button to start the process of creating a new server.

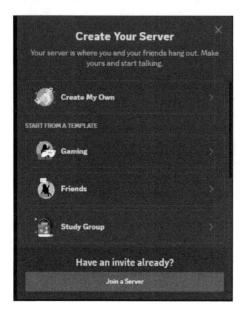

Step 3: Choose Between Creating a New Server or Using a Template

After clicking the "+" button, Discord will give you two options:

- Create My Own – This allows you to build a server from scratch, giving you complete control over setup and customization.

- Start from a Template – Discord offers pre-made templates for gaming, study groups, clubs, friends, and communities to simplify the setup process.

For this guide, we will select "Create My Own" to manually build a fully customized server.

Step 4: Enter Server Details

Now, you need to configure some basic settings for your server:

1. Server Name – Choose a unique and recognizable name that reflects the purpose of your server. (Example: "Tech Enthusiasts Hub" or "Gaming Legends")

2. Server Image (Optional) – Upload a custom server icon to make it visually appealing. This can be a logo, mascot, or any image representing your community.

3. Community Type (Optional) – Discord may ask whether your server is for friends & family or a larger community.

4. Click Create to finalize the initial setup.

Step 5: Adjust Server Settings

Once your server is created, Discord will automatically take you to the **server homepage**, where you can start customizing it. Before inviting members, it's a good idea to configure **key settings** to ensure a smooth user experience.

Essential Initial Server Settings

1. Setting Up Server Regions (Voice & Video Optimization)

Discord automatically selects the best server region based on your location. However, if your community has members from different parts of the world, you might need to manually adjust this setting.

To change the server region:

1. Click on your server name at the top left.

2. Select Server Settings > Overview.

3. Scroll to Server Region and choose the best region for your members (e.g., North America, Europe, Asia).

Setting the right server region ensures low latency and smooth voice/video communication.

2. Creating Default Text and Voice Channels

By default, your server will have a general text channel (#general) and a voice channel (General). You should organize additional channels based on the purpose of your server.

Some common **channel setups** include:

- **#announcements** – For important updates and news.

- **#rules** – A read-only channel where new members can view server guidelines.

- **#introductions** – A place where new members can introduce themselves.

- **#general-chat** – A casual conversation channel.

- **#help-desk** – For questions and troubleshooting.

- 🎙 **Voice Channels** – For group calls, meetings, or gaming sessions.

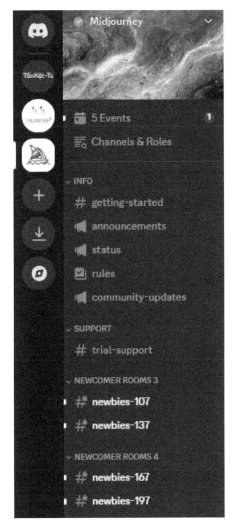

To create a new channel:

1. Click the **"+" button** next to **Text Channels** or **Voice Channels**.

2. Name the channel (e.g., "gaming-chat" or "study-group").

3. Set **permissions** (e.g., making it read-only for announcements).

4. Click **Create Channel**.

3. Setting Up Server Roles and Permissions

Server roles allow you to manage users by assigning them different levels of access. Roles can define who can send messages, manage channels, mute users, or kick members.

To create roles:

1. Go to **Server Settings** > **Roles**.

2. Click **Create Role** and set a name (e.g., "Admin", "Moderator", "Member").

3. Adjust **permissions** (e.g., allow admins to manage the server).

4. Save and **assign roles** to members in the "Members" tab.

Common roles and their permissions:

- **Admin** – Full control over the server.

- **Moderator** – Can mute, kick, or warn users.

- **Member** – Can chat but cannot manage settings.

Properly setting up roles **prevents chaos and ensures smooth moderation**.

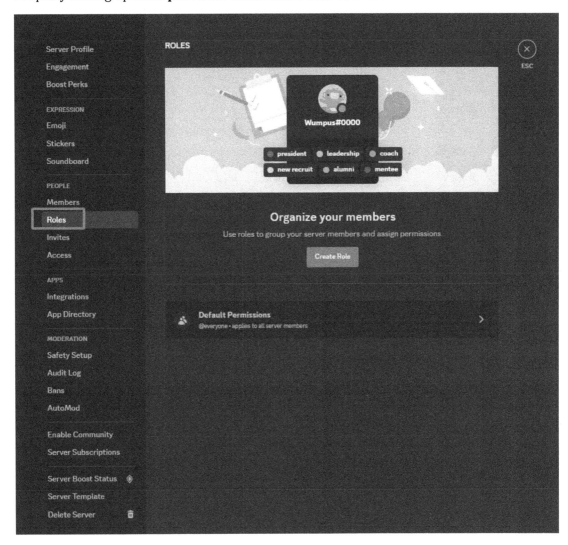

Inviting Members to Your Server

Now that your server is set up, it's time to **invite people**!

To invite members:

1. Click on your server name > **Invite People**.

2. Copy the **invite link** and send it to your friends.

3. (Optional) Set an **expiration time** on the link (e.g., never expire).

You can also create **permanent invite links** with **custom permissions** for specific roles.

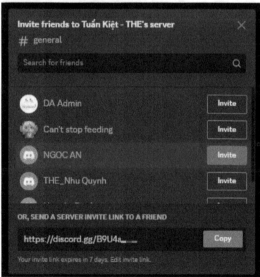

Conclusion

Congratulations! You have successfully created a Discord server from scratch. Your server is now a customized space where members can communicate, collaborate, and build a community.

In the next section (**4.1.2 Choosing Server Templates and Themes**), we'll explore how to customize your server even further with **themes, templates, and advanced settings** to enhance its visual appeal and functionality.

4.1.2 Choosing Server Templates and Themes

Creating a Discord server from scratch can be overwhelming, especially for new users who may not be familiar with all the available settings and customization options. Fortunately, Discord provides **server templates** and **themes** to help users quickly set up a well-structured server suited to their needs.

This section will explore what server templates are, how to use them, the benefits they offer, and how users can customize their server's visual appeal with themes, banners, and branding elements.

What Are Discord Server Templates?

Discord server templates are pre-configured server setups designed to help users quickly create a server with structured channels, roles, and permissions. These templates provide a starting point for various types of communities, making it easier to organize content and manage users.

A **server template** includes:

- Preset channels (e.g., text, voice, announcement, rules).
- Predefined roles and permissions (e.g., admin, moderator, member).
- Category structures to organize discussions.
- Basic settings optimized for the server type.

Instead of manually configuring everything from scratch, users can choose a template that fits their needs and customize it further after creation.

How to Choose and Use Server Templates

1. Accessing Discord's Built-in Templates

Discord provides official server templates for different types of communities. To use a built-in template:

1. Open Discord and go to the Home Screen.
2. Click the "+" (Add a Server) button in the left sidebar.
3. Select "Create My Own" or "Browse Templates".
4. Choose a template from the available categories.
5. Enter a server name and select an icon (optional).
6. Click "Create", and your server will be generated with pre-configured channels and roles.

Official Discord Templates

Discord offers several default templates for common server types:

Template Name	Purpose
Gaming	Designed for gaming communities, with channels for voice chat, matchmaking, and announcements.
Friends & Family	A casual server setup for small groups of friends or family members to chat and share content.
Study Group	Provides text channels for subjects, study resources, and voice rooms for group discussions.
Artists & Creators	Includes galleries for sharing work, critique channels, and collaboration spaces.

Template Name	Purpose
Local Communities	Structured for neighborhood groups, event planning, and local announcements.
Clubs & Organizations	Helps school clubs, nonprofits, and businesses organize discussions and activities.

These templates make it easy to **quickly launch a server** with a structured format suitable for a particular type of community.

2. Using Custom Server Templates from Other Users

In addition to official templates, users can create and share their own custom server templates.

How to Import a Server Template

If someone shares a server template link, you can import it into your Discord:

1. Click the link provided by the template creator.

2. Discord will display a preview of the template, including channel structure, roles, and settings.

3. Click "Create" and choose a server name and icon.

4. Your new server will be created with the imported setup.

Many Discord communities share their templates publicly, making it easy to find well-structured servers for various purposes.

Where to Find Custom Server Templates

You can find pre-made server templates from:

- Discord community forums and subreddits (e.g., r/discordapp).

- Server template directories (websites like Discord.Templates).

- Official Discord partner communities.

Customizing Your Server Theme and Appearance

Once you've chosen a template, the next step is to personalize your server to match its branding or community identity.

1. Setting Up Server Icons and Banners

The server icon and banner help establish the visual identity of a server.

How to Add a Server Icon

A server icon appears next to the server name in the sidebar and should be recognizable and clear. To add an icon:

1. Click the server name in the top left.

2. Select Server Settings > Overview.

3. Click Upload Image under Server Icon.

4. Choose a square image (512x512 pixels recommended).

5. Click Save Changes.

How to Add a Server Banner (Boost Level Required)

If your server reaches Boost Level 2, you can add a custom banner:

1. Go to Server Settings > Overview.

2. Scroll to the Server Banner Background section.

3. Upload an image (960x540 pixels recommended).

4. Click Save Changes.

A banner gives your server a professional and engaging look, especially for large communities.

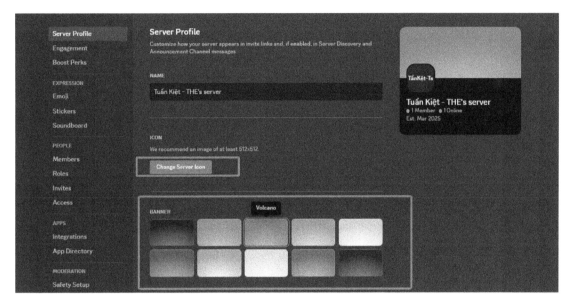

2. Choosing a Server Theme and Layout

While Discord does not currently allow full custom themes, you can modify the layout and appearance using:

Custom Channel and Role Colors

- You can assign unique colors to roles, making it easier to identify admins, moderators, and members.

- To change role colors:

    1. Go to Server Settings > Roles.

2. Select a role and scroll to Role Color.

3. Choose a color and click Save Changes.

Channel Icons and Emojis

- Use Unicode emojis or special characters in channel names to make them stand out (e.g., 🎮│ gaming-chat).

- To edit a channel name:

   1. Click the gear icon next to the channel.

   2. Edit the channel name and insert emojis.

   3. Click Save Changes.

Finalizing Your Server Setup

Once you've chosen a template and customized the theme, take a moment to:

1. Review and modify channels – Rename, delete, or add new channels as needed.

2. Adjust permissions – Ensure admins, moderators, and members have the correct permissions.

3. Enable security settings – Adjust verification levels to prevent spam bots from joining.

Conclusion

Choosing the right server template and theme makes setting up a Discord server fast and efficient, providing an organized structure from the beginning. Whether using Discord's official templates or importing custom ones, templates help users avoid manual setup and focus on building their community.

Additionally, customizing icons, banners, and role colors helps personalize the server and improve user engagement.

In the next section, **4.1.3 Setting Up Server Regions and Boosting**, we'll explore how to **optimize server performance** and **enhance features** through Discord Boosts.

4.1.3 Setting Up Server Regions and Boosting

When creating a Discord server, one of the essential aspects to consider is server performance, including voice quality, latency, and overall responsiveness. Discord provides options to configure server regions, which help optimize connection quality for voice channels. Additionally, Server Boosting allows members to enhance a server's features, unlocking premium perks such as better audio quality, custom banners, and higher upload limits.

In this section, we will explore what server regions are, how they affect performance, how to select the best region, and how Server Boosting works, including its benefits and levels.

1. Understanding Server Regions

What Are Server Regions?

Discord operates data centers in multiple locations worldwide. When a server is created, it is assigned a server region that determines where the server's voice communications are routed. This is particularly important for voice channels, as selecting the right region can reduce latency (ping), packet loss, and voice distortion.

Server regions do not impact text chat, images, or file uploads because these features rely on Discord's global infrastructure rather than a specific location. However, for real-time voice communication, choosing the right server region can improve clarity and reduce lag.

How Server Regions Affect Voice Quality

The server region affects latency, which is the delay in data transmission between a user and the server. The lower the latency, the smoother and clearer the voice communication. Higher latency can result in:

- Choppy audio or delayed responses.

- Robotic or distorted voices due to packet loss.

- Frequent disconnections from voice channels.

If multiple users on a server are experiencing voice lag, changing the server region can help optimize voice communication.

2. How to Change Your Server Region

In early versions of Discord, server owners could manually set the server region. However, since 2021, Discord has implemented automatic region selection, meaning Discord automatically picks the best region based on server members' locations.

While manual server region selection is no longer available, users can still change voice channel regions manually if experiencing issues.

2.1 Changing the Voice Channel Region Manually

If a specific voice channel is experiencing high latency or poor call quality, you can manually adjust its region:

Steps to Change Voice Channel Region:

1. **Go to Your Discord Server.** Open your Discord server where the problematic voice channel exists.

2. **Select the Voice Channel.** Click on the **gear icon** next to the voice channel name to open the settings.

3. **Go to "Region Override".** Scroll down to find the **Region Override** option.

4. **Select a Region.** Choose the best server region based on where most participants are located. Common options include:

   o US East / US West (For North American users)

   o Europe / UK (For European users)

   o Singapore / Hong Kong (For Asian users)

   o Brazil (For South American users)

5. **Save Changes.** Click **Save** and test the new region by having users reconnect to the voice channel.

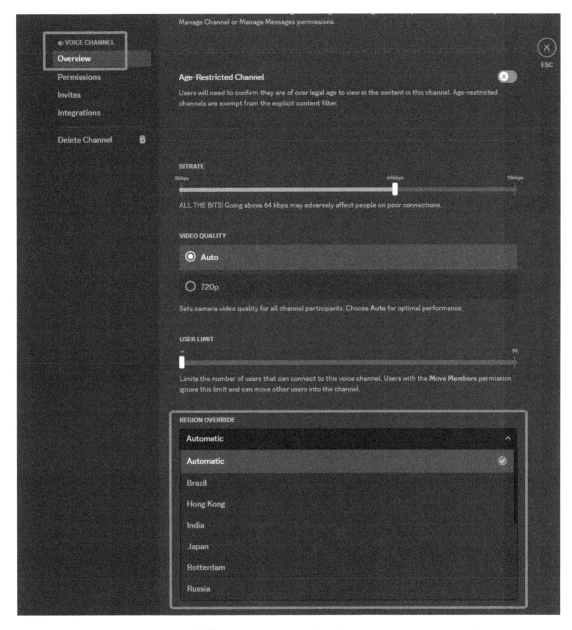

If the problem persists, try a different region or check user internet connections to ensure the issue is not caused by local network problems.

3. Understanding Discord Server Boosting

3.1 What is Server Boosting?

Server Boosting is a premium feature that allows users to contribute to their favorite servers by unlocking additional perks. Unlike Discord Nitro, which provides personal benefits like higher-quality streaming and larger file uploads, Server Boosting enhances server-wide features for all members.

When a user boosts a server, they contribute to the server's boost level, unlocking better functionality such as improved audio quality, more emoji slots, animated banners, and better file-sharing capabilities.

3.2 Server Boosting Benefits by Level

Discord offers three levels of Server Boosting, each providing increasing perks.

Level 1 Boost (Requires 2 Boosts)

✅ 128 Kbps audio quality in voice channels.

✅ Custom server invite background.

✅ 50 additional emoji slots (total: 100).

✅ Animated server icon.

✅ Streaming at 720p, 60 FPS.

Level 2 Boost (Requires 7 Boosts)

✅ 256 Kbps audio quality.

✅ Server banner upload.

✅ More emoji slots (total: 150).

✅ Increased upload limit (50 MB for file sharing).

✅ Streaming at 1080p, 60 FPS.

Level 3 Boost (Requires 14 Boosts)

✅ 384 Kbps audio quality (near lossless audio).

✅ Vanity URL (custom Discord link like discord.gg/yourserver).

✅ More emoji slots (total: 250).

✅ Upload limit increases to 100 MB.

✅ Custom server profile badge.

3.3 How to Boost a Server

To boost a Discord server, follow these steps:

1. **Open Discord.** Navigate to the server you want to boost.

2. **Click on the Server Name.** In the top-left corner, click the server's name to open a dropdown menu.

3. **Select "Server Boost."** Click **"Server Boost"** to open the boost menu.

4. **Choose a Boost.** If you have an available boost (from **Discord Nitro**), you can apply it. Otherwise, you will need to purchase one.

5. **Confirm Purchase.** Follow the payment process to complete the boost.

If a server reaches Level 3 Boosting, it unlocks all premium features, making it highly attractive for large gaming communities, businesses, and content creators.

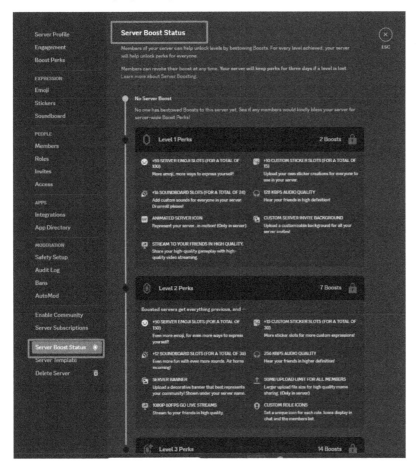

4. Best Practices for Server Regions and Boosting

Choosing the Best Server Region for Your Community

- For global communities, use Discord's automatic region selection to optimize for most users.

- For local communities, manually set voice channel regions based on majority member locations.

- If users experience high ping or robotic voice issues, consider switching to a closer region.

Encouraging Members to Boost the Server

Since Server Boosts are voluntary, consider the following strategies to encourage members to contribute:

- Offer exclusive perks (e.g., special roles, private channels for boosters).

- Recognize boosters with a dedicated role and name color.

- Create an appreciation board to thank members who boost regularly.

Managing Boost Contributions

- Monitor who is boosting your server through Server Settings → Boost Status.

- If your server loses boosts and drops a level, remind members of the lost perks to encourage re-boosting.

- Consider offering community rewards (like giveaways) to keep members engaged.

Conclusion

Setting up a server region correctly ensures smooth voice communication, while Server Boosting enhances server functionality, making it more appealing to members. By understanding how to adjust voice channel regions and how Server Boosting works, you can optimize your server for both performance and engagement.

Next Section: 4.2 Configuring Roles and Permissions

In the next section, we'll dive into setting up roles and permissions to organize your server and maintain security effectively.

4.2 Configuring Roles and Permissions

4.2.1 Creating and Assigning Roles

Managing a Discord server effectively requires organizing users into different roles with specific permissions. Roles allow server owners and administrators to grant or restrict access to certain features, channels, and server functions. By carefully structuring roles, you can create a well-organized community that runs smoothly without constant moderation.

In this section, we will explore what roles are, how to create them, best practices for assigning them, and how they can enhance server management.

Understanding Roles in Discord

A **role** in Discord is a set of **permissions** that can be assigned to a user or group of users. These permissions control what actions users can take within a server, such as sending messages, joining voice channels, or moderating content.

Each Discord server has a **default role** called @everyone, which applies to all members unless additional roles are assigned. You can create custom roles with specific permissions and assign them to users as needed.

Why Roles Are Important

- Security and Organization – Prevent unauthorized actions by limiting permissions.
- Efficient Moderation – Assign moderator roles to help manage the server.
- Custom User Experience – Allow users to unlock features based on their roles.
- Automated Role Management – Bots can assign roles based on user actions or reactions.

Now, let's look at how to create and configure roles in your Discord server.

How to Create Roles in Discord

Step 1: Accessing the Roles Menu

To create a new role:

1. Open your Discord server.

2. Click on the **server name** in the top-left corner.

3. Select **Server Settings** from the dropdown menu.

4. Click on **Roles** in the left-hand menu.

5. Click the **"Create Role"** button.

This opens the role configuration panel, where you can set role names, colors, and permissions.

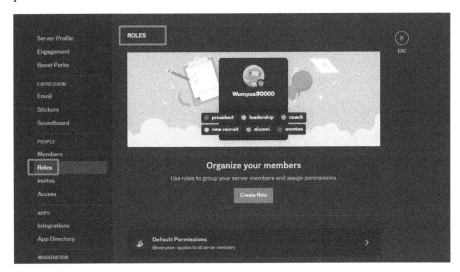

Step 2: Naming and Customizing the Role

When creating a new role, you should:

- Choose a clear and meaningful name (e.g., "Moderator," "VIP," "Content Creator").

- Assign a unique color to distinguish the role from others.

- Set a role icon (optional, available for boosted servers).

Step 3: Configuring Role Permissions

After naming the role, go to the **Permissions** tab to assign its capabilities. Permissions are divided into three categories:

1. General Server Permissions

- Administrator – Grants all permissions (use with caution).

- Manage Server – Allows users to change server settings.

- Manage Channels – Lets users create, delete, and edit channels.

- Manage Roles – Allows users to assign and modify roles.

- Manage Emojis and Stickers – Enables users to upload and remove emojis.

- View Audit Log – Provides access to server activity logs.

2. Text Channel Permissions

- Send Messages – Allows users to type in text channels.

- Manage Messages – Lets users delete or pin messages.

- Embed Links – Allows users to post clickable links.

- Attach Files – Enables file sharing.

- Use External Emojis – Lets users use emojis from other servers.

3. Voice Channel Permissions

- Connect – Allows users to join voice channels.

- Speak – Enables users to talk in voice channels.

- Mute/Deafen Members – Lets users control audio settings for others.

- Use Voice Activity – Allows speaking without push-to-talk.

Once you've configured the necessary permissions, click Save Changes.

Assigning Roles to Members

After creating roles, you need to assign them to members.

Method 1: Assigning Roles Manually

1. Open your server.

2. Click on a **member's name** in the **Members List**.

3. Click the "**+**" icon under **Roles**.

4. Select the desired role from the list.

Method 2: Assigning Roles via Server Settings

1. Go to **Server Settings → Members**.

2. Find the user you want to assign a role to.

3. Click the "**+**" button next to their name.

4. Choose the role you want to assign.

Method 3: Assigning Roles Using Bots

Many servers use bots like MEE6, Dyno, or Carl-bot to automatically assign roles. These bots allow:

- Auto-assign roles when a user joins.

- Reaction-based roles, where users click an emoji to get a role.

- Level-based roles, where users unlock new roles based on activity.

For example, using MEE6:

1. Invite the MEE6 bot to your server.

2. Open the MEE6 dashboard and go to the Auto Role section.

3. Select a role to be assigned automatically.

4. Click Save.

Best Practices for Role Management

1. Use a Clear Role Hierarchy

Roles should follow a logical structure. A typical setup might look like:

- Admin (Full control)

- Moderator (Limited management permissions)

- Verified Member (Basic user access)

- New Member (Limited permissions to prevent spam)

2. Limit Administrator Privileges

Only trusted members should have the Administrator role, as it grants full control over the server.

3. Avoid Overlapping Permissions

Conflicting permissions can create issues where users have unexpected access. Test roles by creating a test account and verifying permissions.

4. Automate Role Assignment

Using bots to assign roles saves time and improves user engagement.

5. Regularly Review and Update Roles

As your community grows, revisit roles to ensure they still serve their intended purpose.

Conclusion

Roles and permissions are the foundation of a well-organized Discord server. By carefully configuring them, you can create a safe, engaging, and well-managed community.

In the next section, we'll explore **Managing Permissions for Channels and Users**, where we'll learn how to fine-tune channel-specific settings to ensure a seamless user experience.

4.2.2 Managing Permissions for Channels and Users

One of the most powerful features of Discord is its role-based permissions system, which allows server owners and administrators to control who can access different parts of a server and what actions they can perform. Properly managing permissions ensures that your Discord server remains organized, secure, and efficient.

In this section, we'll explore how to configure channel permissions, user-specific permissions, and best practices for maintaining a well-structured server.

1. Understanding Discord's Permission System

Discord permissions are divided into two main categories:

1. Server-wide permissions – Assigned through roles and apply to all channels unless overridden.

2. Channel-specific permissions – Allow customization for individual channels, enabling different access levels.

Hierarchy of Permissions

Discord's permissions operate in a hierarchical structure, which means:

- Server Owners and Administrators have the highest level of control.

- Roles can be assigned different permission levels, dictating what users can do.

- Channel permissions can override role permissions, allowing for granular control.

Permissions are divided into three settings:

✅ **Enabled (Green checkmark)** – Grants the permission.

✖ **Disabled (Red X)** – Denies the permission.

━ **Default (Gray Slash)** – Inherits permissions from higher roles or the server settings.

2. Managing Permissions for Channels

Each channel (text or voice) in Discord can have its own set of permissions that determine who can view, send messages, or interact with it.

Step 1: Accessing Channel Permissions

To configure channel permissions, follow these steps:

1. Right-click the channel you want to modify.

2. Click Edit Channel.

3. Navigate to the Permissions tab.

Here, you'll see a list of roles and users, along with specific permissions you can enable or disable.

Step 2: Configuring Basic Permissions for Channels

Each channel has a variety of permission settings, but some of the most important ones include:

For Text Channels

- View Channel – Determines whether users can see the channel.

- Send Messages – Controls whether users can send messages.

- Manage Messages – Allows deletion and pinning of messages.

- Embed Links & Attach Files – Enables sharing of external content.

- Use External Emojis – Lets users use emojis from other servers.

- Mention Everyone – Allows tagging of all members at once.

For Voice Channels

- Connect – Determines whether users can join the voice channel.

- Speak – Allows users to talk in the voice chat.

- Mute/Deafen Members – Grants the ability to control other users' audio.

- Use Voice Activity / Push-to-Talk – Dictates how users activate their microphone.

Step 3: Assigning Role-Specific Channel Permissions

Once you've set up **roles** (covered in **4.2.1**), you can apply role-specific permissions to channels.

For example:

- **"Moderators"** may have the ability to delete messages and manage users.

- **"Verified Members"** may be allowed to send messages but not mention @everyone.

- **"New Users"** might have restricted access to certain channels until they gain a higher role.

Step 4: Creating Private Channels

If you want a private channel (visible only to certain roles), follow these steps:

1. Go to Edit Channel > Permissions.

2. Disable View Channel for @everyone.

3. Enable View Channel only for specific roles (e.g., "Admins" or "VIPs").

This method is useful for staff discussions, VIP lounges, or team-specific channels.

3. Managing Permissions for Individual Users

While roles should handle most permissions, you might sometimes need to set user-specific permissions.

Step 1: Modifying User Permissions in a Channel

1. Open the Edit Channel menu.

2. Go to the Permissions tab.

3. Click Add Members or Roles.

4. Select a specific user and assign custom permissions.

This is useful when:

- You want to grant a specific user access to a restricted channel.

- You need to mute or restrict a user in one channel while allowing normal access elsewhere.

Step 2: Overriding Permissions on a Per-User Basis

- If a user is denied permissions in a role, but granted permissions as an individual, the individual setting takes priority.

- If a user has multiple roles with different permission levels, the highest permission takes effect.

Example: If a user is in both the "Members" role (which can send messages) and the "Muted" role (which cannot), the Muted role takes precedence.

4. Best Practices for Managing Permissions

Use a Hierarchical Role Structure

- Organize roles in a logical order (**Admin > Moderator > Member > New User**).

- Higher roles should have more permissions, while lower roles have restricted access.

Limit the "Administrator" Permission

The Administrator permission grants full control over a server. To prevent abuse:

- Only assign it to trusted users.

- Avoid giving Administrator to bots unless necessary.

Utilize Category Permissions

Instead of setting permissions for each channel manually, configure permissions at the category level to apply them to multiple channels at once.

Restrict Dangerous Permissions

Certain permissions should only be given to trusted roles, including:

- Manage Channels – Prevents unauthorized channel deletion.

- Kick/Ban Members – Ensures only moderators can remove users.

- Mention @everyone – Avoids spam tagging.

Regularly Audit Permissions

Check your permissions setup periodically to ensure:

- No unauthorized users have been granted sensitive permissions.

- Server security remains intact.

Conclusion

Managing permissions for channels and users is essential for maintaining an organized and secure Discord server. By following best practices and utilizing Discord's role-based permission system effectively, you can create a structured environment that enhances user experience while preventing abuse or disruptions.

Next Section: 4.2.3 Using Role Hierarchies and Role Colors

In the next section, we'll explore how role hierarchies affect permissions and how to use role colors to improve server organization.

4.2.3 Using Role Hierarchies and Role Colors

Roles and permissions are fundamental to managing a well-organized Discord server. They allow you to control access to channels, moderate discussions, and create a structured community with different levels of authority. Within Discord's role system, role hierarchies and role colors play a crucial role in distinguishing members and ensuring a smooth experience for all users.

In this section, we will explore how role hierarchies work, the significance of role colors, and best practices for structuring roles in a way that enhances server management and user engagement.

Understanding Role Hierarchies in Discord

What Is a Role Hierarchy?

A role hierarchy in Discord is the order of roles assigned to members within a server. Higher roles have more authority and can override permissions of lower roles. This system allows server administrators to define leadership structures, moderate content, and grant specific privileges to certain users.

The hierarchy is based on role order, which is determined by the position of roles in the server's role settings. The higher a role is placed in the list, the more power and priority it has over lower roles.

How Role Hierarchy Works in Discord

The Discord role system follows a top-down approach, meaning:

- Higher roles can manage lower roles (if granted the necessary permissions).

- Users with higher roles appear above those with lower roles in the member list.

- Permissions granted to higher roles override those of lower roles unless restricted.

Example of a Role Hierarchy

A typical Discord server might have the following role hierarchy:

1. Server Owner (Highest) – Has full control over the server.

2. Administrators – Can manage server settings, channels, and users.

3. Moderators – Can enforce rules and mute, kick, or ban users.

4. Verified Members – Have standard permissions to chat, join voice channels, and react.

5. New Members (Lowest) – Have limited permissions until verified.

The order of these roles determines which members have more influence and which permissions they can control.

Managing Role Hierarchies in Discord

To set up a proper role hierarchy, follow these steps:

1. Access the Role Settings

1. Open your Discord server.

2. Click on the server name at the top-left.

3. Select **"Server Settings"** and then go to **"Roles"**.

2. Arranging Roles in Order

- In the Roles tab, you will see a list of all roles on your server.

- Drag and drop roles to reorder them based on importance.

- The higher a role is, the more authority it has over the ones below it.

3. Assigning Permissions Based on Hierarchy

- Higher roles should have more administrative permissions (e.g., managing channels, banning users).

- Lower roles should have basic permissions (e.g., sending messages, reacting to posts).

For example, a Moderator role should be placed above Member roles to allow moderators to enforce rules without interference from standard members.

Using Role Colors for Organization and Visibility

What Are Role Colors?

Role colors help differentiate user roles visually in a server. When you assign a color to a role, users with that role will have their name displayed in that color in the member list and chat.

Why Role Colors Matter?

- Enhances organization – Helps users quickly identify admins, mods, and members.

- Improves engagement – Makes the server visually appealing.

- Boosts community recognition – Members feel a sense of belonging when they have a distinct role.

How to Assign Role Colors in Discord

1. Open the Role Settings

1. Go to **Server Settings > Roles**.

2. Select a role you want to edit.

2. Choose a Role Color

- Scroll down to the **"Role Color"** section.

- Pick a color from the preset options or **customize your own**.

3. Save the Changes

- Click **"Save Changes"** at the bottom of the screen.

Once assigned, the color will appear next to users' names in the **member list and chat messages**, making them stand out.

Best Practices for Role Colors

1. Use distinct colors for key roles (e.g., Admin = Red, Moderator = Blue, Member = Green).

2. Avoid colors that are too similar to prevent confusion.

3. Use soft colors for general roles and bright colors for leadership roles.

4. Consider accessibility – Avoid colors that are difficult for color-blind users to distinguish.

Best Practices for Setting Up Role Hierarchies and Colors

1. Keep Role Hierarchy Simple

- Don't overcomplicate roles with unnecessary permissions.

- Use broad role categories instead of too many small variations.

2. Restrict Permissions for Lower Roles

- Prevent new users from spamming, tagging everyone, or posting links.

- Only allow trusted roles to moderate or manage channels.

3. Assign Colors Logically

- Administrators should have strong, noticeable colors.

- Moderators should have a different but still noticeable color.

- Regular members should have a more neutral color.

4. Regularly Update and Maintain Roles

- As your server grows, adjust roles to fit new community needs.

- Ensure role permissions align with server rules and policies.

5. Test Role Visibility

- Use an alternate account or ask a friend to check how roles appear in the server.

- Make adjustments based on user feedback.

Conclusion

Using role hierarchies and role colors effectively can greatly improve server management, member engagement, and overall organization. By setting up a clear role structure and assigning distinct colors, you create a server that is easy to navigate and fosters a sense of community.

Next Section: 4.3 Customizing Your Server

In the next section, we'll explore how to add **custom emojis, welcome messages, and server banners** to make your Discord server unique!

4.3 Customizing Your Server

4.3.1 Creating Custom Emojis and Stickers

One of the most exciting aspects of managing a Discord server is the ability to customize it with custom emojis and stickers. These visual elements help make your server more engaging, fun, and personalized to your community's theme or interests. Whether you want to add memes, brand-specific icons, or fun reaction images, Discord provides built-in tools to upload and use custom emojis and stickers effectively.

This section will guide you through everything you need to know about creating, uploading, and managing custom emojis and stickers on your Discord server.

1. Understanding Custom Emojis on Discord

What Are Custom Emojis?

Custom emojis on Discord are user-uploaded images that can be used in messages, reactions, and even in some bot commands. They function just like standard emojis but are unique to your server.

Key features of custom emojis:

- They can be static (PNG, JPG, GIF) or animated (GIF only, for Nitro users).

- Each server can upload up to 50 static emojis (with more slots available via boosts).

- Only Nitro users can use custom emojis across different servers.

- Custom emojis must be 128x128 pixels in size but will be resized to 32x32 pixels when used.

How to Create Custom Emojis

1. Choosing an Image for Your Emoji

Before you upload an emoji, you need an image. Consider the following guidelines:

- **Format:** PNG, JPG, or GIF (GIFs only work for animated emojis).

- **Size:** Recommended size is **120x120 pixels** (Discord will resize it).

- **Transparency:** PNG images with transparent backgrounds work best.

- **Clarity:** Avoid overly detailed images, as they will be resized to 32x32 pixels.

2. Editing and Resizing Your Emoji

To ensure your emoji looks good, you can use image editing tools such as:

- **Adobe Photoshop** (Professional editing)

- **Canva** (Easy-to-use web-based tool)

- **GIMP** (Free alternative to Photoshop)

- **Remove.bg** (For removing backgrounds from images)

Resize your image to **128x128 pixels** and make sure it is visually clear at **32x32 pixels** (since that's how it will appear in chat).

How to Upload Custom Emojis to Your Discord Server

Step 1: Access the Server Settings

1. Open Discord and navigate to your server.

2. Click on the server name at the top-left corner.

3. Select "Server Settings" from the dropdown menu.

Step 2: Go to the Emoji Settings

1. In the left sidebar, click on "Emoji" under the Server Settings section.

2. You'll see a section titled "Custom Emoji" with an upload button.

Step 3: Upload Your Emoji

1. Click the Upload Emoji button.

2. Select the image file from your computer.

3. Assign a short name (e.g., :funnycat:).

4. Click Save Changes.

Your emoji is now available for server members to use!

Note:

- Non-Nitro users can only use these emojis within the server where they were uploaded.

- Nitro users can use custom emojis across multiple servers.

2. Understanding Custom Stickers on Discord

What Are Custom Stickers?

Stickers are larger, more expressive images compared to emojis. Unlike emojis, stickers are designed to convey emotions or reactions in a single image. Discord provides default stickers, but you can also upload custom stickers to your server.

Key features of stickers:

- They must be in PNG, APNG, or Lottie format.

- Recommended size: 512x512 pixels.

- Unlike emojis, stickers cannot be used across different servers (even for Nitro users).

- Requires Level 1 Boost (or higher) to upload custom stickers.

How to Create Custom Stickers

1. Choosing an Image for Your Sticker

To create a high-quality sticker, consider these tips:

- Use a PNG or APNG file for transparency.

- Design for clarity at 512x512 pixels to ensure good visibility.

- Avoid excessive detail, as stickers are meant to be simple but expressive.

2. Using Sticker Design Tools

Some great tools for creating stickers include:

- Adobe Illustrator (For professional vector stickers)
- Procreate (iPad) (For hand-drawn stickers)
- Canva (For simple drag-and-drop sticker creation)
- Sticker Mule's Free Sticker Maker

If you want animated stickers, you'll need APNG format, which can be created using:

- Adobe After Effects + Bodymovin Plugin
- LottieFiles Editor

How to Upload Custom Stickers to Your Discord Server

Step 1: Access the Server Settings

1. Open Discord and go to your server.
2. Click on the **server name** and select **"Server Settings"**.

Step 2: Navigate to Stickers

1. In the left menu, click **"Stickers"**.
2. If your server has **Boost Level 1**, you'll see an **upload section**.

Step 3: Upload Your Sticker

1. Click **"Upload Sticker"**.
2. Select your sticker file (PNG/APNG).
3. Give it a **name** and **emoji association** (for easy access).
4. Click **Save Changes**.

Now, members can use your stickers in chat!

3. Managing and Organizing Your Custom Emojis and Stickers

Renaming or Deleting Emojis and Stickers

- To rename or delete an emoji/sticker, go to Server Settings → Emoji/Stickers and make changes.

- Emojis can be replaced, but stickers need to be deleted and re-uploaded.

Using Bots to Manage Emojis

Several Discord bots can help manage emojis efficiently, such as:

- Emoji.gg Bot (for browsing and adding emojis from an online library)

- NitroBot (to enable Nitro-like features for non-Nitro users)

Expanding Emoji and Sticker Limits

- Base servers get 50 emoji slots and 0 sticker slots.

- Boosting the server unlocks more emoji/sticker slots:

  - Level 1: +50 emojis, +15 stickers

  - Level 2: +100 emojis, +30 stickers

  - Level 3: +200 emojis, +60 stickers

4. Best Practices for Custom Emojis and Stickers

1. Make them relevant – Use emojis and stickers that fit your server's theme.

2. Keep them simple – Complex designs may not be visible at small sizes.

3. Limit animated emojis – Too many can make chat distracting.

4. Regularly update your collection – Keep your community engaged with fresh content.

Conclusion

Custom emojis and stickers add a personal touch to your Discord server, making conversations more engaging and visually expressive. By following this guide, you can create, upload, and manage emojis and stickers that reflect your community's personality.

Next Section: 4.3.2 Setting Up Welcome Messages and Rules

In the next section, we'll explore how to make **new members feel welcome** with automated messages and rules setup.

4.3.2 Setting Up Welcome Messages and Rules

Creating a welcoming environment is crucial for the success of any Discord server. A well-structured server not only provides clear guidelines for behavior but also makes new members feel engaged and included. Two essential aspects of setting up a Discord server are:

- Welcome messages: These help new users understand the purpose of your server and guide them on how to get started.

- Server rules: Establishing clear rules ensures that all members adhere to a common code of conduct, fostering a safe and enjoyable community.

This section will walk you through why welcome messages and rules are important, how to set them up, and best practices to ensure clarity and engagement.

---

1. The Importance of Welcome Messages and Rules

Why Are Welcome Messages Important?

Welcome messages serve multiple purposes:

- Make new members feel valued – A personalized greeting helps create a positive first impression.

- Provide important server information – A well-crafted welcome message can direct users to key channels and resources.

- Encourage interaction – New members may feel overwhelmed in a new server. A friendly welcome can encourage them to participate.

Why Are Server Rules Important?

Rules define the expected behavior within a server and help prevent conflicts, spam, and toxicity. Clear rules:

- Maintain order and structure – Preventing disruptive behavior keeps the server enjoyable for everyone.

- Protect community members – Rules can address safety concerns, such as harassment and hate speech.

- Avoid misunderstandings – Defining expectations prevents conflicts between members and moderators.

Now that we understand their importance, let's dive into how to set up both features effectively.

2. Setting Up a Welcome Message in Discord

Discord allows server owners to automate welcome messages using built-in settings or third-party bots. You can choose to send a welcome message in a dedicated text channel or send a direct message (DM) to new members.

Method 1: Using Discord's Built-in Welcome System

Discord provides a simple, automated welcome message feature. Here's how to set it up:

1. **Go to Server Settings**

   o Click on your server's name in the top-left corner.

   o Select **Server Settings > Overview**.

2. **Enable the Welcome Screen**

   o Scroll down to find the **Welcome Screen** section.

   o Click on **Enable Welcome Screen**.

3. **Customize the Welcome Message**

   o Choose a friendly greeting, such as:

"Welcome to [Server Name]! We're glad to have you here. Check out #rules to get started!"

   o Add links to important channels (e.g., #introductions, #announcements).

4. **Save and Test**

o   Save your settings and create a **test account** to see how the welcome message appears.

Method 2: Using Bots for Custom Welcome Messages

For a more interactive experience, you can use Discord bots to send welcome messages. Some popular bots include:

- MEE6 – Allows personalized welcome messages.
- Dyno – Supports embedding images and assigning roles.
- Carl-bot – Provides reaction-based role assignments.

How to Set Up a Welcome Message Using MEE6

1. **Invite MEE6 to Your Server**

    o   Go to mee6.xyz and log in.

    o   Select your server and grant necessary permissions.

2. **Enable the Welcome Feature**

    o   Click on Welcome & Goodbye in MEE6's dashboard.

    o   Enable Send a message when a user joins the server.

3. **Customize Your Message**

    o   Set the **welcome message** in the designated channel (e.g., #welcome).

    o   Example message:

    o   🎉 Welcome, {user}! 🎉

    o   We're excited to have you in [Server Name].

    o   Check out #rules and introduce yourself in #introductions!

    o   You can use placeholders like {user} to automatically insert the new member's name.

4. **Save and Test**

    o   Try joining with an alternate account to ensure everything works smoothly.

3. Creating and Displaying Server Rules

Once your welcome message is set up, the next step is to establish and display your server rules. Rules should be clear, concise, and easy to find.

Where Should You Display Your Rules?

1. **A Dedicated #rules Channel**

   o Create a text channel named **#rules** or **#server-rules**.

   o Set the channel to **read-only** so that only admins can post.

2. **Use Discord's Membership Screening Feature**

   o Discord allows you to require new members to accept rules before interacting in the server.

   o Go to **Server Settings > Membership Screening > Enable**.

   o Add your rules and enable **"I agree"** verification.

How to Write Effective Server Rules

Here are some key guidelines when drafting your rules:

- Keep them short and simple – Avoid long, complex legal jargon.

- Use a positive tone – Instead of "No spam," say "Keep conversations meaningful."

- Make expectations clear – Use examples to clarify what is allowed and what isn't.

- Be specific – Instead of "Be respectful," explain what constitutes disrespect.

Example of a Well-Formatted Rules List

📜 Welcome to [Server Name]! Please follow these rules:

1. **Be respectful** – Treat all members with kindness. No hate speech, racism, or harassment.

2. **No spamming** – Avoid excessive messages, emojis, or @mentions.

3. **Use the correct channels** – Keep discussions relevant to the channel topics.

4. **No NSFW content** – This is a safe space. No inappropriate images or discussions.

5. **Follow Discord's TOS** – You must comply with Discord's Community Guidelines. /https://discord.com/guidelines

💡 *Breaking these rules may result in warnings or bans. Thank you for helping us keep this community friendly!*

Using Bots to Enforce Rules

If you want to automate rule enforcement, consider bots like:

- Dyno – Auto-moderates chat and issues warnings.

- Carl-bot – Allows reaction-based rule agreements.

- MEE6 – Automatically bans repeated offenders.

4. Best Practices for Effective Welcome Messages and Rules

To ensure that your welcome system and rules are effective, follow these best practices:

Do's

✓ Use a friendly and inviting tone in your welcome message.
✓ Include links to important channels like #introductions or #faq.
✓ Keep rules concise and clear—nobody likes to read an essay.
✓ Regularly update your rules to address new challenges or issues.
✓ Use Discord's built-in features to streamline the experience.

Don'ts

✗ Overload new users with information in the welcome message.
✗ Use vague rules like "Be nice" without explaining what that means.
✗ Make rules too strict—keep the community fun and engaging.
✗ Ignore enforcement—rules mean nothing if they aren't enforced.

Conclusion

Setting up welcome messages and rules is a vital part of managing a successful Discord server. A well-crafted welcome message helps new members feel at home, while clear and structured rules ensure a safe and enjoyable experience for everyone.

By leveraging Discord's built-in features and bots, you can create a welcoming and well-moderated community that fosters engagement, participation, and long-term growth.

Next Section: 4.3.3 Using Server Banners and Icons

In the next section, we'll explore how to visually enhance your Discord server using **custom banners, icons, and branding elements**.

4.3.3 Using Server Banners and Icons

Customizing a Discord server is an essential step in creating a unique and engaging community. One of the most effective ways to personalize your server is by using server banners and icons, which help define your server's identity and make it visually appealing to members. In this section, we will explore the importance of server banners and icons, how to set them up, and best practices for designing them.

1. Understanding Server Banners and Icons

What Are Server Banners?

A server banner is a large image displayed at the top of your server's channel list. It serves as a branding element and can be used to set the theme of your community. The banner is only available to servers that have Server Boost Level 2 or higher, meaning your community must either contribute enough boosts or be subscribed to Discord Nitro.

Key Features of Server Banners:

- Visible to all members at the top of the server.

- Helps set the tone and personality of the server.

- Can be updated anytime to match events, holidays, or community changes.

- Available in Server Boost Level 2 or higher servers.

What Is a Server Icon?

A server icon is the small, circular image that represents your server in the server list. This is the first visual element users see when browsing their joined servers, making it crucial for server recognition.

Key Features of Server Icons:

- Appears on the server list and invites.

- Helps members easily identify the server.

- Can be an image, logo, or animated icon (with Nitro Boost Level 1 or higher).

2. How to Set Up a Server Icon

Setting a server icon is simple and requires no boosts. Follow these steps to upload or change your server icon:

Step 1: Access Server Settings

1. Open Discord and navigate to your server.

2. Click on the server name in the top-left corner.

3. Select "Server Settings" from the dropdown menu.

Step 2: Upload Your Server Icon

1. Under the "Overview" tab, locate the Server Icon section.

2. Click on the current icon (or blank icon) to upload a new image.

3. Select an image from your device (recommended size: 512x512 pixels).

Step 3: Adjust and Save

1. Crop the image if needed to fit the circular shape.

2. Click **"Save Changes"** to update your icon.

Tips for Choosing a Server Icon:

✓ Use a recognizable image, such as a logo or mascot.
✓ Keep the background transparent for a cleaner look.

✓ Ensure the image is high quality and not pixelated.

✓ If your server is boosted to Level 1 or higher, you can upload an animated GIF icon.

3. How to Set Up a Server Banner

Unlike icons, server banners require Level 2 boosting. If your server qualifies, follow these steps to upload a banner:

Step 1: Check Your Server Boost Level

1. Go to your Server Settings > Server Boost Status.

2. Ensure your server has reached Level 2 or higher.

Step 2: Upload Your Banner

1. Navigate to Server Settings > Overview.

2. Scroll down to the Server Banner Background section.

3. Click on Upload Banner and select an image from your device.

Step 3: Adjust and Save

1. The recommended size for banners is 960x540 pixels.

2. Make sure the image is within the 8MB file limit.

3. Click Save Changes to apply your new banner.

4. Designing an Eye-Catching Server Banner

Choosing the Right Colors and Style

- Match Your Theme: If your server is about gaming, use vibrant and energetic colors. If it's a business or professional server, opt for clean and minimalistic designs.

- Maintain Consistency: Use colors that complement your server icon and general branding.

Adding Text and Logos

- You can include your server's name, slogan, or social media handles on the banner.

- Keep text simple and readable, avoiding excessive clutter.

Using Graphics and Effects

- Add subtle patterns or gradients to create depth.

- Avoid overly complex designs that distract from the main purpose of the banner.

Tools for Creating Banners and Icons

If you don't have a graphic design background, you can use these tools:

- Canva (Free & Paid) – Easy drag-and-drop interface for beginners.

- Adobe Photoshop (Paid) – Advanced editing options for professionals.

- Figma (Free & Paid) – Great for collaborative design.

5. Best Practices for Updating Server Banners and Icons

Keeping It Fresh and Engaging

- Update your banner for special events, such as holidays, anniversaries, or major server milestones.

- Rotate designs occasionally to keep members engaged.

Avoiding Common Mistakes

⊘ Low-Quality Images: Use high-resolution images to prevent pixelation.
⊘ Excessive Text: Keep text minimal and ensure it's readable.
⊘ Overcomplicated Designs: Simple and clean banners are often the most effective.

6. Advanced Features: Animated Icons and Banners

If your server has Server Boost Level 3, you can upload an animated GIF banner to make your server stand out even more.

How to Upload an Animated Server Icon

1. Ensure your GIF is 512x512 pixels and under 8MB.

2. Upload it under Server Settings > Overview > Server Icon.

How to Upload an Animated Server Banner

1. Your animated banner must be in GIF format.

2. Upload it under Server Settings > Overview > Server Banner Background.

Conclusion

Server banners and icons are essential branding elements that help define your Discord community. A well-designed icon makes your server easily recognizable, while a custom banner enhances its visual appeal. By following the best practices outlined in this guide, you can create a visually engaging environment that attracts new members and keeps existing ones engaged.

In the next section, we will explore how to set up welcome messages and rules to improve member onboarding.

CHAPTER V
Enhancing Your Server with Bots and Integrations

5.1 Introduction to Discord Bots

5.1.1 What Are Bots and How Do They Work?

Introduction

As Discord servers grow in size and complexity, managing them manually can become time-consuming and challenging. This is where Discord bots come into play. Bots are automated programs designed to perform various tasks within a Discord server, such as moderating chats, playing music, generating memes, integrating third-party services, and much more.

In this section, we will explore what Discord bots are, how they work, and why they are essential for enhancing your server's functionality and user experience.

What Are Discord Bots?

A Discord bot is an automated script or program that interacts with Discord's API to perform specific functions within a server. Bots can:

- Automate repetitive tasks (e.g., welcoming new members, assigning roles).
- Moderate the server by filtering spam, detecting rule violations, and managing bans.
- Enhance user engagement by adding games, trivia, polls, or giveaways.

- Integrate with external platforms like Twitch, YouTube, Reddit, or Google Docs.

Essentially, bots help reduce the workload of server administrators while making the community experience more interactive and enjoyable.

How Do Discord Bots Work?

1. Discord API and Bot Tokens

Discord provides an API (Application Programming Interface) that allows developers to create bots that interact with servers. To function properly, each bot requires:

- A bot token: A unique identifier provided by Discord when the bot is registered.

- Permissions and roles: Specific access levels granted by server administrators.

- A hosting environment: Bots need to run on a server, cloud platform, or local machine.

Once set up, bots connect to Discord servers and execute commands based on user inputs or automated triggers.

2. Command-Based vs. Automated Bots

There are two main types of Discord bots:

a) Command-Based Bots

- Require users to enter specific prefix commands (e.g., !play for music bots).

- Usually respond with a message, action, or data output.

- Example: !ban @user – A moderation bot may issue a ban when this command is used.

b) Automated Bots

- Operate based on event triggers instead of commands.

- Example: A bot automatically assigns a "New Member" role when someone joins the server.

Many bots combine both command-based and automated functionalities for flexibility.

Common Features of Discord Bots

1. Moderation and Administration Bots

Bots help keep servers organized and safe by:

- Filtering spam, offensive language, and NSFW content.
- Automatically banning or muting rule violators.
- Logging deleted messages and actions for admins to review.

Example Bots:

- MEE6 – Custom moderation rules, automated messages, and role assignments.
- Dyno Bot – Advanced moderation, auto-responses, and custom commands.

2. Music and Entertainment Bots

Music bots allow users to:

- Stream music from YouTube, Spotify, or SoundCloud.
- Create playlists and share music with friends.

Example Bots:

- Hydra – A high-quality music bot with an interactive interface.
- Chip Bot – Plays music with bass boost and audio filters.

3. Gaming and Fun Bots

Bots can make servers more entertaining by adding:

- Mini-games (e.g., word puzzles, trivia, casino games).
- Memes, GIF generators, and custom reactions.
- XP-based leveling systems for active users.

Example Bots:

- Dank Memer – Meme creation, currency system, and random fun commands.
- Pokétwo – A Pokémon-catching bot for Discord.

4. Productivity and Utility Bots

Bots improve workflow by integrating with:

- Google Calendar, Trello, and Notion for task management.
- GitHub and Jira for software development teams.
- Reddit, Twitter, and RSS feeds for automated news updates.

Example Bots:

- Tatsumaki – A productivity bot with reputation and leaderboard tracking.
- Carl-bot – Custom automated messages and logs.

5. Streaming and Content Creation Bots

For streamers and content creators, Discord bots help by:

- Notifying server members when a stream goes live.
- Automatically posting YouTube video links.
- Managing fan engagement with giveaways and polls.

Example Bots:

- Streamcord – Sends automatic live stream alerts for Twitch and YouTube.
- Nightbot – Moderation and automated chat responses for streamers.

Why Should You Use Discord Bots?

1. Automation Saves Time

- Instead of manually assigning roles, approving members, or deleting spam, bots handle these tasks instantly.

2. Improved Server Engagement

- Gamification features like XP leveling and mini-games encourage members to stay active.

3. Better Moderation and Security

- Bots prevent raids, spam, and inappropriate content with automated moderation tools.

4. Enhanced User Experience

- Music, memes, and interactive features make servers more enjoyable and dynamic.

5. Seamless Integration with Other Platforms

- Whether you're a gamer, student, or professional, bots connect Discord to tools like YouTube, Twitch, GitHub, and Google Drive.

How Do You Get a Discord Bot?

There are three main ways to add a bot to your Discord server:

1. Using Pre-Made Bots

- Websites like Top.gg, Discord Bot List, and Bots on Discord provide thousands of ready-to-use bots.
- Simply invite the bot to your server, grant permissions, and start using it.

2. Creating a Custom Bot

- Developers can build their own bots using Discord's API and programming languages like:
    - Python (discord.py)
    - JavaScript (discord.js)
    - Go, C#, and Java
- Custom bots allow for unique features tailored to your server's needs.

3. Using Bot Hosting Services

- Platforms like Heroku, Replit, and AWS provide cloud hosting for bot scripts.
- Helps keep bots online 24/7 without running them on a local PC.

Conclusion

Discord bots revolutionize server management by automating tasks, enhancing moderation, and providing entertainment. Whether you're looking for a music bot, a moderation bot, or a productivity tool, there's a bot for every need.

In the next section (**5.1.2 Popular Discord Bots for Different Purposes**), we will explore the **best bots available**, their features, and how they can improve your Discord experience.

5.1.2 Popular Discord Bots for Different Purposes

Discord bots are an essential tool for enhancing server functionality, automating tasks, and improving user experience. Whether you're managing a gaming community, a study group, or a business workspace, bots can help streamline operations and add engaging features to your server. In this section, we'll explore some of the most popular Discord bots across different categories, including moderation, entertainment, productivity, and custom bot development.

---

1. Moderation Bots: Keeping Your Server Safe and Organized

Moderation bots are crucial for managing communities and ensuring that server rules are followed. These bots can automatically enforce rules, ban or mute disruptive members, and prevent spam. Below are some of the most widely used moderation bots:

1.1 MEE6

◆ **Features:**

- Automatic moderation (banning, muting, kicking).

- Custom welcome messages and announcements.

- Leveling system with XP rewards.

- Custom commands and reaction roles.

- Auto-moderation to detect spam, links, and bad language.

◆ **Best For:**
Gaming communities, large public servers, and professional communities that require strict moderation.

◈ **How to Use:**

- Visit the MEE6 website and log in with your Discord account.

- Select your server and authorize the bot.

- Configure moderation settings from the dashboard.

1.2 Dyno

◈ **Features:**

- Auto-moderation with customizable settings.

- Logging system for tracking user activity.

- Custom commands and role management.

- Integration with Twitch, YouTube, and Reddit.

◈ **Best For:**
Servers that need advanced moderation while integrating with social media platforms.

1.3 Carl-bot

◈ **Features:**

- Auto-moderation with anti-spam filters.

- Reaction roles for easy member management.

- Logging and auditing features.

- Customizable commands and automation tools.

◈ **Best For:**
Communities that require detailed logging and custom role management.

2. Entertainment Bots: Making Discord More Fun

Entertainment bots add fun and engaging features like music playback, memes, trivia games, and AI chat capabilities.

2.1 Rythm (Music Bot - No Longer Available, But Alternatives Exist)

◆ **Features:**

- High-quality music streaming from YouTube, SoundCloud, and Spotify.

- Playlist support and song queueing.

- Customizable audio settings and volume control.

◆ **Alternatives:**

- **Hydra** – Multi-platform music bot with playlist support.

- **FredBoat** – Open-source bot with reliable music streaming.

2.2 Dank Memer

◆ **Features:**

- Generate memes with a built-in meme creator.

- Virtual currency system with gambling and heist features.

- Fun commands like image manipulation and random jokes.

◆ **Best For:**
Servers that enjoy casual fun and interactive community activities.

2.3 Pokétwo (Pokémon-Themed Bot)

◆ **Features:**

- Allows users to catch, trade, and battle Pokémon.

- Encourages community engagement through collection challenges.

- Regular updates and new Pokémon additions.

◆ **Best For:**
Pokémon fan servers and communities that love interactive mini-games.

3. Productivity Bots: Enhancing Server Efficiency

Productivity bots help manage tasks, schedule events, and integrate external services.

3.1 Apollo (Event Scheduling Bot)

◈ Features:

- Create and manage scheduled events.

- Users can RSVP to events directly in Discord.

- Integrates with Google Calendar.

◈ Best For:
Servers that host regular meetings, game nights, or study sessions.

3.2 Reminder Bot

◈ Features:

- Set reminders for individuals or the entire server.

- Customizable alert messages and repeat reminders.

- Easy-to-use command system for scheduling tasks.

◈ Best For:
Students, businesses, and communities that require event coordination.

3.3 Discord Translator

◈ Features:

- Automatic translation between multiple languages.

- Supports over 100 languages.

- Custom translation channels for multilingual servers.

◈ Best For:
Global communities that need real-time translation services.

4. Customization Bots: Personalizing Your Server

Customization bots allow you to create unique user experiences with reaction roles, automation, and custom commands.

4.1 YAGPDB (Yet Another General Purpose Discord Bot)

◆ **Features:**

- Custom role assignment through reaction roles.

- Extensive automation options.

- Logging and anti-spam moderation tools.

◆ **Best For:**
Servers that need highly customizable features with automation.

4.2 Tatsu

◆ **Features:**

- Leveling system with leaderboards.

- Reputation and economy features.

- Custom profile cards for members.

◆ **Best For:**
Communities that want to encourage participation through a ranking system.

---

5. AI and Chatbots: Adding Smart Conversations

AI-powered bots can simulate conversations, answer FAQs, and provide smart automation.

5.1 ChatGPT Discord Bot

◆ **Features:**

- AI-generated responses based on OpenAI's ChatGPT.

- Can answer questions, tell stories, and generate text.

- Customizable chatbot behavior.

◆ **Best For:**
Servers that want an interactive chatbot for entertainment or support.

5.2 AI Image Generator Bot

◆ **Features:**

- Generates AI-powered images based on text prompts.

- Allows users to create artwork in real-time.

- Supports multiple AI art styles.

◆ **Best For:**

Creative communities and artists who want on-demand AI-generated images.

6. Gaming Bots: Enhancing Multiplayer Experiences

Gaming bots add features for matchmaking, leaderboards, and interactive gameplay.

6.1 Chess Bot

◆ **Features:**

- Play chess with other members or AI.

- Supports different time controls and rating systems.

- Saves game history for analysis.

◆ **Best For:**

Chess enthusiasts looking to challenge members within Discord.

6.2 Mudae (Anime and Manga Bot)

◆ **Features:**

- Collect and trade anime characters.

- Interactive gacha system.

- Trivia and minigames related to anime and manga.

◆ **Best For:**

Anime fans and otaku communities.

Conclusion

Discord bots are powerful tools that can improve server engagement, automate tasks, and enhance user experience. Whether you need moderation, entertainment, productivity, or AI-based chat features, there is a bot available to meet your needs.

In the next section, we will learn how to find and add these bots to your server, ensuring you get the most out of Discord's automation and customization capabilities.

5.1.3 How to Find and Add Bots to Your Server

Discord bots are an essential part of managing and enhancing a server, automating tasks, moderating users, and adding interactive features like games, music, and custom commands. If you want to take your server to the next level, learning how to find and install the right bots is crucial.

In this section, we will explore:

- Where to find reliable Discord bots

- How to add bots to your server

- Setting up permissions and ensuring security

By the end of this chapter, you will have a clear understanding of how to integrate bots into your Discord server and fully utilize their features.

---

1. Where to Find Reliable Discord Bots

There are thousands of bots available online, but not all of them are trustworthy or effective. Choosing the right bot requires careful consideration of its functionality, reputation, and security. Here are some of the most reliable sources for finding Discord bots:

1.1 Popular Discord Bot Directories

1.1.1 Top.gg

Top.gg is one of the most popular websites for discovering Discord bots. It provides:

- A large collection of verified bots

- User ratings and reviews

- Categories such as music, moderation, gaming, and economy

To find a bot on Top.gg:

1. Visit https://top.gg.

2. Use the search bar to find bots by keyword (e.g., "music bot," "moderation bot").

3. Browse by category to discover bots suited for specific needs.

4. Check reviews, ratings, and the number of servers using the bot to evaluate its quality.

1.1.2 Discord Bot List

Discord Bot List is another reputable bot directory that categorizes bots based on functionality. It offers:

- Bot descriptions with usage instructions

- Active community feedback

- A user-friendly interface for browsing and filtering bots

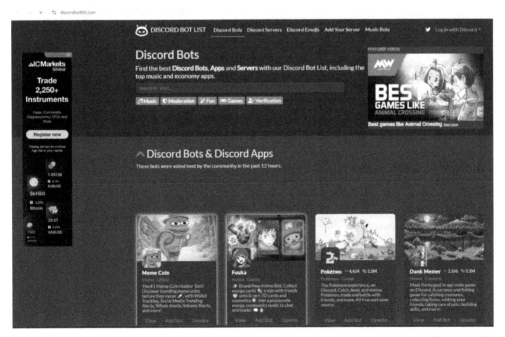

1.1.3 Bots on GitHub and Developer Websites

Many developers create custom bots and open-source projects on GitHub. Searching "Discord bot" on GitHub can lead to unique bots that are not available in mainstream directories. However, these bots require some technical knowledge to host and configure.

To find bots on GitHub:

1. Go to https://github.com.

2. Use the search query "Discord bot" to browse repositories.

3. Read the bot's documentation to see installation instructions.

If you prefer custom-built solutions, hiring a bot developer from platforms like Fiverr or Upwork is an option.

1.2 Official Discord Bot Verification Badge

To ensure security, Discord provides an **Official Bot Verification Badge** for bots with over 100 servers. A verified bot means:

- It meets Discord's security guidelines.

- It has been reviewed by Discord's Trust & Safety team.

- It is less likely to be malicious or contain harmful code.

When choosing a bot, look for the verified badge to avoid security risks.

2. How to Add a Bot to Your Discord Server

Once you have selected a bot, the next step is adding it to your server. Follow these steps:

Step 1: Make Sure You Have the Right Permissions

To add a bot, you must have either:

- Administrator permissions OR

- The "Manage Server" permission

If you are not the server owner, ask an admin to grant you these permissions.

Step 2: Get the Bot's Invite Link

Most bot directories provide a direct **"Add to Server"** or **"Invite"** button. If you are adding a bot manually, use this link format:

https://discord.com/oauth2/authorize?client_id=BOT_CLIENT_ID&scope=bot&permissions=PERMISSION_NUMBER

Replace:

- BOT_CLIENT_ID with the actual bot's ID.

- PERMISSION_NUMBER with the required permissions.

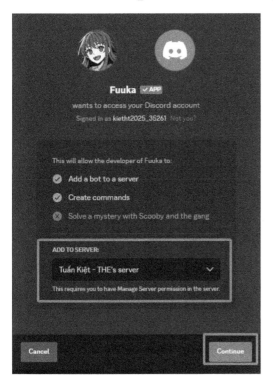

Step 3: Select Your Server

1. Clicking the bot's invite link will open Discord's authorization page.

2. Select the server where you want to add the bot.

3. Click "Continue" and grant the necessary permissions.

4. Click "Authorize" to complete the process.

Step 4: Verify That the Bot Has Joined

After authorization, go to your Discord server and check:

- The member list (the bot should appear under "Online").

- The bot's commands (some bots require a prefix like !help or /help to function).

3. Setting Up Bot Permissions and Ensuring Security

Adding a bot is just the first step. You must also manage its permissions to ensure it doesn't disrupt your server or create security risks.

3.1 Understanding Bot Permissions

When adding a bot, you will see a list of permissions it requests, such as:

- Administrator – Full control over the server (not recommended for most bots).

- Manage Channels – Allows the bot to create, edit, or delete channels.

- Kick/Ban Members – Required for moderation bots.

- Read & Send Messages – Essential for any bot that interacts with users.

Always review the requested permissions carefully. If a bot asks for admin rights but doesn't need them, reconsider using it.

3.2 Restricting Bot Access with Roles

To limit a bot's power:

1. Go to Server Settings > Roles.

2. Create a new role (e.g., Bot Role).

3. Assign only the necessary permissions.

4. Move the bot to this role and disable unwanted permissions.

This prevents bots from deleting channels, banning users, or accessing private areas.

3.3 Removing or Replacing Bots

If a bot is malfunctioning or no longer needed:

1. Right-click the bot's name in the server list.

2. Click Kick (removes the bot temporarily) or Ban (prevents rejoining).

3. If replacing a bot, find an alternative with similar functionality.

Conclusion

Adding bots to your Discord server enhances functionality, automation, and engagement. However, it's essential to:

- Choose bots from reputable sources (e.g., Top.gg, Discord Bot List).

- Grant only necessary permissions to protect server security.

- Regularly monitor and update bots to ensure they function properly.

With the right bots in place, your Discord server can run more efficiently, provide better moderation, and offer interactive features for your community.

Next Section: 5.2 Managing and Configuring Bots

In the next section, we will explore **how to set up bot permissions, customize bot behavior, and troubleshoot common issues**.

5.2 Managing and Configuring Bots

5.2.1 Setting Up Bot Permissions and Roles

Adding bots to a Discord server is only the first step in enhancing your server's functionality. To ensure that bots work effectively while maintaining security and control, it's crucial to configure their permissions and roles properly. Misconfigured bot permissions can lead to security risks, spam issues, and unwanted disruptions in your server. This section will guide you through the process of setting up bot roles, assigning permissions, and managing access levels to create a secure and efficient server environment.

Understanding Discord's Role and Permission System

Before diving into bot-specific permissions, it's essential to understand how Discord's role system works.

- Roles: These are sets of permissions that can be assigned to users or bots. Each role determines what actions a member (or bot) can perform.

- Permissions: These dictate what a role can and cannot do, such as sending messages, managing channels, or kicking members.

- Hierarchy: Roles are arranged in a hierarchy, meaning that higher roles have control over lower roles. Bots will generally operate based on the highest role assigned to them.

Bots function just like server members, meaning they need roles and permissions to perform actions within your server.

Step-by-Step Guide to Setting Up Bot Permissions and Roles

Step 1: Creating a Role for the Bot

Rather than assigning permissions to a bot directly, it's best to create a **dedicated bot role**. This ensures better organization and security.

1. **Open Your Server Settings**

   o   Click on your server's name in the **top-left corner**.

   o   Select **Server Settings > Roles**.

2. **Create a New Role**

   o   Click the **Create Role** button.

   o   Name the role something descriptive, such as "Bot Manager" or "Automated Assistant".

   o   Choose a **role color** (optional) to visually differentiate bot roles from regular user roles.

3. **Set Basic Role Permissions**

   o   Under the **Permissions** tab, configure general permissions for the bot.

   o   **Common permissions for bot roles include**:

      ▪   ✅ Manage Messages → Allows bots to delete spam messages.

      ▪   ✅ Read Messages → Lets the bot read messages in the channels it operates in.

      ▪   ✅ Send Messages → Allows the bot to respond to users.

      ▪   ✅ Embed Links → Enables the bot to send rich embedded content.

      ▪   ✅ Use External Emojis → Lets the bot use emojis from other servers.

      ▪   ✖ Administrator → Generally **not recommended**, as it grants full control over the server.

Step 2: Assigning the Role to the Bot

Once the bot role is created, it must be assigned to the bot.

1.   Go to Server Settings > Members.

2.   Find the bot in the member list (bots have a "BOT" label next to their name).

3. Click the + icon next to the bot's name and select the role you created.

4. The bot will now inherit the permissions assigned to that role.

💡 **Tip**: If you have multiple bots, consider **separating roles** (e.g., "Moderation Bots," "Music Bots") to prevent permission conflicts.

Fine-Tuning Bot Permissions for Specific Channels

Bots may not need full access to every channel. You can **customize permissions** per channel to control where bots can and cannot operate.

Step 3: Restricting Bot Permissions in Channels

1. Go to Your Server's Channel List.

2. Right-click a channel where you want to limit bot access and select Edit Channel.

3. Click the Permissions tab.

4. Under "Roles/Members," select the bot's assigned role.

5. Adjust permissions per channel:

   o Allow the bot in moderation channels but deny access to private staff chats.

   o Enable bots to send messages in a help desk channel but disable message sending in an announcements channel.

   o Mute bots in voice channels where they aren't needed.

💡 **Example Use Case**: If you're using a **music bot**, it should only have access to a **"Music Room"** channel rather than the entire server.

Common Bot Permissions and Their Uses

Below is a breakdown of the most frequently used bot permissions and what they control.

Permission	Function	Recommended for Bots?
Manage Channels	Allows the bot to create, edit, or delete channels.	✖ Not recommended (Security risk)
Manage Roles	Lets the bot assign or remove roles.	✖ Use with caution
Kick Members	Enables the bot to kick users from the server.	✔ For moderation bots
Ban Members	Allows the bot to ban users permanently.	✔ For anti-spam bots
Manage Messages	Lets the bot delete or pin messages.	✔ For chat cleanup bots
Send Messages	Allows the bot to post in text channels.	✔ Essential for all bots
Embed Links	Enables the bot to send rich embedded content.	✔ Useful for announcement bots
Use External Emojis	Lets the bot use emojis from other servers.	✔ For fun bots
Connect to Voice	Allows the bot to join voice channels.	✔ For music bots

💡 **Security Tip**: Avoid giving bots **"Administrator"** rights unless absolutely necessary. Instead, assign only the permissions required for their function.

Troubleshooting Bot Permission Issues

Even after setting up permissions correctly, you may encounter problems where a bot is not functioning as expected. Below are common issues and their solutions:

Issue 1: The Bot Isn't Responding

- Check if the bot is online (some bots may be temporarily offline due to maintenance).

- Ensure the bot has the correct role and is assigned to the correct channels.

- Verify the bot's command prefix (some bots use !, others use ? or /).

Issue 2: The Bot Can't Send Messages in a Channel

- Check channel permissions and allow "Send Messages" for the bot role.
- Ensure the bot isn't muted in that channel.

Issue 3: The Bot is Kicking/Banning Members Incorrectly

- Review bot settings to ensure anti-spam or auto-moderation features aren't too aggressive.
- Adjust bot commands to require manual approval for bans/kicks.

Conclusion

Setting up bot permissions and roles correctly is essential to maintaining security, functionality, and efficiency in your Discord server. By carefully assigning permissions, restricting bot access to specific channels, and troubleshooting common issues, you can ensure that your bots enhance your server without causing disruptions.

Next Section: 5.2.2 Using Commands and Customizing Bot Behavior

In the next section, we will explore how to use bot commands, customize bot responses, and set up automation features to make the most out of your Discord bots.

5.2.2 Using Commands and Customizing Bot Behavior

Discord bots are an essential part of managing and enhancing a server, offering automation, moderation, entertainment, and utility functions. However, to get the most out of your bots, you need to understand how to use their commands and customize their behavior to fit your server's needs. This section will cover:

- How bot commands work
- Common command structures and syntax
- Using bot commands effectively
- Customizing bot responses and behaviors

- Advanced configuration for automation

By mastering bot commands and customization, you can create a more efficient and engaging server experience.

1. Understanding Bot Commands

What Are Bot Commands?

Bot commands are instructions given to a bot in Discord to trigger specific actions. These commands can be used for a variety of tasks, such as:

- Moderating a server (e.g., banning or muting users)

- Playing music in a voice channel

- Assigning roles automatically

- Fetching information (e.g., game stats, weather updates)

- Running fun interactions (e.g., memes, trivia games)

Most Discord bots operate through text commands entered in a server's chat. However, with the introduction of **slash commands**, Discord has made bot interactions more user-friendly and organized.

Types of Bot Commands

There are two main types of bot commands:

1. **Prefix-Based Commands**

   o Traditional bot commands require a prefix (e.g., !, ?, .) followed by a keyword.

   o Example: !ban @user (to ban a user).

   o The prefix varies depending on the bot and can often be customized.

2. **Slash Commands (/commands)**

   o Introduced by Discord to improve bot security and usability.

   o Displayed as a list when typing /, allowing users to select a command.

- o Example: /ban @user (to ban a user).

- o More structured and prevent conflicts between multiple bots.

Most modern bots now support **slash commands**, as they provide better security and prevent bot abuse.

2. Using Bot Commands Effectively

To use bot commands efficiently, you need to:

Check the Bot's Prefix or Slash Commands

- If a bot uses prefix-based commands, check what prefix it requires. Common prefixes include !, ?, and ..

- If a bot supports slash commands, simply type / in a chat to view all available commands.

Find a List of Available Commands

Most bots provide a help command, such as:

- !help or /help – Displays a list of commands and descriptions.

- !commands or /commands – Shows available functions of the bot.

For example, if you have **MEE6**, typing /help will show all moderation and automation commands available.

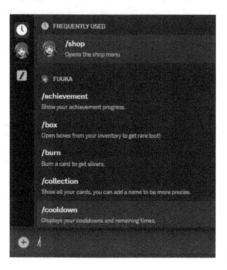

Using Bot Commands in Different Channels

- Some bots require specific permissions to work in certain channels.

- Moderation commands typically need Administrator or Manage Server permissions.

- Entertainment bots, such as music bots, may require Voice Channel permissions.

Commonly Used Bot Commands

Here are some common commands used in different types of bots:

1. Moderation Commands

Command	Function	Example
/ban @user	Bans a user	/ban @John123
/mute @user	Mutes a user	/mute @John123
/kick @user	Kicks a user from the server	/kick @John123
/clear [number]	Deletes messages in a channel	/clear 10

2. Music Bot Commands

Command	Function	Example
/play [song name]	Plays a song in a voice channel	/play Imagine Dragons
/pause	Pauses the music	/pause
/resume	Resumes playback	/resume
/skip	Skips the current song	/skip

3. Fun and Utility Commands

Command	Function	Example
/meme	Generates a random meme	/meme
/weather [city]	Shows the weather of a city	/weather New York
/quote	Generates a random quote	/quote

3. Customizing Bot Behavior

Many bots allow users to customize their behavior by modifying their settings. This can be done through:

1. Adjusting Bot Prefixes

- Some bots allow users to change their prefix to avoid conflicts with other bots.
- Example: !prefix ? (Changes the bot's command prefix to ?).

2. Customizing Auto-Responses

- Some bots, like MEE6 and Dyno, allow users to create custom commands.
- Example: Setting up /rules to display a custom set of server rules.

3. Managing Permissions for Bots

- To prevent bots from spamming or being misused, set proper permissions in:
  - Server settings → Roles → Bot Role

> o   Allow or deny specific actions, such as banning users or sending messages in certain channels.

4. Creating Automated Actions with Bots

- Use bots like Dyno or MEE6 to set up automatic welcome messages, role assignments, and moderation alerts.

- Example:

  > o   Auto-role assignment: Assigns roles to new users automatically.

  > o   Auto-moderation: Deletes messages with certain banned words.

4. Advanced Bot Customization

For more advanced users, some bots allow scripting and coding for full customization.

1. Using Webhooks for Automation

- Webhooks allow bots to send automated messages from other platforms (Trello, GitHub, etc.).

- Example: Sending real-time updates to a Discord channel when a new GitHub issue is created.

2. Using APIs to Extend Bot Functionality

- Developers can use Discord's API to create custom bots using Python or JavaScript.

- Example: A bot that tracks stock prices and updates users automatically.

5. Troubleshooting Bot Commands

If bot commands are not working, check the following:

1. Ensure the Bot Has Proper Permissions

- Go to **Server Settings** → **Roles** and check if the bot has permission to send messages and manage roles.

2. Check if the Bot is Online

- Some bots may go offline due to server downtime. Check the bot's status on its official website or Discord server.

3. Verify the Correct Prefix or Slash Command

- Ensure you're using the correct command format (/command for slash commands, !command for prefix-based bots).

4. Restart the Bot or Re-add It to the Server

- Sometimes, removing and re-adding a bot can resolve issues.

Conclusion

Using bot commands and customizing their behavior can greatly enhance the efficiency and engagement of your Discord server. By understanding how commands work, adjusting bot settings, and troubleshooting issues, you can create a well-managed and interactive community.

Next Section: 5.2.3 Troubleshooting Bot Issues

In the next section, we will cover how to diagnose and fix common bot-related issues to ensure smooth operation on your server.

5.2.3 Troubleshooting Bot Issues

Discord bots are powerful tools that can enhance your server's functionality, automate tasks, and improve community engagement. However, like any software, they are not immune to issues. Whether a bot is unresponsive, malfunctioning, or causing unintended problems, effective troubleshooting is key to ensuring your server runs smoothly.

This section will guide you through common bot issues, their causes, and step-by-step solutions to resolve them.

1. Understanding Common Discord Bot Issues

Before jumping into solutions, it's essential to recognize the types of problems you might encounter with Discord bots. Some of the most common issues include:

Bot Is Offline or Unresponsive

- The bot does not respond to commands.
- The bot appears as "Offline" in the member list.
- The bot was working before but suddenly stopped.

Bot Does Not Execute Commands Properly

- The bot responds with an error message.
- The bot does not recognize specific commands.
- The bot executes commands incorrectly.

Permission and Role Issues

- The bot does not have access to certain channels.
- The bot cannot assign roles or perform actions on users.
- The bot cannot delete messages, mute users, or ban members.

API and Rate Limit Problems

- The bot reaches Discord's rate limits and stops working temporarily.
- The bot experiences delays in executing commands.
- The bot fails to fetch data from external services (e.g., Twitch, YouTube, or Google).

Integration and Third-Party Errors

- The bot does not sync properly with other platforms.
- External services (e.g., Twitch, Spotify, or YouTube) fail to connect.
- Webhooks and automated notifications stop working.

2. Troubleshooting Steps for Common Bot Issues

Now that we have identified the most frequent problems, let's go through a step-by-step troubleshooting guide for each one.

Fixing an Offline or Unresponsive Bot

If a bot appears offline or is not responding to commands, try these solutions:

✅ Check the Bot's Status on Its Official Website or Dashboard

- Some bots, especially popular ones like MEE6, Dyno, or Carl-bot, have dedicated status pages that indicate if their servers are down.

- If the bot's service is experiencing downtime, you may need to wait until the issue is resolved by the bot developers.

✅ Ensure the Bot Is Added to Your Server

- Sometimes, server owners or administrators accidentally remove a bot. To verify:

  1. Open Discord and go to your server.

  2. Click Server Settings > Members and check if the bot is still present.

  3. If the bot is missing, invite it again using its official invite link.

✅ Check the Bot's Required Permissions

- If the bot lacks essential permissions, it might fail to perform actions or appear inactive.

- To fix this:

  1. Go to Server Settings > Roles and select the bot's role.

  2. Ensure the bot has permissions like Send Messages, Read Message History, Manage Roles, and Use Voice Activity.

  3. If necessary, create a separate bot role with all required permissions and assign it to the bot.

✅ Restart the Bot

- If you are using a self-hosted bot, restart it by stopping and re-running its script.

- If you are using a bot hosted by a third-party service, visit the bot's dashboard and restart it from there.

✅ Reinvite the Bot

- Sometimes, simply removing and reinviting the bot can resolve issues.

- To do this:

    1. Remove the bot from your server using Server Settings > Members.

    2. Reinvite the bot using its official link and grant it proper permissions.

Fixing Command Execution Problems

If the bot does not respond to commands correctly, follow these steps:

✅ **Check the Command Prefix**

- Some bots use a default prefix like !, ?, or /.

- If multiple bots are in a server, their prefixes might conflict.

- To check or change a bot's prefix:

    1. Look for the bot's help command (!help, ?help, etc.).

    2. If the bot allows it, set a new prefix (!setprefix %).

✅ **Verify If the Bot Has the Necessary Role**

- If the bot lacks "Administrator" or "Manage Messages" permissions, it may not work properly.

- Go to Server Settings > Roles and ensure the bot's role is positioned above the roles it needs to manage.

✅ **Check Bot Logs for Errors**

- Some bots provide logs in a log channel or error console.

- If a bot has a dedicated website or dashboard, check its logs for error messages.

✅ **Update the Bot**

- If you are hosting a bot, ensure it is running the latest version.

- If the bot is outdated, update its code using git pull or by downloading the latest release.

2.3 Fixing API and Rate Limit Issues

✅ Reduce the Number of Commands Sent in a Short Time

- Discord has rate limits to prevent spam.
- If a bot sends too many messages quickly, it may be temporarily blocked.
- Solutions:
  - Reduce excessive bot usage.
  - Use bot cooldowns to limit command frequency.

✅ Check API Keys and Authentication

- If a bot fetches data from external platforms (e.g., YouTube, Twitch), check:
  - API keys are correctly entered.
  - The service is not down.

✅ Restart the Bot After a Timeout

- If Discord rate-limits the bot, wait a few minutes and restart it.

2.4 Fixing Integration and Third-Party Errors

✅ Reconnect External Services

- If your bot is linked to Twitch, Spotify, or Google, disconnect and reconnect the accounts from the bot's dashboard.

✅ Check Webhooks

- If webhook notifications fail:
  - Ensure the webhook URL is correct.
  - Delete and **recreate the webhook in Server Settings > Integrations.**

✅ Verify API Token Permissions

- Some APIs require special **read/write** permissions.

- Go to the bot's **developer portal** and ensure API keys are properly set.

Conclusion

Troubleshooting Discord bot issues requires a systematic approach. By identifying the problem type—whether it's an offline bot, incorrect command execution, permission issues, API errors, or integration failures—you can apply the right fix efficiently.

If all else fails, contact the bot's developer support, check Discord's official bot documentation, or seek help from Discord communities like r/Discord_Bots on Reddit or Discord API Developer Forums.

With a well-maintained bot, your server can benefit from automation, security, and engagement, making it a more dynamic and enjoyable place for your members.

5.3 Integrating Discord with Other Platforms

5.3.1 Linking Discord with Twitch and YouTube

Discord is widely used by content creators, streamers, and online communities to engage with their audience in real time. By integrating Discord with **Twitch** and **YouTube**, streamers can provide exclusive perks to their subscribers, automate notifications for new content, and create a seamless interaction between their live streams and their Discord servers.

This section will guide you through the process of linking your Discord account with **Twitch and YouTube**, setting up automated notifications, managing subscriber roles, and leveraging these integrations to enhance your community.

---

1. Why Link Discord with Twitch and YouTube?

Benefits for Streamers and Content Creators

Integrating Discord with Twitch and YouTube offers multiple advantages, including:

- Automated Notifications: Notify your Discord server members when you go live on Twitch or upload a new YouTube video.

- Subscriber Perks: Automatically assign special roles to Twitch subscribers and YouTube members.

- Enhanced Engagement: Allow fans to interact with you and other viewers in real-time.

- Community Growth: Convert Twitch and YouTube followers into active Discord members.

- Monetization Support: Encourage more subscriptions by offering exclusive Discord access.

Benefits for Viewers and Fans

For viewers, a Discord community linked to a Twitch or YouTube channel provides:

- Exclusive content: Access to private chatrooms, behind-the-scenes content, and early releases.

- Real-time updates: Immediate notifications about live streams, premieres, and new uploads.

- Direct interaction: An opportunity to chat with the creator and fellow fans in a dedicated space.

2. How to Link Your Discord Account with Twitch and YouTube

Before setting up automation and subscriber roles, you need to connect your Discord account to Twitch or YouTube.

2.1 Linking Discord with Twitch

Step 1: Open Discord Settings

1. Open Discord and click on the User Settings (⚙☐) icon in the bottom-left corner.

2. Navigate to Connections in the left-hand menu.

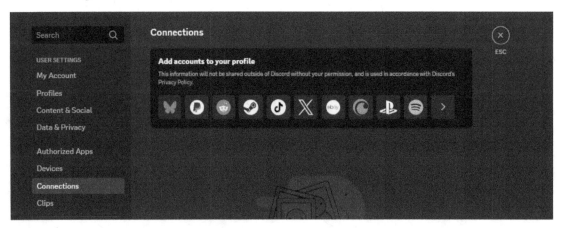

Step 2: Connect Your Twitch Account

1. In the Connections tab, find the Twitch option and click on it.

2. A pop-up will appear asking you to log into your Twitch account.

3. Sign in with your Twitch credentials and authorize Discord to access your Twitch account.

Step 3: Enable Twitch Integration on Your Server

1. Go to **Server Settings** (only available if you own or manage a server).

2. Click on **Integrations** and select **Twitch**.

3. Enable **Sync** to allow Discord to automatically recognize your Twitch subscribers.

4. You can now create **special roles** for Twitch subscribers and assign them permissions (e.g., access to exclusive chatrooms).

2.2 Linking Discord with YouTube

Step 1: Open Discord Settings

1. Click on the User Settings (⚙⬜) icon in Discord.

2. Navigate to Connections in the left-hand menu.

Step 2: Connect Your YouTube Account

1. In the Connections tab, find the YouTube option and click on it.

2. A pop-up will appear prompting you to log into your Google account.

3. Sign in with the YouTube channel account you want to connect.

4. Grant Discord permission to access your YouTube account.

Step 3: Enable YouTube Integration on Your Server

1. Open your Discord server settings.

2. Go to Integrations and select YouTube.

3. Enable Sync to allow Discord to recognize YouTube channel members (subscribers who have joined as paid members).

4. Assign exclusive roles to YouTube members for perks like access to private channels and special badges.

3. Automating Stream Notifications in Discord

Once you've linked Discord with Twitch and YouTube, you can automate notifications to alert your community when you go live or upload a new video.

3.1 Setting Up Auto-Notifications for Twitch

Discord can automatically post notifications in a designated channel when you go live on Twitch.

Using Discord's Built-in Integration

1. Go to Server Settings > Integrations > Twitch.

2. Enable Live Stream Announcements.

3. Choose a text channel where you want live notifications to appear.

Using a Bot (e.g., MEE6 or Streamcord)

For more advanced notifications, you can use a bot:

1. Invite a bot like MEE6 or Streamcord to your Discord server.

2. Use the bot's dashboard to connect your Twitch account.

3. Configure the bot to post live stream notifications in a specific channel.

4. Customize the message format and mention roles to notify subscribers.

3.2 Setting Up Auto-Notifications for YouTube

Using Discord's Built-in Integration

1. Go to Server Settings > Integrations > YouTube.

2. Enable New Video Announcements.

3. Select a text channel where notifications will be posted.

Using a Bot (e.g., MEE6 or YAGPDB)

To automate YouTube upload notifications, you can use bots like MEE6:

1. Invite MEE6 to your Discord server.

2. Go to the MEE6 Dashboard and select YouTube.

3. Link your YouTube channel and set up automatic notifications.

4. Customize the message format and ping specific roles if needed.

4. Managing Subscriber Roles and Exclusive Access

One of the best benefits of linking Twitch and YouTube with Discord is subscriber-exclusive roles. This allows you to grant special permissions to paying subscribers.

Creating Subscriber Roles

1. Open Server Settings > Roles.

2. Click Create Role and name it (e.g., Twitch Subscriber or YouTube Member).

3. Assign special permissions (e.g., access to VIP channels, custom emojis, priority voice chat).

4. Enable Auto-Sync so that Twitch or YouTube members automatically receive the role.

Setting Up Exclusive Channels

To create private chat rooms for subscribers:

1. Go to Server Settings > Channels > Create Channel.

2. Select Text Channel or Voice Channel.

3. In Permissions, restrict access to only subscriber roles.

4. Customize settings (e.g., slow mode, message reactions, pinned content).

Conclusion

Linking Discord with Twitch and YouTube is an excellent way for content creators to enhance their community engagement. By integrating these platforms, you can:

✅ Automatically notify members when you go live or upload a video.

✅ Reward subscribers with exclusive perks and roles.

✅ Foster an interactive and engaged fanbase.

With these integrations in place, your Discord server becomes more than just a chatroom—it transforms into an interactive hub where fans and followers can stay connected, receive updates, and support your content.

Next Section: 5.3.2 Using Webhooks for Automations

In the next section, we'll explore **how to use Discord Webhooks** to automate messages, connect external apps, and enhance your server functionality.

5.3.2 Using Webhooks for Automations

In the world of online communication, automation plays a crucial role in streamlining workflows, improving efficiency, and reducing manual effort. **Discord Webhooks** are one of the most powerful tools for automating notifications, integrating external services, and sending messages from external applications into your Discord server.

In this section, we will explore:

- What webhooks are and how they work in Discord.

- The benefits of using webhooks for automation.

- How to create, configure, and manage webhooks.

- Real-world examples of webhooks in action.

What Are Webhooks in Discord?

A webhook is a mechanism that allows applications to send real-time data to a specific endpoint (a URL) when a particular event occurs. In Discord, webhooks are unique URLs that allow external services to send messages directly into a channel without requiring a bot.

Unlike traditional API calls, which require an application to frequently check for updates (polling), webhooks work on a push-based system, meaning that they send updates automatically when an event occurs.

How Webhooks Work in Discord

- A Discord webhook is created inside a specific text channel on a server.

- The webhook is assigned a unique URL that can receive JSON payloads from external sources.

- When an event happens in the connected application (e.g., a new post on a blog, a GitHub commit, a Twitch stream going live), the application sends data to the webhook URL.

- Discord receives this data and posts it in the designated channel.

This makes webhooks an ideal solution for automating updates, notifications, and integrations without requiring a complex bot setup.

Benefits of Using Webhooks in Discord

Using webhooks provides several advantages:

1. Real-Time Notifications

Webhooks allow instant updates from external services, reducing the need for users to manually check for new information. For example:

- A webhook connected to GitHub can notify a development team about new commits or pull requests.

- A webhook linked to Twitch can alert a Discord server when a streamer goes live.

2. Simplified Integration Without Bots

Many automation tasks that typically require a bot can be accomplished with webhooks, saving time and resources. Unlike bots, webhooks do not require hosting, authentication tokens, or complex configurations.

3. Improved Workflow Automation

Businesses, developers, and content creators can automate routine tasks by integrating webhooks with productivity tools like Trello, Google Sheets, or Zapier. This helps streamline workflows and ensures important information is shared automatically.

4. Customizable Message Formatting

Discord webhooks support **rich embeds**, which allow messages to include:

- Titles and descriptions

- Images and thumbnails

- Color-coded sidebars

- Hyperlinks and formatted text

This ensures that notifications are clear, visually appealing, and easy to read.

How to Create and Configure Webhooks in Discord

Setting up a webhook in Discord is a straightforward process. Follow these steps to create and configure a webhook in your server.

Step 1: Creating a Webhook in Discord

1. Open Discord and navigate to the server where you want to set up the webhook.

2. Click on the Server Settings (⚙▢) from the server name dropdown.

3. Select Integrations from the left-hand menu.

4. Under Webhooks, click Create Webhook.

5. Give your webhook a name and select a channel where it will send messages.

6. Click Copy Webhook URL—this will be used to send data to Discord.

7. Click Save Changes.

Step 2: Sending a Test Message via Webhook

To test the webhook, you can use cURL or an online request tool like Postman.

Using cURL (in Command Prompt or Terminal):

```
curl -H "Content-Type: application/json" \
   -X POST \
   -d '{"content": "Hello, Discord! This is a webhook test."}' \
   https://discord.com/api/webhooks/YOUR_WEBHOOK_URL
```

If configured correctly, this message will appear in your Discord channel.

Step 3: Formatting Webhook Messages with Embeds

Instead of sending plain text messages, you can format your webhook messages using Discord's embed format.

Example JSON payload:

```
{
  "embeds": [{
    "title": "New Blog Post Published!",
    "description": "Check out our latest article on Discord automation.",
    "url": "https://example.com/blog",
    "color": 16711680,
    "thumbnail": {
      "url": "https://example.com/image.jpg"
    },
    "footer": {
      "text": "Powered by Webhooks"
    }
  }]
}
```

This will produce a rich-embed message in Discord with a clickable title, description, and an image thumbnail.

Practical Use Cases for Webhooks in Discord

Now that you know how to create and format webhooks, let's explore real-world scenarios where webhooks can be useful.

1. GitHub Notifications for Developers

Webhooks can be used to notify a Discord server when:

- A new commit is pushed.

- A pull request is opened or merged.

- An issue is created or closed.

To set up:

- Go to your GitHub repository's settings.

- Under Webhooks, click Add Webhook.

- Enter the Discord webhook URL and choose events to track.

2. Twitch or YouTube Live Stream Alerts

For streamers, webhooks can notify a Discord community when a live stream starts.

- Twitch and YouTube offer webhook integrations through Streamlabs, Muxy, or Nightbot.

- These services send an automatic message to a Discord channel when a stream goes live.

3. Automated News and RSS Feeds

If you run a news or blogging server, you can set up webhooks to send:

- Updates from an RSS feed (e.g., new articles from a website).

- Latest posts from Twitter, Reddit, or other social media platforms.

Services like Zapier, IFTTT, and Integromat allow you to connect RSS feeds to Discord webhooks.

4. Business and Productivity Notifications

For businesses and remote teams, webhooks can:

- Notify a Discord channel when a Trello card is updated.

- Send Google Calendar event reminders.

- Alert a team when a new support ticket is created in platforms like Zendesk or Jira.

5. Cryptocurrency and Stock Market Updates

Webhooks can be used to send automated alerts for:

- Bitcoin price fluctuations from CoinGecko or Binance.

- Stock market updates from Yahoo Finance or TradingView.

Managing and Securing Webhooks

While webhooks are useful, they can also be vulnerable if not managed properly. Here are some best practices:

1. Keep Webhook URLs Private – Never share webhook URLs publicly, as anyone with access can send messages to your Discord server.

2. Use Role-Based Channel Restrictions – Restrict webhook access to admin-only channels.

3. Monitor Webhook Activity – Regularly review Discord's audit logs to track webhook activity.

4. Regenerate Webhook URLs If Compromised – If a webhook URL is leaked, delete it and create a new one.

Conclusion

Webhooks are a powerful and flexible way to automate updates and integrate external applications with Discord. Whether you're a developer, streamer, or business owner, webhooks allow you to connect Discord with third-party services effortlessly.

By leveraging webhooks, you can enhance your Discord server, keep members informed, and streamline workflows without needing complex bot development.

Next Section: 5.3.3 Connecting Discord to Productivity Tools

In the next section, we'll explore how to integrate Discord with productivity tools like Slack, Trello, and Google Calendar for **team collaboration and workflow automation**.

5.3.3 Connecting Discord to Productivity Tools

Discord is not just for gaming and community interaction; it is also a powerful tool for businesses, remote teams, and productivity-focused individuals. By integrating Discord with various productivity tools, you can streamline communication, automate tasks, and create a more efficient workflow for your team or community.

In this section, we will explore why integrating Discord with productivity tools is beneficial, the most useful tools to connect with Discord, and the step-by-step process of integrating them into your server.

Why Integrate Discord with Productivity Tools?

Whether you are managing a business, running a study group, or coordinating a remote team, integrating Discord with productivity tools offers several advantages:

1. **Streamlined Communication** – Keep all discussions, updates, and notifications in one place, reducing the need to switch between multiple apps.

2. **Task Automation** – Automate repetitive tasks like meeting reminders, project tracking, and file sharing.

3. **Centralized Work Management** – Use Discord as a hub for managing tasks, schedules, and workflows across multiple platforms.

4. **Improved Team Collaboration** – Allow team members to access shared documents, track project progress, and receive real-time updates without leaving Discord.

5. **Enhanced Organization** – Keep important information structured using Discord bots and integrations, preventing clutter and lost data.

With these benefits in mind, let's explore some of the most popular productivity tools you can integrate with Discord.

Popular Productivity Tools to Connect with Discord

There are many productivity tools that can be linked with Discord, but some of the most useful include:

1. Trello (Task and Project Management)

Trello is a visual project management tool that helps teams organize tasks using a simple Kanban board system. By integrating Trello with Discord, you can:

- Receive notifications for task updates and due dates.

- Create and assign tasks directly from Discord.

- Sync task progress across Trello and Discord channels.

♠ **Integration Method:** Use the Trello Discord bot or Webhooks to sync notifications with a dedicated channel.

2. Notion (Note-Taking and Collaboration)

Notion is a powerful all-in-one workspace that combines note-taking, project management, and databases. With a Discord-Notion integration, you can:

- Share real-time updates from Notion pages into Discord.

- Sync meeting notes and documentation with your server.

- Create to-do lists that notify team members in Discord.

♠ **Integration Method:** Use Zapier or Webhooks to connect Notion and Discord for automated updates.

3. Google Workspace (Docs, Sheets, and Calendar)

Google's suite of tools is widely used for team collaboration. Integrating Google Workspace with Discord allows you to:

- Get notifications for document edits and comments in Google Docs.

- Sync Google Calendar with Discord to send event reminders.

- Share Google Drive files easily within Discord channels.

♠ **Integration Method:** Use Discord bots like "Zapier" or "GCal Bot" to sync updates.

4. Slack (Business Communication)

For teams that use Slack for internal communication, integrating it with Discord can help bridge the gap between different teams or departments. You can:

- Sync important Slack messages with a Discord channel.

- Send automated notifications from Slack to Discord.

- Allow cross-platform communication between Slack and Discord users.

◆ **Integration Method:** Use Zapier or Webhooks to create automatic message forwarding.

5. Asana (Task and Workflow Management)

Asana is another popular task management tool that allows teams to track progress on projects. Connecting it to Discord enables:

- Automated reminders for task deadlines.

- Status updates from Asana to Discord channels.

- The ability to create new tasks directly from Discord.

◆ **Integration Method:** Use the Asana Bot for Discord or automation services like Zapier.

How to Connect Productivity Tools to Discord

Now that we've covered some of the most useful productivity tools, let's walk through the step-by-step process of integrating them with your Discord server.

Method 1: Using Discord Bots

The easiest way to connect productivity tools to Discord is by using bots designed specifically for those services.

Steps to Add a Productivity Bot to Discord:

1. **Find a Bot** – Visit a bot marketplace like top.gg or the official website of the tool (e.g., Trello's bot page).

2. **Invite the Bot to Your Server** – Click **"Invite"** or **"Add to Discord"**, then select your server.

3. **Grant Necessary Permissions** – Ensure the bot has permission to send messages, manage webhooks, and access relevant channels.

4. **Configure the Bot** – Follow the bot's setup guide to link it with your productivity tool.

5. **Test the Integration** – Send test commands to check if the bot is working properly.

♦ **Example:** To add a **Trello bot**, you can use the command:

!trello setup

This will guide you through connecting your Trello account to Discord.

Method 2: Using Webhooks

Webhooks allow you to send real-time updates from productivity apps to Discord without needing a bot.

Steps to Set Up a Webhook:

1. Go to Server Settings – In Discord, open your server and navigate to "Integrations" > "Webhooks".

2. Create a Webhook – Click "New Webhook" and name it appropriately (e.g., "Trello Updates").

3. Copy the Webhook URL – You'll need this URL to send data from your productivity tool.

4. Connect the Webhook to a Productivity Tool – In the tool's settings, find the Webhook option and paste your Discord Webhook URL.

5. Test the Connection – Perform a sample action in your productivity tool to check if notifications appear in Discord.

♦ **Example:** In Trello, go to "Automation" > "Webhooks", paste the Discord Webhook URL, and choose which updates should be sent to your Discord channel.

Method 3: Using Third-Party Automation Services

If a direct bot or webhook isn't available, you can use automation tools like Zapier or Automate.io to connect Discord with nearly any productivity platform.

Steps to Use Zapier for Discord Integration:

1. Create a Zapier Account – Sign up on Zapier.com.

2. Create a New Zap – Select a trigger app (e.g., Notion, Google Calendar, Asana).

3. Choose an Action for Discord – Set up the automation (e.g., "Send a message to Discord when a new Google Calendar event is created").

4. Connect Your Accounts – Log in to both services and authorize Zapier to access them.

5. Test and Enable the Zap – Run a test to ensure the automation works properly.

Conclusion

By integrating Discord with productivity tools, you can enhance team collaboration, automate workflows, and create an efficient digital workspace. Whether you're managing tasks in Trello, scheduling events with Google Calendar, or sharing notes via Notion, Discord can serve as a centralized hub for communication and productivity.

With the right integrations, your Discord server can transform from a simple chat platform into a powerful productivity tool that keeps your community, business, or team organized and connected.

Next Section: 6.1 Boosting Your Server with Discord Nitro

In the next chapter, we will explore **Discord Nitro**, how it enhances your server, and how to manage server boosts effectively.

CHAPTER VI
Advanced Discord Features

6.1 Boosting Your Server with Discord Nitro

6.1.1 What is Discord Nitro and How It Works?

Introduction to Discord Nitro

Discord Nitro is Discord's premium subscription service that enhances the user experience by providing exclusive perks, such as higher-quality streaming, animated emojis, larger file uploads, and server boosts. It is a paid service designed for users who want to support Discord's development while unlocking premium features for both personal use and community engagement.

Discord Nitro comes in two main tiers:

1. Discord Nitro (Full Version) – The premium plan with all features.

2. Discord Nitro Basic – A more affordable option with limited perks.

Additionally, Discord offers Server Boosts, which allow users to contribute towards improving their favorite servers. Server boosting grants special benefits to a community, such as better audio quality, custom banners, and more emoji slots.

History and Evolution of Discord Nitro

Discord Nitro was introduced in 2017 as a way to generate revenue without relying on ads. Initially, it offered a game subscription service similar to Xbox Game Pass, where users could play a rotating library of premium games. However, this approach didn't gain traction, and in 2019, Discord removed the gaming library and focused purely on premium perks like HD streaming, better emojis, and server boosting.

Since then, Nitro has become a major part of Discord's business model, helping to fund server maintenance, security improvements, and new feature development.

Key Features of Discord Nitro

1. Enhanced Personal Features

◆ **Higher-Quality Streaming (HD Video and Screen Sharing)**

Nitro users can stream at 1080p (Full HD) or even 4K at 60 FPS, compared to free users who are limited to 720p at 30 FPS. This is particularly useful for:

- Gamers who live-stream their gameplay on Discord.

- Professionals who share high-resolution presentations.

- Artists and designers who demonstrate their creative process.

◆ **Bigger File Upload Limits**

- Free users have a 25MB file upload limit, which can be restrictive.

- Nitro Basic increases this to 50MB per file.

- Full Nitro users can upload files up to 500MB!

This is ideal for:
✓ Sharing high-quality images, videos, and animations.
✓ Sending large PDF files or design projects.
✓ Uploading gameplay clips or work documents without compression.

◆ **Animated and Custom Emojis**

- Free users can only use static emojis within the server they belong to.

- Nitro users get access to animated emojis and can use custom emojis across all servers and DMs.

This allows for more expressive communication and personalization.

◆ **Custom Profile Features**

With Nitro, users can:

✓ Set an animated profile picture (GIFs).

✓ Choose a custom Discord tag (e.g., JohnDoe#0001 instead of a random number).

✓ Set unique profile banners to showcase their personality.

2. Server Boosting and Community Perks

One of the biggest Nitro benefits is Server Boosting, which allows users to support their favorite communities.

◆ What is a Server Boost?

- Boosts are special contributions that improve a server's features.

- Unlike standard Nitro perks (which are personal), boosts enhance the entire server.

- Each server unlocks more features as it receives more boosts.

◆ Server Boost Levels and Their Benefits

Boost Level	Requirements	Key Perks Unlocked
Level 1	2 Boosts	+50 Emoji Slots, 128 Kbps Audio, Custom Server Banner
Level 2	7 Boosts	+50 More Emojis, 256 Kbps Audio, 50MB Upload Limit
Level 3	14 Boosts	+100 More Emojis, 384 Kbps Audio, 100MB Upload, Vanity URL

This encourages communities to work together to improve their server experience.

◆ How Nitro Users Get Free Server Boosts

- Full Nitro subscribers receive 2 free boosts every month that they can use on any server.

- Users can purchase additional boosts separately.

How to Subscribe to Discord Nitro

1. Subscription Plans and Pricing

Plan	Monthly Cost	Annual Cost	Key Benefits
Nitro Basic	$2.99/month	$29.99/year	50MB Upload, HD Video (720p 60FPS)
Full Nitro	$9.99/month	$99.99/year	500MB Upload, 4K Streaming, 2 Server Boosts

Users can subscribe through:

- Discord's website (https://discord.com/nitro)

- The Discord app (under "Nitro" settings)

- Gift Cards available online

2. How to Activate Nitro

1. Go to Settings > Nitro in Discord.

2. Choose a subscription plan.

3. Enter payment details (Credit card, PayPal, or gift card).

4. Click Subscribe, and enjoy Nitro perks immediately!

How Discord Nitro Compares to Other Premium Services

Discord Nitro vs. Twitch Turbo

Feature	Discord Nitro	Twitch Turbo
Streaming Quality	4K 60FPS	1080p 60FPS
Ad-Free Experience	No	Yes
Custom Emojis	Yes	No
Price	$9.99/month	$8.99/month

Discord Nitro vs. Slack and Microsoft Teams

- Slack and Teams are work-focused, while Discord Nitro is entertainment and community-focused.

- Nitro enhances personal and community features, while Slack charges for business collaboration tools.

Is Discord Nitro Worth It?

Who Should Get Discord Nitro?

✓ Gamers who stream and want higher-quality video and voice chat.

✓ Community managers looking to boost their server.

✓ Users who love using emojis and customization.

Who Might Not Need Nitro?

✗ Casual users who don't need premium perks.

✗ Those who only use Discord for basic text chatting.

Conclusion

Discord Nitro is a powerful way to upgrade your Discord experience, providing users with better video quality, higher file limits, custom emojis, and server boosts. Whether you're a hardcore gamer, content creator, or just someone who enjoys personalizing their profile, Nitro offers plenty of value.

If you want to enhance your Discord usage and support the platform's growth, Nitro is worth considering!

Next Section: 6.1.2 Benefits of Server Boosting

In the next section, we'll explore how **Server Boosting works**, how it improves community engagement, and whether it's worth investing in for your favorite servers.

6.1.2 Benefits of Server Boosting

Server Boosting is one of the most exciting and beneficial features of Discord Nitro, allowing users to contribute directly to their favorite servers by unlocking various perks and enhancements. By boosting a server, members can improve audio and video quality, gain access to exclusive customization options, and unlock powerful community management features. In this section, we will explore the key benefits of Server Boosting, how it enhances the overall server experience, and why it is an important feature for community growth.

1. What is Server Boosting?

Before diving into the benefits, let's clarify what Server Boosting actually means.

1.1 How Server Boosting Works

- Any Discord user with a Nitro or Nitro Basic subscription can choose to boost a server.

- Boosting provides various benefits that enhance the server for all members.

- Each boost is counted towards a total "Boost Level", unlocking more perks as the number of boosts increases.

- Unlike traditional Nitro perks (which apply to an individual user), Server Boosting upgrades an entire community, making it ideal for gaming clans, content creators, businesses, and social groups.

1.2 Server Boosting Tiers

- **Level 1** – Requires **2 Boosts**

- **Level 2** – Requires **7 Boosts**

- **Level 3** – Requires **14 Boosts**

Each higher level unlocks progressively better perks, which we will explore in detail below.

2. Key Benefits of Server Boosting

2.1 Higher Audio and Voice Channel Quality

One of the most immediate improvements that boosting provides is higher quality voice channels. This is essential for communities that use voice chat frequently, whether for gaming, business meetings, or casual discussions.

- Level 1 – Increases audio quality to 128 kbps, resulting in clearer communication.

- Level 2 – Enhances quality further to 256 kbps, delivering studio-level voice chat.

- Level 3 – Unlocks the highest voice quality at 384 kbps, which is ideal for professional-grade conversations and musicians or podcasters who want crystal-clear audio.

For communities that host large events, live streams, or competitive gaming sessions, these upgrades significantly improve the experience.

2.2 Better Video Streaming and Screen Sharing

Discord allows users to stream games, presentations, and videos directly within servers. However, non-boosted servers have limitations on quality and frame rates.

With Server Boosting:

- Level 1 – Unlocks 720p 60 FPS streaming for all members.

- Level 2 – Enables 1080p 60 FPS streaming, ensuring smoother, high-definition content.

- Level 3 – Grants the ability to stream in 4K Ultra HD quality, making it perfect for professional content creators, streamers, and movie-watching parties.

If your server frequently hosts live streams, study sessions, gaming meetups, or movie nights, higher video quality creates a more immersive experience.

2.3 Increased File Upload Size

Non-boosted servers limit file uploads to 8 MB, which can be frustrating when sharing images, GIFs, videos, and documents. Boosting removes this restriction:

- Level 1 – Raises the limit to 25 MB, allowing for larger images, short videos, and music files.

- Level 2 – Increases the limit to 50 MB, making it easier to share gameplay clips, higher-resolution media, and longer voice recordings.

- Level 3 – Unlocks 100 MB file uploads, perfect for designers, musicians, and developers who need to share large assets and projects.

For creative communities, educational groups, and business teams, higher upload limits eliminate the need for third-party file-sharing services.

2.4 Customization and Branding Enhancements

Server Boosting allows communities to personalize their servers, making them more visually appealing and unique.

Custom Invite Links

- At Level 1, servers can create a custom invite URL (e.g., discord.gg/yourservername), making it easier for members to find and join.

- This is especially useful for businesses, content creators, and large public communities.

Animated Server Icons and Banners

- Level 2 – Allows animated server icons, making the server stand out and look more professional.

- Level 3 – Unlocks custom server banners, allowing server owners to add branded designs or themed visuals.

Extra Emoji Slots

- Non-boosted servers have a 50-slot limit for custom emojis.

- Boosting expands this to 100, 150, and 250 slots at Levels 1, 2, and 3, respectively.

- Great for fan groups, streamers, and businesses that use branded emojis for engagement.

These branding features help make servers more recognizable, professional, and visually engaging.

2.5 Larger Community and Increased Member Limit

- By default, Discord servers can support up to 250,000 members.

- With Level 3 Boosting, this limit doubles to 500,000, making it essential for massive public communities, esports teams, and large-scale online groups.

- Boosting also increases the number of pinned messages, voice channels, and simultaneous connections, ensuring smooth performance even in crowded servers.

2.6 Dedicated Server Banner and Vanity URL

At Level 3, Discord grants servers a dedicated splash banner and vanity URL, making the server more attractive and easier to access.

- Vanity URL: Instead of a random invite link, the server gets a permanent custom URL (e.g., discord.gg/yourbrand).

- Splash Banner: A custom full-screen banner appears when users join the server.

These perks enhance server branding and help attract new members, making them particularly useful for businesses, gaming communities, and influencer groups.

3. Why Server Boosting is Worth It

Now that we've explored the benefits, here's why Server Boosting is valuable for any community:

✅ Improves overall user experience – Clearer voice chat, higher video quality, and faster file sharing.

✅ Makes servers more attractive – Custom icons, banners, and vanity URLs help with branding.

✅ Enhances engagement – More emoji slots, better media sharing, and smoother streaming.

✅ Supports large communities – Increased member limits and server features keep communities thriving.

For gaming clans, study groups, businesses, content creators, and large communities, Server Boosting is an investment that enhances both functionality and aesthetics.

Conclusion

Server Boosting is more than just a luxury feature—it significantly improves the experience for both server owners and members. Whether you're running a small group or a massive online community, unlocking Boost Levels creates a smoother, more engaging, and professional environment.

In the next section (**6.1.3 Managing Server Boost Levels**), we'll explore how to track Boost progress, encourage members to boost, and maintain perks efficiently.

6.1.3 Managing Server Boost Levels

Discord Server Boosting is one of the most effective ways to enhance a server by unlocking premium features. Whether you are managing a community server, a gaming group, or a professional workspace, understanding how to manage Server Boost levels can help you optimize your server's performance and provide exclusive perks to members. In this section, we will explore how Server Boost levels work, how to manage them efficiently, and best practices to encourage community participation in boosting.

Understanding Server Boost Levels

When a Discord server is boosted, it gains access to various perks that enhance the user experience. Boosts accumulate to increase the server's boost level, unlocking additional benefits. Discord has three boost levels, with each level providing progressively better rewards.

Breakdown of Server Boost Levels

Boost Level	Required Boosts	Perks
Level 1	2 Boosts	- 128 Kbps Audio Quality

- Custom Server Invite Background

- Animated Server Icon

- Additional Emoji Slots (+50)

- Streaming at 720p 60FPS | | **Level 2** | 7 Boosts | - 256 Kbps Audio Quality

- More Emoji Slots (+50, total 150)

- 1080p 60FPS Streaming

- Server Banner Image

- 50MB File Upload Limit | | **Level 3** | 14 Boosts | - 384 Kbps Audio Quality

- 250 Emoji Slots (Total)

- 100MB File Upload Limit

- Vanity URL

- Even Higher Stream Quality |

Each level improves the server experience, making the community more appealing for existing and new members.

How to Manage Server Boosts

As a server owner or administrator, monitoring and managing boosts is crucial to ensure your community maintains its current boost level and encourages continued contributions from members.

Checking Your Server's Boost Status

To check your server's boost level and see how many boosts are currently active:

1. Open Your Server – Navigate to the Discord server you manage.

2. Go to Server Settings – Click on your server name in the top-left corner and select Server Settings.

3. Click on "Server Boost Status" – This section provides details on the current boost level, number of active boosts, and which members have boosted the server.

This panel allows you to track how close you are to the next boost level and recognize members who contribute boosts.

Encouraging Members to Boost Your Server

Since Server Boosting requires a Discord Nitro subscription, not all users will be willing to contribute. However, there are effective strategies to encourage participation.

Offering Incentives for Boosters

One of the best ways to encourage members to boost your server is by offering exclusive perks. Some common incentives include:

- Exclusive Roles & Permissions – Create a "Booster" role with unique name colors and access to VIP channels.

- Custom Emoji & Stickers – Allow boosters to suggest and add their own emojis.

- Private Channels – Provide private voice/text channels for boosters to interact.

- Early Access to Content – If your server is for content creation (e.g., streaming, YouTube, game development), allow boosters early access to content before the general audience.

- Personalized Name Tags – Give boosters the option to have custom name tags with unique fonts or icons.

Hosting Special Booster-Only Events

Creating exclusive events for server boosters can encourage more members to contribute. Some examples include:

- Monthly Booster Giveaways – Raffles where only boosters can win prizes such as game codes, merchandise, or Discord Nitro subscriptions.

- VIP Q&A Sessions – Special Q&A sessions with server leaders, content creators, or developers.

- Priority Support – Boosters can receive priority support for any questions or issues within the community.

Using Automated Messages & Reminders

Setting up automated messages to remind users of the benefits of boosting can be an effective strategy. Bots like MEE6, Carl-bot, or Dyno can be used to send messages in a #server-updates channel whenever a new boost is received.

A sample booster message might look like this:

🌟 [Username] just boosted the server! 🌟
Thank you for supporting our community! Boosters gain access to **VIP chat, custom emojis, and more!** Want to join them? Click **Server Boost** in the top-right corner! 🚀

Maintaining Server Boost Levels

Since Server Boosts are subscription-based, boosts can expire if a member cancels their Nitro subscription. This means servers may lose their boost level over time.

Tracking Expiring Boosts

To prevent your server from dropping a level, actively monitor boosts and plan ahead.

- Use the Server Boost Panel – Check how many boosts are set to expire.

- Engage with Boosters – If a key booster's Nitro subscription is about to end, consider reaching out and thanking them for their contribution.

- Prepare a Contingency Plan – If multiple boosts are set to expire soon, you can run a special promotion encouraging new boosters to step in.

Reaching Out to Boosters Directly

Building personal connections with your boosters can help retain them long-term. Consider:

- **Sending Personal Thank-You Messages** – A simple DM like:

"Hey [Username], thanks so much for boosting our server! Your support helps us unlock awesome perks for everyone. Let us know if there's anything we can do to make the server even better for you!"

- **Creating a Hall of Fame** – A permanent **"Booster Wall"** in the server where booster names are recognized.

Using Bots to Manage Boosters Efficiently

Bots can automate the tracking of boosts and notify server admins when boosts are set to expire. Some useful bots include:

- **Statbot** – Provides detailed analytics on server boosts.

- **Carl-bot** – Sends reminders when a boost is about to expire.

- **MEE6** – Can automatically grant and remove booster roles.

Server Boosts vs. Discord Nitro Boosting

Some users may be confused between Server Boosting and Nitro Boosting. It's important to educate members on how boosting works:

- Nitro Classic ($4.99/month) – No boosts included.

- Nitro ($9.99/month) – Includes two Server Boosts that can be used on any server.

Encouraging members to get Nitro instead of purchasing standalone boosts can be a cost-effective way to maintain your server's boost level.

Final Thoughts

Managing Server Boost Levels effectively requires active monitoring, community engagement, and incentives. By keeping track of your boosts, offering exclusive rewards, and maintaining strong relationships with boosters, you can sustain and grow your server's boost level over time.

In the next section, we will explore how to use Discord for streaming and gaming, covering everything from going live with game streaming to optimizing voice chat settings for the best performance.

6.2 Using Discord for Streaming and Gaming

6.2.1 Going Live with Game Streaming

Streaming has become an essential part of online entertainment, and Discord offers a powerful yet simple way to broadcast your gameplay to friends, community members, or even the public. Whether you're a casual gamer who wants to share a fun session with friends or an aspiring content creator looking to build an audience, Discord's Go Live feature provides a seamless solution for low-latency game streaming.

In this section, we'll explore:

- How to set up and start streaming on Discord.

- The technical requirements for smooth performance.

- Key streaming settings and customization options.

- Tips for optimizing quality and engagement.

- Troubleshooting common streaming issues.

1. What is Discord's Go Live Feature?

Discord's Go Live is a built-in streaming feature that allows users to broadcast their screen or a specific game directly within a voice channel. Unlike platforms like Twitch or YouTube, where streams are publicly accessible, Discord streaming is more private, making it ideal for small groups or communities.

Key Features of Go Live

- Low Latency Streaming – Ensures minimal delay between the streamer and viewers.

- Up to 1080p, 60 FPS Streaming (with Nitro for higher quality).

- Stream to a Voice Channel – Only people in the channel can view.

- Game Detection – Automatically recognizes supported games.

- Screen Share Mode – Allows users to share their entire screen instead of just a game.

Go Live is not designed for large-scale broadcasting like Twitch but is perfect for private gaming sessions, tutorials, or community hangouts.

2. How to Start Streaming on Discord

Step 1: Join a Voice Channel

1. Open Discord and navigate to your server.

2. Join any Voice Channel where you want to stream.

3. Ensure your microphone and audio settings are properly configured.

Step 2: Launch Your Game

- Discord's Game Detection automatically recognizes many games.

- If your game isn't detected, you can manually add it in User Settings → Registered Games.

Step 3: Start Streaming

1. Once your game is running, click the Go Live button near your profile in the voice channel.

2. Choose your streaming quality (e.g., 720p, 1080p, 30 FPS, 60 FPS).

3. Click Go Live to begin broadcasting.

Step 4: Inviting Others to Watch

- Members in the same voice channel can see a "Live" badge and join your stream.

- You can directly invite people by clicking the "Invite" button on your stream window.

Step 5: Stopping the Stream

- Click the Stop Streaming button or simply exit the voice channel.

3. Customizing Streaming Settings for Better Performance

Streaming Resolution & Frame Rate

- Free Users: 720p at 30 FPS.

- Discord Nitro Users: 1080p at 60 FPS, or 4K resolution with Nitro Boost.

Optimizing Audio Settings

- Enable Krisp Noise Suppression to reduce background noise.

- Adjust voice sensitivity in User Settings → Voice & Video for clearer communication.

- Set up Push-to-Talk to avoid accidental noise in your stream.

Enhancing Video Settings

- Enable Hardware Acceleration to reduce lag.

- If streaming multiple screens, select the specific window to avoid privacy leaks.

Adjusting Stream Privacy

- Ensure that only trusted members have access to your voice channel by modifying channel permissions.

- Use Roles and Permissions to control who can view or interact with your stream.

4. How to Stream Non-Gaming Content on Discord

While Go Live is designed for game streaming, it also supports general screen sharing, making it useful for:

- Tutorials and Walkthroughs (e.g., coding, software demos).

- Movie or Video Watching Parties (check copyright policies!).

- Collaborative Work and Presentations.

To stream non-gaming content, simply:

1. Click Screen Share instead of Go Live.

2. Select the window or entire screen you want to share.

3. Start streaming and adjust settings for clarity.

5. Best Practices for an Engaging Discord Stream

Engaging with Viewers

- Interact through voice chat to make the stream more dynamic.

- Use polls or viewer suggestions to keep engagement high.

- Enable text chat alongside your stream for audience participation.

Optimizing Performance for Smooth Streaming

- Use a wired connection to avoid network fluctuations.

- Close unnecessary applications that may cause lag.

- Adjust bitrate settings for optimal quality based on your internet speed.

Enhancing the Experience with Bots & Overlays

- Bots like MEE6 or Dyno can help notify users when you go live.

- Integrate OBS Studio for additional overlays and customization.

6. Troubleshooting Common Streaming Issues

Issue 1: Game Not Detected by Discord

✓ Solution: Add it manually in User Settings → Registered Games.

Issue 2: Viewers Can't Hear Game Audio

✅ Solution:

- Ensure audio output is selected correctly.

- If using Windows, enable "Stereo Mix" in sound settings.

Issue 3: Stream Quality is Low or Laggy

✅ Solution:

- Lower resolution and frame rate.

- Close bandwidth-heavy applications (e.g., YouTube, downloads).

- Upgrade to Discord Nitro for higher streaming quality.

Issue 4: Black Screen When Streaming

✅ Solution:

- Disable Hardware Acceleration in browser settings.

- Run Discord in Administrator Mode.

7. Comparing Discord Streaming with Other Platforms

Feature	Discord Go Live	Twitch	YouTube Live	Facebook Gaming
Audience	Private (Server Members)	Public/Followers	Public/Followers	Public/Friends
Latency	Low	Medium	Medium	Medium
Monetization	No	Yes (Ads, Subs)	Yes (Ads, Super Chat)	Yes (Stars, Ads)
Max Resolution	4K (Nitro)	4K	4K	1080p
Ease of Use	Very Easy	Moderate	Moderate	Moderate

Conclusion

Discord's Go Live feature is a simple, effective, and low-latency way to stream your gameplay or screen to a private audience. Whether you're playing casually with friends or running a gaming community, mastering Discord streaming can enhance your experience and engagement.

In the next section (**6.2.2 Optimizing Discord for Low Latency Voice Chat**), we'll explore how to fine-tune your voice settings for **crystal-clear communication** while gaming or streaming! 🚀

6.2.2 Optimizing Discord for Low Latency Voice Chat

Discord is widely recognized for its low-latency voice chat, making it an essential tool for gamers, streamers, and remote teams. Whether you are coordinating strategies in a competitive game, chatting with friends, or running a live event, optimizing Discord's voice settings ensures crystal-clear audio with minimal delay.

This section will guide you through configuring Discord for the best voice chat performance, covering:

- Understanding latency in Discord voice channels.

- Adjusting Discord's voice and audio settings for minimal delay.

- Optimizing your network connection for stable voice communication.

- Using advanced features like Quality of Service (QoS) and regional servers.

1. Understanding Latency in Discord Voice Channels

What is Latency in Voice Chat?

Latency refers to the delay between when you speak and when others hear you. In an ideal scenario, voice communication should feel instantaneous, but network congestion, server distance, and device settings can cause noticeable lag.

How Discord Maintains Low Latency

Discord is designed to keep voice latency low by using:

- Dedicated, region-based voice servers to reduce distance-related delay.

- Opus audio codec to compress voice data efficiently without losing quality.

- WebRTC technology to minimize the time voice data travels between users.

- Real-time adjustments based on network performance.

However, high ping, unstable connections, or incorrect settings can still cause audio delays, making optimization necessary.

2. Adjusting Discord's Voice and Audio Settings

Discord provides several customization options to **fine-tune voice performance**. Here's how you can optimize your voice chat experience:

Step 1: Selecting the Right Input and Output Devices

1. Open Discord Settings (⚙ gear icon in the bottom-left corner).

2. Go to Voice & Video under the App Settings section.

3. Choose your preferred Input Device (microphone) and Output Device (headphones or speakers).

4. Adjust Input Volume and Output Volume to ensure clear audio without distortion.

📌 *Tip:* If you use a USB microphone or external sound card, ensure it is selected as the default input device in both Discord and your operating system.

Step 2: Enabling Push-to-Talk (PTT) or Voice Activation

- Voice Activity Detection: If you prefer hands-free communication, make sure the sensitivity is adjusted correctly.

- Push-to-Talk (PTT): Helps eliminate background noise and accidental mic activations, reducing unnecessary data transmission.

To set up Push-to-Talk:

1. Navigate to Voice & Video Settings.

2. Select Push to Talk under Input Mode.

3. Assign a convenient PTT key.

4. Adjust the Release Delay (shorter delays improve responsiveness).

Step 3: Fine-Tuning Advanced Voice Settings

- Echo Cancellation & Noise Suppression: Helps reduce background noise and improve clarity.

- Automatic Gain Control: Adjusts mic sensitivity dynamically, useful for varying input levels.

- Enable High Packet Priority: Ensures Discord prioritizes your voice data over other background processes.

3. Optimizing Your Network Connection

A stable and fast internet connection is crucial for low-latency voice chat. Here's how you can enhance your network settings:

Step 1: Choosing the Right Internet Connection

- **Wired (Ethernet) vs. Wireless (Wi-Fi):**

  o Ethernet offers a more stable connection with less interference.

  o Wi-Fi can be unstable, especially if multiple devices share the network.

★ *Tip:* If you must use Wi-Fi, position your router closer to your PC or use a Wi-Fi extender.

- **Check Your Internet Speed:**

  o A ping below 50ms is ideal for real-time voice chat.

  o A download speed of at least 5 Mbps ensures smooth communication.

  o Use speed test tools like Speedtest.net to check your connection.

Step 2: Reducing Network Congestion

- Close background applications that consume bandwidth (e.g., streaming services, large downloads).

- Limit other devices using the same network (especially gaming consoles, streaming devices, and smart TVs).

- Enable Quality of Service (QoS) settings in your router to prioritize Discord traffic.

Step 3: Switching to the Best Discord Server Region

Discord automatically selects a voice server based on your location, but manual selection can improve latency.

To change your server region:

1. Open Server Settings (for server owners/admins).

2. Navigate to the Overview tab.

3. Select the closest region under Server Region.

✦ *Tip:* If you experience lag, try switching to a different region temporarily and see if performance improves.

4. Using Discord's Advanced Low-Latency Features

Quality of Service (QoS) Packet Priority

Discord includes a Quality of Service (QoS) High Packet Priority setting, which tells your router to prioritize voice packets over other internet traffic.

To enable QoS:

1. Open Discord Settings → Voice & Video.

2. Scroll down to Quality of Service.

3. Toggle Enable Quality of Service High Packet Priority.

✦ *Note:* Some ISPs or routers block QoS packets, so if enabling this setting causes issues, try disabling it.

Enabling Hardware Acceleration (Optional)

If you use a modern gaming PC, enabling Hardware Acceleration in Discord can improve performance by offloading processing tasks to the GPU.

To enable Hardware Acceleration:

1. Open Discord Settings → Advanced.

2. Toggle Hardware Acceleration ON.

✦ *Note:* This may cause frame drops in some systems, so test its impact on your performance.

Using Low Latency Mode for Streaming & Gaming

- If you stream while using Discord, disable hardware encoding in your streaming software to reduce system load.

- If gaming, enable Game Mode on Windows or Performance Mode on macOS to allocate more resources to Discord.

Conclusion

Optimizing Discord for low-latency voice chat enhances the overall communication experience, whether you're gaming, streaming, or collaborating with a team.

By adjusting voice settings, improving network stability, and leveraging Discord's advanced features, you can significantly reduce lag and enjoy crystal-clear, real-time conversations.

Key Takeaways:

✓ Select the correct input/output devices for the best sound quality.
✓ Adjust voice activity settings or use Push-to-Talk for better control.
✓ Ensure a stable internet connection, preferably with Ethernet over Wi-Fi.
✓ Reduce network congestion by limiting bandwidth-heavy activities.
✓ Manually select the best Discord voice server region for lower latency.
✓ Enable QoS High Packet Priority for optimized network performance.

By following these steps, you'll maximize Discord's low-latency voice chat capabilities, ensuring a smooth and uninterrupted communication experience for all your gaming, streaming, and social interactions.

Next Section: 6.2.3 Syncing Discord with Steam and Other Platforms

In the next section, we'll explore how to connect Discord with other gaming platforms like Steam, Xbox, and PlayStation, allowing seamless integration for cross-platform communication and enhanced gaming experiences.

6.2.3 Syncing Discord with Steam and Other Platforms

Discord is more than just a chat platform—it's a hub for gamers, streamers, and content creators. One of its most powerful features is the ability to sync with external gaming and social platforms like Steam, Xbox, PlayStation, Twitch, and YouTube. This integration enhances the gaming experience by displaying your activity, enabling cross-platform communication, and making it easier to connect with friends and communities.

In this section, we'll explore:

- The benefits of syncing Discord with Steam and other platforms.

- Step-by-step guides on how to link your accounts.

- How to manage synced accounts and troubleshoot common issues.

Why Sync Discord with Other Platforms?

Syncing your gaming and social accounts with Discord offers several advantages:

1. Rich Presence and Activity Status

- When you link platforms like Steam or Xbox, Discord automatically displays your current game activity in your profile.

- Friends can see what you're playing and even join your game directly from Discord if the game supports it.

- Some games have custom Discord integrations, showing additional details like match stats, in-game location, or team members.

2. Improved Friend Connectivity

- Syncing allows Discord to automatically find friends who also have linked accounts, making it easier to connect.

- It enables cross-platform messaging, so you can chat with PlayStation, Xbox, or Steam friends without switching apps.

3. Seamless Streaming and Broadcasting

- If you link Twitch or YouTube, Discord can automatically notify your server when you go live.

- Xbox and PlayStation integrations allow you to stream gameplay directly into Discord voice channels.

4. Unlocking Special Server Features

- Some Discord servers offer exclusive roles or channels for members who have linked their Twitch, YouTube, or Patreon accounts.

- Steam-linked accounts can verify ownership of certain games, granting access to game-specific Discord communities.

How to Sync Steam with Discord

Steam is one of the most popular gaming platforms, and linking it with Discord enhances the social gaming experience.

Step 1: Open Discord User Settings

1. Launch Discord and click the gear icon next to your username in the bottom-left corner.

2. Navigate to the Connections tab in the left menu.

Step 2: Link Your Steam Account

3. In the Connections menu, you'll see a list of platforms you can sync with Discord. Click the Steam icon.

4. A browser window will open, prompting you to log in to your Steam account.

5. Once logged in, confirm that you want to allow Discord to access your Steam data.

Step 3: Adjust Privacy and Visibility Settings

6. After linking, go back to Discord > Connections and check if Steam is successfully connected.

7. Customize the following settings:

   o *Display on Profile:* If enabled, your Steam account will be visible on your Discord profile.

   o *Display Game Activity:* When turned on, friends can see what Steam game you're currently playing.

Step 4: Verify the Connection

8. Open Steam and launch a game.

9. In Discord, check your status—your game should now be displayed under your username.

10. Invite friends to join your game directly from Discord if the game supports it.

Syncing Discord with Other Gaming Platforms

Linking Xbox with Discord

Benefits:

- Show your Xbox game activity on your Discord profile.

- Join voice chats through Discord directly from Xbox Series X/S and Xbox One.

Steps:

1. Go to Discord Settings > Connections and select the Xbox logo.

2. Sign in with your Microsoft account.

3. Allow Discord to access your Xbox activity.

4. Customize settings to show your Xbox games on Discord.

Tip: If you have an Xbox Series X/S, you can join Discord voice chats from the Xbox dashboard without needing a PC or phone.

Linking PlayStation with Discord

Benefits:

- Display your PlayStation activity in your Discord profile.

- Join cross-platform gaming communities more easily.

Steps:

1. Open Discord > Settings > Connections and select PlayStation Network.

2. Log in to your PlayStation account.

3. Grant permission for Discord to access your PlayStation activity.

4. Adjust visibility settings (e.g., who can see what you're playing).

Note: PlayStation does not yet support native Discord voice chat, but this feature is expected in future updates.

Connecting Discord with Twitch and YouTube

If you're a streamer, linking your Discord with Twitch or YouTube unlocks special server features:

- Auto-sync your subscribers or members with your Discord server.

- Create subscriber-only channels for premium supporters.

- Allow Discord to auto-notify followers when you go live.

How to Link Twitch:

1. Open Discord > Settings > Connections.

2. Select Twitch and log in to your account.

3. Choose if you want to show your Twitch link on your profile.

4. If you own a server, enable Twitch Integration for subscriber-only perks.

How to Link YouTube:

1. Follow the same steps as Twitch, but select YouTube instead.

2. If you're a YouTube streamer, enable "Notify my Discord server when I go live."

3. Sync YouTube memberships with Discord roles for premium users.

Managing Synced Accounts and Troubleshooting Issues

Managing Multiple Connections

If you've linked multiple platforms to Discord, you can:

- Reorder connections in the Connections tab to prioritize certain accounts.

- Toggle visibility settings for each platform individually.

- Unlink accounts if needed by clicking the Disconnect button.

Common Issues and Fixes

Issue	Solution
My Steam game isn't showing on Discord	Ensure "Display Game Activity" is enabled in Settings > Activity Status.
Discord isn't detecting my Xbox or PlayStation	Make sure your console's privacy settings allow third-party app access.

Twitch or YouTube auto-notifications aren't working	Check if your Discord server has the correct Twitch/YouTube roles and permissions enabled.
Can't link accounts due to login errors	Try logging out and back in or disabling two-factor authentication temporarily.

Conclusion

Syncing Discord with platforms like Steam, Xbox, PlayStation, Twitch, and YouTube significantly enhances your gaming and streaming experience. It helps you:

✅ Showcase your game activity.

✅ Easily connect with friends across platforms.

✅ Enable Twitch/YouTube perks in Discord servers.

✅ Improve your streaming and content-sharing workflow.

By integrating these platforms, Discord transforms into a central hub for gaming, socializing, and content creation. Whether you're looking to build a streaming career, manage a gaming community, or just have fun with friends, syncing your accounts is a great way to get the most out of Discord.

Next Section: 6.3 Security and Moderation Tools

In the next chapter, we'll explore how to **protect your Discord server** with moderation bots, auto-moderation tools, and security best practices.

6.3 Security and Moderation Tools

6.3.1 Setting Up Moderation Bots

Moderation is a crucial aspect of managing a Discord server, ensuring that the community remains safe, respectful, and free from spam or harmful behavior. One of the most effective ways to automate and streamline moderation tasks is by using Discord moderation bots. These bots help enforce rules, filter inappropriate content, manage spam, and assist with administrative tasks. In this section, we will explore the importance of moderation bots, how to set them up, and the best practices for configuring them to enhance your Discord server's security.

1. Understanding Moderation Bots

What Are Moderation Bots?

Moderation bots are automated programs designed to help server administrators and moderators maintain order in a Discord server. These bots can perform a wide range of tasks, including:

- Detecting and removing spam messages

- Filtering offensive language

- Enforcing rules with warnings, mutes, kicks, and bans

- Preventing raids (mass spam attacks from malicious users)

- Logging user activity and infractions for server admins

Using moderation bots reduces the workload on human moderators, allowing them to focus on building a positive and engaging community rather than constantly monitoring for rule violations.

Popular Moderation Bots

Several powerful moderation bots are widely used across Discord communities. Here are some of the best options:

1. **MEE6** – A versatile bot that provides advanced moderation, custom commands, and auto-moderation features.

2. **Dyno** – One of the most popular moderation bots, offering role management, anti-spam filters, and logging.

3. **Carl-bot** – A feature-rich bot that includes auto-moderation, reaction roles, and custom logging.

4. **Automod** – A simple yet effective bot for filtering offensive content and managing spam.

5. **Gaius** – A powerful bot designed for advanced rule enforcement and moderation.

Each bot has its own strengths, and the best choice depends on your server's size, needs, and the level of automation you require.

2. How to Set Up a Moderation Bot

Setting up a moderation bot involves adding it to your server, configuring permissions, and customizing its settings to fit your server's rules and policies. Below are the step-by-step instructions to get started.

Step 1: Inviting a Moderation Bot to Your Server

Most moderation bots are available on platforms like top.gg, Discord Bots List, and GitHub. To invite a bot:

1. **Choose a Bot**

   o Visit a bot listing website (e.g., https://top.gg/) and search for a moderation bot such as MEE6 or Dyno.

   o Click on the bot's profile to view its details.

2. **Generate an Invite Link**

   o Click the "Invite" or "Add to Server" button.

- o Log in to your Discord account if prompted.

- o Select the server where you want to add the bot.

3. **Grant Necessary Permissions**

- o Bots require certain permissions to function correctly, such as "Manage Roles," "Kick Members," "Ban Members," "Read Messages," and "Send Messages."

- o Always review the permissions before approving.

4. **Authorize the Bot**

- o Click "Authorize" to complete the process.

- o You may need to complete a CAPTCHA verification to confirm you're not a bot.

Once added, the bot will appear in your server's member list, usually with a special bot tag next to its name.

Step 2: Configuring Moderation Bot Permissions

To ensure your moderation bot works correctly without unwanted side effects, you need to configure its permissions.

1. **Create a Dedicated Moderation Role**

- o Go to Server Settings > Roles and click "Create Role."

- o Name the role (e.g., Moderator Bot).

- o Assign the bot to this role to ensure it has appropriate permissions.

2. **Set Channel-Specific Permissions**

- o Navigate to Server Settings > Roles > Permissions.

- o Assign or restrict bot actions based on the needs of your server.

     o For example, you may allow the bot to manage messages in general chat but restrict it in private channels.

3. **Limit Administrative Privileges**

     o Avoid giving full administrator rights to bots unless necessary.

     o Disable permissions like "Administrator" and "Manage Server" unless required for advanced features.

Step 3: Configuring Auto-Moderation Features

Most moderation bots have an auto-moderation system that helps detect and remove inappropriate content automatically.

Common Auto-Moderation Features

- Spam Protection – Blocks users from sending multiple messages too quickly.

- Word Filters – Censors specific words or phrases.

- Link & File Blocking – Prevents users from posting unwanted links or files.

- Raid Prevention – Detects and bans mass bot accounts joining the server.

Setting Up Auto-Moderation in MEE6 (Example)

1. Type /moderation in a channel where the bot is active.

2. Click on "Auto-Moderation" settings in the MEE6 dashboard.

3. Toggle on features such as anti-spam, bad words filter, and link blocker.

4. Customize the warning, mute, or ban system for rule violations.

5. Save your settings and test with a sample message to ensure everything works correctly.

3. Best Practices for Using Moderation Bots

While bots automate many tasks, they should be used alongside human moderators to ensure fairness and adaptability. Below are some best practices:

1. Set Clear Server Rules

- Publish a "Rules & Guidelines" channel where users can see what is allowed.
- Use a bot like MEE6 to automatically warn users who break the rules.

2. Use Logs to Track Moderation Actions

- Enable logging features in moderation bots to keep track of bans, kicks, and infractions.
- Review these logs periodically to identify false positives or mistakes.

3. Fine-Tune Anti-Spam and Filter Settings

- Be careful with overly aggressive spam filters, as they can wrongfully mute active users.
- Regularly update your banned words list to reflect evolving community standards.

4. Maintain a Balance Between Automation and Human Moderation

- Moderation bots should handle routine tasks, but sensitive issues (e.g., harassment reports) should be reviewed by human moderators.
- Assign a moderator team to manually review complex situations.

5. Train Your Moderators to Work with Bots

- Educate staff on how to use bot commands and log systems.
- Assign different moderator levels (e.g., junior mod, senior mod) for handling bot overrides.

Conclusion

Setting up a moderation bot is an essential step in managing a successful Discord server. By choosing the right bot, properly configuring its permissions, and setting up effective auto-moderation tools, you can create a safe and engaging community while reducing the workload on your moderators.

In the next section, **6.3.2 Using Auto-Moderation and Spam Filters**, we will explore advanced spam protection techniques, automated mute and ban settings, and strategies to prevent malicious attacks on your server.

6.3.2 Using Auto-Moderation and Spam Filters

Maintaining a healthy and respectful environment in a Discord server is crucial for keeping members engaged and ensuring that conversations remain productive. As servers grow in size, managing spam, inappropriate content, and disruptive behavior manually becomes increasingly difficult. This is where auto-moderation and spam filters come into play.

Discord provides built-in moderation tools, and many third-party bots offer advanced filtering options to automate moderation tasks. In this section, we'll explore how auto-moderation works, how to configure spam filters, and the best practices for keeping your server safe.

---

1. Understanding Auto-Moderation on Discord

Auto-moderation is a system that automatically detects and takes action against spam, inappropriate content, and rule violations. Instead of requiring human moderators to constantly monitor the chat, auto-moderation tools can automatically:

- Delete messages containing banned words.
- Detect and limit excessive message spam.
- Prevent users from sending links, images, or specific types of content.
- Take action against users who repeatedly break the rules (e.g., mute, kick, or ban them).

Why Auto-Moderation is Important

Without moderation, servers can quickly become **chaotic and toxic**, driving away members and damaging the community's reputation. Auto-moderation:

- Reduces workload for human moderators.

- Prevents spam and harmful content from disrupting conversations.

- Creates a safer space for members, especially younger audiences.

- Maintains a professional and welcoming atmosphere.

Discord's Built-In Auto-Moderation Features

Discord provides some basic auto-moderation tools in Server Settings → AutoMod that allow server admins to:

- Block harmful words and phrases.

- Prevent excessive mentions (spam).

- Detect and filter links from unknown sources.

However, these built-in tools have limitations, so many server owners use moderation bots for more control and customization.

2. Setting Up Discord's Built-In AutoMod

In August 2022, Discord introduced AutoMod, a built-in system that allows server admins to set up rules and filters without needing third-party bots.

Enabling AutoMod on Your Server

To enable AutoMod on your Discord server:

1. Open Server Settings: Click on your server name at the top left and select Server Settings.

2. Go to AutoMod: Navigate to the AutoMod tab in the settings menu.

3. Set Up Rules: Click Create Rule and choose from the available moderation filters.

AutoMod Rule Options

AutoMod provides several pre-set rule options:

- "Commonly Flagged Words" Filter – Blocks offensive language from appearing in chat.

- Custom Keyword Filters – Allows you to add specific words or phrases that should be blocked.

- Mention Spam Filter – Limits excessive tagging of users to prevent mention spam.

- Link Filtering – Restricts users from sharing suspicious or external links.

When a rule is triggered, AutoMod can delete the message, warn the user, or notify moderators for further action.

Adjusting AutoMod Actions

For each rule, you can specify what should happen when a violation occurs:

- Delete Message: Automatically removes the offending message.

- Send an Alert Message: Notifies moderators in a private channel.

- Timeout User: Prevents the user from sending messages for a set period.

These settings ensure that moderation is handled efficiently without constant manual oversight.

3. Using Bots for Advanced Auto-Moderation

While Discord's built-in AutoMod is useful, third-party moderation bots provide even greater flexibility and customization. Popular bots include:

- MEE6 – Provides auto-moderation, spam filters, and customizable warnings.

- Dyno Bot – Allows for automatic banning, muting, and message filtering.

- Carl-bot – Offers custom filters, anti-spam tools, and auto-responses.

- Nightbot – Commonly used for Discord and Twitch integration with moderation features.

Setting Up a Moderation Bot

To set up a bot for auto-moderation:

1. Choose a Bot – Visit the bot's official website (e.g., mee6.xyz, dynobot.net).

2. Invite the Bot to Your Server – Click Add to Discord and select your server.

3. Grant Permissions – Ensure the bot has the necessary Manage Messages and Kick/Ban Members permissions.

4. Configure Moderation Settings – Use the bot's dashboard or commands to set up filters.

Customizing Spam Filters with Bots

Most moderation bots allow you to create custom spam filters that detect:

- Excessive message flooding (too many messages in a short time).

- Repeated identical messages (copy-pasting).

- Random character spam (nonsense text like "asdklfjaksd").

- Excessive emoji or capital letters.

For example, in MEE6, you can set up anti-spam rules by:

1. Opening the MEE6 Dashboard.

2. Navigating to the Moderation Plugin.

3. Enabling Anti-Spam Detection.

4. Adjusting Sensitivity Settings.

When triggered, the bot can warn, mute, or ban users based on the severity of the spam.

---

4. Best Practices for Using Auto-Moderation and Spam Filters

Avoid Over-Moderation

While auto-moderation is useful, excessive restrictions can frustrate users. It's important to:

- Allow normal conversation flow without too many automatic deletions.

- Regularly review banned words and spam filters to prevent false positives.

- Give trusted users and moderators permissions to bypass auto-filters.

Educate Your Community on Server Rules

Users should understand what behavior is expected. Some ways to communicate rules effectively:

- Create a #rules channel with clear guidelines.

- Use a welcome bot that sends rules to new members.

- Enable slow mode in high-traffic channels to reduce spam.

Monitor Moderation Logs

Most bots and Discord's AutoMod provide moderation logs that store details of every filtered message. Reviewing these logs helps identify false positives and adjust settings accordingly.

To access AutoMod logs:

1. Go to Server Settings → AutoMod.

2. Click View Logs to see all recent moderation actions.

For bots, use commands like !modlogs (Dyno Bot) or check the bot's dashboard.

---

5. Conclusion

Auto-moderation and spam filters are essential tools for maintaining a safe, welcoming, and organized Discord community. Whether using Discord's built-in AutoMod or third-party moderation bots, automating moderation reduces the workload for admins and ensures that conversations remain respectful and spam-free.

By implementing custom filters, setting up proper bot permissions, and regularly reviewing moderation logs, server owners can create a balanced and enjoyable environment for all members.

Next Section: 6.3.3 Handling Bans, Kicks, and Mutes

Now that we have covered **auto-moderation and spam filters**, the next section will focus on **how to handle bans, kicks, and mutes** to enforce server rules effectively.

6.3.3 Handling Bans, Kicks, and Mutes

Discord servers thrive on a sense of community, but with any open platform, there will always be situations where moderation is required. Whether you are dealing with spam, harassment, or other rule violations, knowing how to enforce server rules effectively is essential for maintaining a healthy and welcoming environment.

Three of the most commonly used moderation actions in Discord are banning, kicking, and muting users. Each action serves a different purpose, and understanding how and when to use them can help you manage your community efficiently.

1. Understanding Bans, Kicks, and Mutes in Discord

Before diving into how to use these tools, let's define what they mean:

- **Ban** – A ban permanently removes a user from the server, preventing them from rejoining unless the ban is lifted.

- **Kick** – A kick removes a user from the server, but they can rejoin with a new invite unless additional restrictions are in place.

- **Mute** – A mute prevents a user from speaking in voice channels or sending messages in text channels, but they remain in the server.

Each of these actions is useful in different situations, depending on the severity of a user's behavior.

When to Use Bans, Kicks, and Mutes

Moderation Action	When to Use It	Example Scenarios
Ban	Permanent removal from the server	- Severe rule violations (e.g., hate speech, doxxing, hacking). - Repeated offenses after multiple warnings. - Bot accounts or spam attacks.
Kick	Temporary removal from the server	- First-time offenses or minor disruptions. - A user who is being disrespectful but may improve. - A warning before issuing a ban for repeat behavior.
Mute	Temporary or indefinite restriction on communication	- Spamming messages or voice chat disruptions. - A user needs a "cooling-off" period. - Preventing communication without removing access.

By applying these actions appropriately, you can maintain a positive server environment without being too harsh on first-time offenders.

2. How to Ban, Kick, and Mute Users in Discord

Discord provides several ways to moderate users: manual actions via the user interface, using moderation bots, or configuring role permissions.

2.1 Banning a User from Your Discord Server

A ban in Discord prevents a user from rejoining the server unless explicitly unbanned. Here's how to issue a ban:

Method 1: Banning via the Discord UI

1. Right-click the user's name in the server member list or chat window.

2. Select "Ban [username]" from the dropdown menu.

3. A ban confirmation window will appear. Choose:

   o Delete message history (if needed).

   o Specify a reason (this will be logged for admins).

4. Click "Ban" to confirm.

Method 2: Using Slash Commands

If you have administrative permissions, you can use Discord's built-in commands:

/ban @username reason

For example:

/ban @TrollUser Spamming links in general chat

This method is quicker, especially for large servers.

Method 3: Using Moderation Bots (e.g., MEE6, Dyno, Carl-bot)

Bots provide additional control, such as temporary bans or automatic bans based on violations.

- Example with Dyno bot:

- ?ban @username 7d Spamming and harassment

This bans the user for 7 days, after which they can rejoin.

2.2 Kicking a User from Your Discord Server

Kicking a user removes them from the server, but they can rejoin with an invite unless additional measures (such as bans or verification steps) are in place.

Method 1: Kicking via the Discord UI

1. Right-click the user's name in the server member list or chat window.

2. Select "Kick [username]" from the dropdown menu.

3. A confirmation window will appear.

4. Optionally, add a reason for the kick.

5. Click "Kick" to confirm.

Method 2: Using Slash Commands

/kick @username reason

Example:

/kick @User123 Disruptive behavior in voice chat

Method 3: Using Moderation Bots

Bots allow for **automatic kicks** based on behavior patterns. For example, MEE6 can kick users automatically if they receive multiple warnings. Example command for Dyno bot:

?kick @username Being disruptive

2.3 Muting a User in Discord

Muting is useful when a user is spamming messages, shouting in voice chat, or needs a temporary restriction without being removed from the server.

Method 1: Manually Muting via Discord UI

- **For voice channels:**

  1. Right-click the user's name.

  2. Select "Mute" from the menu.

  3. This prevents them from speaking in voice chat.

- **For text channels:**

  1. Modify the user's role permissions:

     - Go to Server Settings > Roles > [Select Role].

     - Disable Send Messages in text channels.

  2. Assign the muted role to the user.

Method 2: Using Slash Commands

/mute @username 10m Flooding general chat

This mutes the user for 10 minutes.

Method 3: Using Moderation Bots

Bots like Dyno, MEE6, and Carl-bot allow automated mutes. Example with MEE6:

!mute @username 30m excessive pinging

This mutes the user for 30 minutes.

3. Best Practices for Effective Moderation

To ensure that bans, kicks, and mutes are used fairly, consider these best practices:

1. Set Clear Server Rules

- Create a rules channel outlining acceptable behavior.
- Pin important guidelines to general chat or new members' channels.

2. Issue Warnings Before Harsh Actions

- Many servers use a three-strike system (e.g., warning > mute > kick > ban).
- Automate warnings using bots like MEE6 (!warn @username command).

3. Use Moderation Logs

- Enable Discord's Audit Log (in Server Settings) to track actions.
- Set up mod-log channels to document bans, kicks, and mutes.

4. Prevent Ban Evasion

- Turn on 2FA for server moderation.
- Enable higher verification levels (e.g., requiring email/phone verification).
- Use IP bans if a user keeps returning under different accounts.

Conclusion

Handling bans, kicks, and mutes is an essential part of server moderation. By using these tools effectively, you can ensure your community remains safe, organized, and enjoyable for all members.

In the next section, we will explore "6.4 Handling Disruptive Users and Conflict Resolution," where we discuss de-escalation techniques, community management, and handling difficult situations without resorting to bans.

CHAPTER VII
Privacy, Safety, and Best Practices

7.1 Protecting Your Account

7.1.1 Enabling Two-Factor Authentication (2FA)

Security is a crucial aspect of using any online platform, and Discord is no exception. With the rise of cyber threats such as hacking, phishing, and account takeovers, it is essential to protect your Discord account from unauthorized access. One of the most effective ways to enhance your account security is by enabling Two-Factor Authentication (2FA).

What is Two-Factor Authentication (2FA)?

Two-Factor Authentication (2FA) is an additional layer of security that helps protect your account by requiring two forms of verification before granting access. Instead of relying solely on a password, 2FA requires a secondary verification method, such as:

- A unique time-sensitive code generated by an authentication app.

- A backup code provided by Discord when setting up 2FA.

- A security key (for advanced users who use hardware authentication devices).

With 2FA enabled, even if a hacker manages to steal your password, they will still need access to your second verification method to log in, significantly reducing the risk of unauthorized access.

Why is 2FA Important on Discord?

1. Prevents Unauthorized Logins

Cybercriminals often use phishing techniques to trick users into revealing their passwords. Without 2FA, a compromised password can give hackers full access to your Discord account. Enabling 2FA ensures that only **you** can log in, even if someone obtains your password.

2. Protects Your Personal Information

Your Discord account may contain sensitive information, such as private messages, billing details (if you have Discord Nitro), and personal data. With 2FA, you add an extra layer of defense to prevent unauthorized users from accessing your personal details.

3. Enhances Server Security

If you are an administrator or moderator of a Discord server, enabling 2FA is even more critical. Many Discord servers require moderators and administrators to enable 2FA before they can manage server settings. This helps prevent malicious actors from hijacking a server by compromising a high-level user's account.

4. Prevents Account Takeovers

Account takeovers occur when cybercriminals gain access to an account and use it for spamming, scamming, or distributing malware. By enabling 2FA, you significantly reduce the risk of your account being hijacked and used for malicious activities.

How to Enable 2FA on Discord

Enabling 2FA on Discord is a simple process that requires an authentication app and access to your Discord account. Follow these steps to enable 2FA and secure your account.

Step 1: Open Discord and Access Account Settings

1. Launch the Discord app on your desktop or mobile device.

2. Click on the gear icon (⚙▢) in the bottom-left corner next to your username to open User Settings.

3. In the left-hand menu, navigate to the "My Account" section.

Step 2: Begin the 2FA Setup Process

1. Scroll down to the Two-Factor Authentication section.

2. Click on the "Enable Two-Factor Auth" button.

Step 3: Download and Install an Authentication App

To proceed, you will need an authentication app to generate time-sensitive 2FA codes. Some of the most commonly used authentication apps include:

- Google Authenticator (Available on iOS and Android)

- Authy (Recommended for multi-device syncing)

- Microsoft Authenticator

- LastPass Authenticator

If you don't have an authentication app installed, download one from the **Apple App Store** or **Google Play Store** before proceeding.

Step 4: Scan the QR Code or Enter the Key Manually

1. Open your authentication app and choose the option to add a new account.

2. Use the app's QR code scanner to scan the QR code displayed on Discord.

   o If you cannot scan the QR code, Discord provides a manual setup key that you can enter into the authentication app.

3. Once added, your authentication app will generate a 6-digit time-sensitive code that refreshes every 30 seconds.

Step 5: Enter the Authentication Code

1. In Discord, enter the 6-digit code generated by your authentication app.

2. Click "Activate" to complete the setup.

At this stage, Two-Factor Authentication is now enabled for your Discord account.

Setting Up Backup Codes

Since 2FA requires access to an authentication app, you may run into issues if you lose your phone or the app becomes inaccessible. To prevent getting locked out, Discord provides backup codes that can be used as a secondary login method.

How to Generate and Save Backup Codes

1. After enabling 2FA, click on "View Backup Codes" in your Discord settings.

2. Discord will generate a list of one-time-use backup codes.

3. Save these codes in a secure location, such as:

- o   A password manager (e.g., LastPass, 1Password).

- o   A secure note on your computer (not in plain text).

- o   A printed copy stored safely.

Important: If you lose access to your authentication app and don't have backup codes, you will need to contact Discord Support to recover your account.

Enabling SMS-Based 2FA (Optional)

For additional security, you can enable SMS-based 2FA as a secondary method. This sends a verification code to your mobile number when you log in. While SMS 2FA is not as secure as authentication apps, it serves as a useful backup option.

How to Enable SMS 2FA

1. Go to User Settings → My Account → Enable SMS Authentication.

2. Enter your phone number and verify it with the code sent via SMS.

Once enabled, if you lose access to your authentication app, you can request a backup login code via SMS.

How to Disable 2FA If Needed

If you ever need to disable 2FA, follow these steps:

1. Navigate to User Settings → My Account.

2. Scroll to the Two-Factor Authentication section.

3. Click "Remove 2FA" and enter a verification code from your authentication app.

Warning: Disabling 2FA removes the extra layer of protection from your account, making it more vulnerable to attacks. Only disable 2FA if absolutely necessary.

Common Issues and Troubleshooting

Issue 1: Lost Access to 2FA Codes

- Use a backup code to log in.

- If you have enabled SMS 2FA, request a code via SMS.

- If neither option is available, contact Discord Support for recovery.

Issue 2: 2FA Code Not Working

- Ensure that your device's date and time settings are accurate (incorrect time settings can cause desynchronization).

- Try generating a new code from your authentication app.

- Restart your device and attempt the login process again.

Issue 3: Phone Lost or Reset

- If you still have access to backup codes, use them to log in.

- Set up 2FA again on a new device as soon as possible.

Conclusion

Enabling Two-Factor Authentication (2FA) is one of the most effective ways to secure your Discord account. By requiring a secondary authentication method, you protect your account from unauthorized logins, phishing attacks, and cyber threats.

To maximize your security:
✓ Always keep your backup codes in a safe place.
✓ Use an authentication app instead of SMS for stronger protection.
✓ Ensure 2FA is enabled for your server moderators and administrators.

By taking these steps, you safeguard your personal information, Discord servers, and online presence.

Next Section: 7.1.2 Recognizing and Avoiding Scams

In the next section, we will explore common scams on Discord and how to protect yourself from phishing attempts, fake giveaways, and account hijacking.

7.1.2 Recognizing and Avoiding Scams

Discord, like many other online platforms, is a prime target for scammers. With millions of users engaging daily in text chats, voice calls, and video communications, it has become an attractive environment for cybercriminals looking to steal personal information, distribute malware, or commit fraud.

In this section, we will explore the most common scams on Discord, how to identify potential threats, and the best practices to protect yourself from falling victim to these scams.

1. Common Types of Scams on Discord

1.1 Phishing Scams

Phishing is one of the most prevalent scams on Discord. It involves cybercriminals impersonating legitimate individuals, businesses, or Discord staff to trick users into revealing their login credentials, personal information, or financial details.

How It Works:

- A scammer sends a message claiming to be from Discord Support, asking you to verify your account or confirm suspicious activity via a provided link.

- The link leads to a fake login page that looks identical to Discord's official site.

- Once you enter your credentials, the scammer steals your username and password, potentially gaining full access to your account.

Warning Signs of Phishing Attempts:

- Unsolicited messages claiming urgent action is required.

- Links that look suspicious or contain misspellings (e.g., "díscord.com" instead of "discord.com").

- Requests to input your password or enable special permissions.

- Messages that create a sense of panic or urgency (e.g., "Your account will be banned unless you act now!").

Example of a Phishing Message:

"Hello, we detected unauthorized activity on your Discord account. Please verify your details immediately by clicking this link: [fake-website.com] to avoid permanent suspension."

1.2 Fake Giveaways and Nitro Scams

Scammers often use fake giveaways or Discord Nitro scams to trick users into revealing sensitive information or downloading malware.

How It Works:

- A scammer impersonates Discord staff, popular influencers, or bots to claim you have won a Discord Nitro subscription, gaming currency, or other rewards.

- They provide a malicious link that either asks for your login credentials or downloads malware onto your device.

- Some scams involve fake QR codes, asking you to scan them with your Discord mobile app, allowing the scammer to hijack your account.

Warning Signs of Fake Giveaways:

- Receiving a random direct message (DM) saying you won a prize.

- Links that redirect to an unfamiliar website.

- Requests to enter your login details or scan a QR code to claim the reward.

- Unrealistic giveaways (e.g., "You won $1000 in Nitro credits!").

Example of a Fake Giveaway Message:

"Congratulations! You have been randomly selected to receive 3 months of free Discord Nitro! Click here to claim your reward: [fake-link.com]. Act fast before this offer expires!"

1.3 Impersonation Scams (Fake Moderators, Bots, and Staff)

Some scammers pretend to be Discord administrators, moderators, or bot services to manipulate users into giving up sensitive information.

How It Works:

- A scammer creates a fake profile that looks identical to a Discord staff member or bot (e.g., "Discord Verification Bot").

- They send messages claiming you need to verify your account or submit information for security purposes.

- They ask for login credentials, payment details, or 2FA codes.

- Sometimes, they threaten users with account bans or server removals to pressure them into complying.

Warning Signs of Impersonation Scams:

- Discord never sends direct messages (DMs) to users for verification purposes.

- Legitimate Discord staff members have a blue "Discord Staff" badge next to their username.

- Requests for personal information or payment details through DMs.

- Claims that you must verify your account to avoid being banned.

Example of an Impersonation Scam Message:

"Hello, I am a Discord Moderator. Your account has been flagged for suspicious activity. Please verify your details here: [fake-link.com] or your account will be permanently banned."

1.4 Malware and Trojan Attacks

Scammers may attempt to distribute malicious software (malware) through links, attachments, or file downloads. These malicious files can:

- Steal your Discord credentials and other personal data.

- Take control of your device.

- Use your account to spread the malware further.

How It Works:

- A scammer sends a message with an attachment (e.g., "game hack," "exclusive mod," or "Discord enhancement tool").

- When you download and execute the file, malware is installed on your system.

- Your passwords, personal files, and browser history may be exposed to the attacker.

Warning Signs of Malware Scams:

- Random users sending executable (.exe) files or ZIP archives.

- Claims that the file will improve your gaming experience or unlock premium Discord features for free.

- Links that redirect to strange domains.

2. How to Protect Yourself from Scams on Discord

Now that you are aware of common scams, here are essential tips to keep your account safe:

Enable Two-Factor Authentication (2FA)

Always enable 2FA on your Discord account. This adds an extra layer of security by requiring a verification code from an authentication app (e.g., Google Authenticator) when logging in. Even if a scammer steals your password, they won't be able to access your account without the 2FA code.

Avoid Clicking Suspicious Links

- Do not click on links from unknown users or suspicious messages.

- Verify the URL before logging in—only use "discord.com" or "discordapp.com".

- If a link looks slightly misspelled or unfamiliar, assume it's a scam.

Never Share Your Login Credentials

- Discord staff will never ask for your password or 2FA codes.

- Be cautious if someone claims they need your login information for security reasons.

Block and Report Scammers

- If you receive a suspicious message, block the sender immediately.

- Use Discord's built-in report feature to alert moderators and Discord Trust & Safety.

Verify Official Discord Communications

- If you receive a message claiming to be from Discord, check their official support website (support.discord.com).

- Official Discord staff have a blue badge next to their username.

Conclusion

Scams on Discord are constantly evolving, but by staying informed and vigilant, you can protect yourself from fraudsters. Always be skeptical of unsolicited messages, fake giveaways, and suspicious links. Enabling 2FA, blocking scammers, and reporting suspicious activity are crucial steps in keeping your Discord experience safe.

In the next section, we will explore **7.1.3 Managing Blocked Users and Privacy Settings**, where we discuss how to configure **privacy controls, manage blocked users, and enhance security settings** to prevent unwanted interactions on Discord.

7.1.3 Managing Blocked Users and Privacy Settings

Ensuring your privacy and security on Discord is essential, whether you use it for gaming, work, or community engagement. Discord offers a variety of privacy settings and tools that allow you to control who can interact with you, block unwanted users, and manage your overall safety on the platform. This section will cover how to block users, what happens when you block someone, how to manage privacy settings, and tips for maintaining a secure and comfortable experience on Discord.

Blocking Users on Discord

Blocking someone on Discord is a simple yet effective way to prevent unwanted interactions. Whether you are dealing with harassment, spam, or simply wish to avoid specific users, blocking ensures they cannot contact you directly.

How to Block a User

Blocking a user can be done through different methods, depending on where you encounter them.

Blocking from a Direct Message (DM)

1. Open Discord and navigate to the **Direct Messages** section.

2. Select the conversation with the person you want to block.

3. Click on their **profile picture** or **username** to open their profile.

4. Click the **three-dot menu (⋮)** in the top-right corner.

5. Select **Block** from the dropdown menu.

Blocking from a Server

1. Go to the Discord server where the user is a member.

2. Locate their username in the **member list** or within a chat message.

3. Right-click on their name to open a menu.

4. Select **Block**.

Blocking from a Friend List

1. Open your **Friends** list.

2. Find the user you want to block.

3. Click on their profile and select **Block**.

What Happens When You Block Someone?

Blocking someone on Discord affects your interaction with them in several ways:

- **No Direct Messages (DMs):** The blocked user cannot send you direct messages, and any existing conversation will be removed from your DM list.

- **Invisible Messages in Shared Servers:** If you share a server with the blocked user, you will no longer see their messages. Instead, you will see a notification that says, "Blocked Message."

- **They Can't Add You as a Friend:** The blocked user will be unable to send you a friend request.

- **Voice and Video Communication Blocked:** If you are in a voice channel with a blocked user, you won't hear them speaking, and they won't hear you.

- **No Notifications or Mentions:** The blocked user cannot mention your username or ping you in a shared server.

However, blocking someone does not remove them from shared servers, and they can still see your messages unless they block you as well. If you want to completely remove someone from your environment, consider leaving the server or asking an admin to intervene.

Managing Privacy Settings on Discord

Discord offers a range of privacy and security settings that allow you to customize your experience. These settings help you control who can message you, add you as a friend, or see your activity.

Accessing Your Privacy Settings

1. Open **Discord** and click on the **gear icon** ⚙☐ next to your username (bottom-left corner) to open **User Settings**.

2. Scroll down to the **Privacy & Safety** tab on the left menu.

3. From here, you can adjust various settings related to your privacy and interactions.

Key Privacy Settings

1. Safe Direct Messaging

This setting automatically scans and filters direct messages from people who are not your friends. Options include:

- Keep Me Safe – Scans all direct messages, even from friends.

- My Friends Are Nice – Scans DMs only from non-friends.

- Do Not Scan – No filtering of messages.

For the best security, Keep Me Safe is the recommended setting.

2. Friend Request Settings

This controls who can send you friend requests:

- Everyone – Anyone can send a friend request.
- Friends of Friends – Only mutual friends can send a request.
- Server Members – Only members of shared servers can send a request.

For better privacy, disable "Everyone" to avoid spam requests.

3. Server Privacy Settings

You can manage who can message you from servers you are in:

- Toggle Allow Direct Messages from Server Members – Disabling this prevents members of shared servers from DMing you unless they are friends.
- Adjust Who Can Add You as a Friend – You can choose to limit friend requests to only mutual friends or people in shared servers.

4. Activity Status and Rich Presence

By default, Discord displays your activity status (e.g., what game you are playing or what app you are using). You can turn this off to maintain privacy:

1. Go to User Settings > Activity Privacy.
2. Toggle off "Display Current Activity as a Status Message."
3. You can also disable Rich Presence to prevent apps from showing detailed activity.

5. Read Receipts and Typing Indicators

Discord shows when you are typing in a chat. If you prefer more privacy:

1. Open User Settings > Text & Images.
2. Toggle off "Show Typing Indicator" to disable this feature.

6. Who Can Mention You

Mentions can be used to get your attention, but they can be misused for spam. You can:

1. Open User Settings > Notifications.
2. Adjust @mention settings to limit who can tag you.

For public servers, it's advisable to disable mentions from @everyone, @here, and @roles to reduce spam.

Tips for Maintaining a Secure and Private Discord Experience

1. Regularly Review Your Privacy Settings – Check your settings periodically to ensure they align with your preferences.

2. Avoid Accepting Random Friend Requests – Be cautious about adding unknown users to your friend list.

3. Use Strong and Unique Passwords – Combine letters, numbers, and special characters to secure your account.

4. Enable Two-Factor Authentication (2FA) – Adds an extra layer of security.

5. Report Suspicious Users – If you encounter harassment or suspicious activity, report the user to Discord moderators or admins.

6. Be Wary of External Links and Bots – Scammers often use bots or links to phishing websites. Avoid clicking unfamiliar links.

7. Customize Server-Specific Privacy Settings – Some settings are server-wide. Adjust them based on the type of community you are in.

Conclusion

Managing your blocked users and privacy settings is an essential part of having a safe and enjoyable experience on Discord. By blocking unwanted users, adjusting privacy settings, and staying vigilant against scams and harassment, you can maintain a secure and comfortable space while engaging in online conversations.

In the next section, we will discuss server safety, Discord's Terms of Service, and how to create a secure community environment.

7.2 Server Safety and Community Guidelines

7.2.1 Understanding Discord's Terms of Service

Discord is a widely used communication platform that connects people across different communities, interests, and industries. As with any online service, Discord has a Terms of Service (ToS) agreement that outlines the rules, responsibilities, and rights of users and the platform itself. Understanding these terms is crucial for server owners, moderators, and general users to ensure compliance, maintain a safe environment, and avoid penalties such as account bans or server deletions.

This section will provide a detailed breakdown of Discord's Terms of Service, its importance, and how users can adhere to it while managing or participating in servers.

1. What Are Discord's Terms of Service?

The Terms of Service (ToS) is a legal agreement between Discord and its users that defines how the platform should be used. By creating a Discord account and using the platform, every user automatically agrees to these terms. The ToS covers topics such as acceptable use, prohibited content, user rights, privacy policies, and penalties for violations.

Discord's official Terms of Service can be found on their website: https://discord.com/terms.

The ToS is legally binding, meaning that violating any terms can result in account suspension or permanent bans. Server owners and moderators should familiarize themselves with these rules to prevent violations and protect their communities.

2. Key Sections of Discord's Terms of Service

Below are some of the most important sections of Discord's ToS that users should be aware of:

2.1 Age Requirements

- Discord requires users to be at least 13 years old (or the minimum legal age in their country).

- In certain jurisdictions (such as the European Union), users under 16 years old may require parental consent to use the service.

- Creating an account while underage violates Discord's terms and can lead to an account ban.

- Server owners should implement age-restricted roles and channels to prevent younger users from accessing inappropriate content.

2.2 Prohibited Activities

Discord strictly prohibits harmful or illegal activities, including:

1. **Harassment, Bullying, and Hate Speech**

   o Targeting individuals or groups based on race, gender, religion, sexuality, or disability is strictly forbidden.

   o Encouraging violence or discrimination violates Discord's Community Guidelines.

2. **Threats, Self-Harm, and Suicide Promotion**

   o Threats of harm, doxxing (exposing private information), and blackmail are not allowed.

   o Discussions promoting self-harm or suicide should be handled responsibly—users should be directed to mental health resources instead.

3. **Illegal Activities and Content**

   o Sharing, promoting, or discussing illegal substances, hacking, fraud, or criminal activities is forbidden.

   o Piracy (e.g., sharing cracked software, illegal streaming links, or copyright violations) is not allowed.

4. **Malware, Scams, and Phishing**

- o Sending links to malicious websites, viruses, or phishing scams can result in immediate account termination.

- o Server admins should enable link filters and educate users on spotting suspicious messages.

5. **Explicit Content and NSFW Material**

- o Discord allows NSFW (Not Safe for Work) channels, but they must be properly labeled with age restrictions.

- o Sharing pornography, graphic violence, or extreme gore in non-NSFW areas violates Discord's rules.

- o Users under 18 years old should not have access to NSFW content.

2.3 Spam, Bots, and Automation Rules

- Mass spamming, including excessive messages, friend requests, and advertising, is prohibited.

- Self-bots (bots running on personal accounts) are not allowed.

- Any bots used in a server must comply with Discord's Developer Terms.

3. Consequences of Violating the Terms of Service

Violating Discord's ToS can lead to various **penalties**, depending on the severity of the infraction:

3.1 Warnings and Temporary Bans

- Minor infractions (e.g., mild spam or inappropriate language) may result in a warning or temporary mute from a server.

- Discord may issue a temporary account ban if a user violates minor rules repeatedly.

3.2 Account Suspension or Termination

- Serious violations (e.g., hate speech, illegal activities, or hacking attempts) can result in a permanent ban from Discord.

- Banned accounts cannot be recovered, and users must create a new account to rejoin the platform.

3.3 Server Deletion

- If a server consistently violates ToS, Discord may suspend or delete the entire server.

- Server owners who fail to enforce the rules risk losing their communities.

4. How to Ensure Compliance with Discord's Terms of Service

For Server Owners and Moderators

- Read and understand Discord's Terms of Service before creating a server.

- Set clear community guidelines that align with Discord's rules.

- Use moderation bots (such as MEE6, Dyno, or Carl-bot) to enforce rules.

- Monitor activity and report violations to Discord if necessary.

For General Users

- Avoid sharing personal information to protect your privacy.

- Think before posting—do not share illegal, offensive, or misleading content.

- Report violations if you encounter spam, scams, or harmful content.

5. Reporting Violations and Seeking Help

How to Report a User or Server

If you come across a ToS violation, you can report it directly to Discord:

1. **For individual users**

     o   Right-click on the user's name and select **"Report"**.

     o   Provide evidence (screenshots, message links) when submitting a report.

2. **For servers**

     o   Use the Discord Trust & Safety Form: https://dis.gd/report.

     o   Reports are reviewed by Discord's moderation team before action is taken.

Contacting Discord Support

- If you have questions about Discord's ToS, visit: https://support.discord.com.

- Use Discord's Help Center for troubleshooting and safety concerns.

Conclusion

Understanding Discord's Terms of Service is essential for maintaining a safe, compliant, and enjoyable experience on the platform. Whether you are a server owner, moderator, or casual user, following these guidelines prevents bans, protects privacy, and fosters a positive online environment.

In the next section (**7.2.2 Reporting Violations and Harmful Content**), we'll cover how to effectively report rule-breaking users and manage safety concerns within a Discord server.

7.2.2 Reporting Violations and Harmful Content

Discord is designed to be a safe and welcoming platform for communities of all kinds. However, like any online space, Discord can sometimes be misused for harmful behavior, including harassment, hate speech, scams, and illegal activities. To ensure that Discord remains a secure and enjoyable environment, it is important for users and server administrators to recognize violations, understand the reporting process, and take proactive measures to maintain a positive community.

This section will guide you through the different types of violations, how to report harmful content effectively, and best practices for handling problematic behavior on Discord.

Understanding Discord's Community Guidelines and Terms of Service

Before reporting a violation, it's essential to understand what constitutes a breach of Discord's Community Guidelines and Terms of Service (ToS). Discord enforces strict policies against harmful behavior to protect its users.

Common Violations on Discord

The following behaviors are explicitly prohibited on Discord:

1. **Harassment and Bullying** – Targeting users with threats, insults, or unwanted messages.

2. **Hate Speech and Discrimination** – Promoting violence or hatred based on race, ethnicity, gender, religion, disability, or sexual orientation.

3. **Spam and Scams** – Sending mass unsolicited messages, phishing links, or fraudulent promotions.

4. **Illegal Content** – Sharing or discussing illegal activities, including drug sales, piracy, and child exploitation.

5. **Self-Harm and Suicide Promotion** – Encouraging self-harm, eating disorders, or suicide.

6. **Doxxing and Privacy Violations** – Sharing personal information without consent.

7. **Malicious Software and Hacking** – Distributing viruses, malware, or engaging in hacking activities.

8. **NSFW Content in Public Spaces** – Sharing explicit or adult content in non-designated areas.

If you encounter any of these violations, you should take immediate action by reporting them to server moderators, Discord staff, or both, depending on the severity.

How to Report Violations on Discord

1. Reporting to Server Moderators

If a violation occurs within a private server, the server moderators and administrators should be your first point of contact. Here's how you can report an issue within a server:

Step 1: Identify the Moderation Team

- Look for users with special roles such as "Moderator," "Admin," or "Staff."

- Some servers have a dedicated channel for reporting issues, like #report-violations or #moderator-help.

Step 2: Collect Evidence

When reporting a violation, provide clear evidence to help moderators take appropriate action. This includes:

- Screenshots of offending messages or behavior.

- Usernames and Discord IDs (to avoid confusion with similar names).

- Timestamps and context of the incident.

Step 3: Submit the Report

- Use the server's designated reporting system, such as a bot command (!report @username reason).

- If no system is in place, message a moderator directly.

- Some servers use moderation bots like Dyno, MEE6, or Carl-bot, which have built-in reporting tools.

2. Reporting Direct Messages (DMs) and Harassment

If someone is harassing you in private messages, you can report them directly to Discord's Trust & Safety team.

Step 1: Block the User

- Right-click their username and select **Block** to prevent further messages.

Step 2: Enable Message Requests (Optional)

- If you don't want random users messaging you, go to: User Settings → Privacy & Safety → Allow direct messages from server members (toggle off).

Step 3: Report the User to Discord

- If the behavior is severe (e.g., threats, scams, or illegal content), report them to Discord.

- **How to Report a User:**

  1. Right-click their username and click Copy ID (you must enable Developer Mode for this in User Settings).

  2. Right-click the message you want to report and click Copy Message Link.

  3. Go to Discord's Trust & Safety Center (https://dis.gd/report) and fill out the form.

3. Reporting Harmful Content in Public Servers

For public servers, especially large ones with thousands of members, you can report violations directly to Discord staff if moderators fail to act.

What You Need to Report

- The server name and invite link (if accessible).

- Screenshots or message links of the harmful content.

- The user's ID and tag (Username#1234).

To report a public server, visit the Trust & Safety Center and choose the Report a Server option.

What Happens After You Submit a Report?

Once you report a user, message, or server, Discord's Trust & Safety team will investigate the issue. Here's what you can expect:

1. Reviewing the Report

- Reports are prioritized based on severity (e.g., threats of violence get immediate attention).

- Discord does not share the results of the investigation for privacy reasons.

2. Possible Actions Taken by Discord

- Warning – A user may receive a warning for minor violations.

- Temporary Ban – The user may be temporarily suspended from Discord.

- Permanent Ban – Severe offenders can be permanently removed from the platform.

- Server Removal – If a server is dedicated to illegal or harmful activities, Discord may shut it down.

Best Practices for Handling Violations in Your Server

If you are a server administrator or moderator, you have an important role in maintaining a safe community. Here's how you can prevent and handle violations effectively:

1. Set Up Clear Server Rules

- Create a #rules channel with guidelines on acceptable behavior.

- Use bots like Dyno or MEE6 to automatically warn users who break rules.

2. Use Moderation Bots

- AutoMod (built-in Discord tool) – Detects and removes harmful messages.

- Carl-bot / Dyno / MEE6 – Allows keyword filtering, auto-muting, and logging reports.

3. Appoint Responsible Moderators

- Choose moderators who understand Discord's terms of service and best practices.

- Train them to handle reports fairly and efficiently.

4. Encourage Users to Report Issues

- Have a clear reporting system in place.

- Offer anonymous reporting options for users who fear retaliation.

5. Monitor Server Activity Regularly

- Check audit logs for suspicious activities (Server Settings → Audit Log).

- Review message history in public channels for inappropriate content.

Conclusion

Reporting violations is crucial to maintaining a safe and positive Discord experience. By understanding what constitutes a violation, how to report harmful content, and best practices for server moderation, you can contribute to a healthier online community.

If you ever feel unsafe or witness illegal activity on Discord, do not hesitate to take action. Your report could help protect not only yourself but also many others in the community.

Next Section: 7.2.3 Creating a Safe and Inclusive Community

In the next section, we'll explore how to foster a welcoming environment, set up community guidelines, and promote inclusivity within your server.

7.2.3 Creating a Safe and Inclusive Community

Discord servers are powerful spaces where people gather to communicate, collaborate, and build meaningful connections. Whether you're running a gaming community, a professional workspace, or a fan club, fostering a safe and inclusive environment is crucial for the success of your server. A welcoming atmosphere encourages engagement, trust, and long-term participation from members.

In this section, we will explore best practices for creating a safe and inclusive community on Discord, covering server moderation strategies, diversity and inclusivity measures, conflict resolution techniques, and essential tools to maintain a healthy community.

1. Establishing Clear Community Guidelines

Every successful server starts with well-defined rules and expectations. Having clear community guidelines helps prevent misunderstandings, minimizes conflicts, and ensures that all members know what behavior is acceptable.

How to Create Effective Community Rules

When drafting your community guidelines, consider the following:

1. Be Clear and Concise – Use straightforward language to explain acceptable and unacceptable behavior.

2. Cover Key Areas – Address harassment, hate speech, spamming, self-promotion, NSFW content, and other potential issues.

3. Promote Respect and Inclusivity – Emphasize the importance of treating all members with kindness and respect.

4. Outline Consequences – Clearly state what actions will be taken against rule-breakers (e.g., warnings, temporary mutes, bans).

5. Pin or Post Rules in a Readable Format – Use a dedicated #rules or #community-guidelines channel where all members can easily access them.

Example of a Simple Set of Rules

1. Be respectful – No harassment, discrimination, or personal attacks.

2. No hate speech – Any form of racism, sexism, homophobia, or derogatory remarks will not be tolerated.

3. No spamming – Avoid excessive messaging, emoji spam, and self-promotion without permission.

4. Keep it appropriate – No NSFW content, political debates, or illegal discussions.

5. Follow Discord's Terms of Service – Violations of Discord's official policies will result in immediate action.

2. Promoting Diversity and Inclusion

Creating an inclusive community means ensuring that all members, regardless of their background, feel safe, valued, and respected.

How to Foster an Inclusive Environment

1. **Use Gender-Neutral Language** – Encourage the use of terms like "everyone" instead of "guys" to make the space welcoming to all genders.

2. **Respect Pronouns** – Allow members to share their pronouns and avoid assuming gender identities. You can use a pronoun role system where members can select their pronouns through reaction roles.

3. **Celebrate Cultural and Regional Diversity** – Be mindful of global time zones, languages, and cultural differences. Consider adding multilingual channels if your server has a diverse audience.

4. **Ensure Accessibility** – Use descriptive text for images, minimize excessive use of flashing GIFs (to accommodate those with epilepsy), and provide alternative ways for members to engage (such as voice and text options).

5. **Zero Tolerance for Discrimination** – Take reports of racism, sexism, homophobia, ableism, and other forms of discrimination seriously and take swift action when necessary.

3. Moderation Strategies for a Safe Community

A well-moderated community ensures that negative behavior is addressed quickly while allowing positive discussions to thrive.

Setting Up a Moderation Team

- Assign trusted and responsible moderators who understand the server rules and enforce them fairly.

- Use role permissions to give mods access to tools like kicking, banning, and muting users.

- Train moderators on handling conflicts professionally and dealing with reports objectively.

Using Moderation Bots

Bots can help automate moderation tasks and ensure **consistent enforcement of rules**. Some of the most popular moderation bots include:

- Dyno – Auto-moderation, anti-spam, logging, and role management.

- MEE6 – Custom moderation commands, automatic rule enforcement, and logging.

- Carl-bot – Reaction roles, auto-moderation, and logging features.

Example of auto-moderation capabilities:
✓ Auto-detect spam and mute spammers.
✓ Filter inappropriate language and delete messages.
✓ Flag potential harassment for moderator review.

Handling Rule Violations

When a rule is broken, it's important to address the situation calmly and professionally. Here's a recommended approach:

1. Issue a Warning – A simple reminder of the rules can resolve minor offenses.

2. Temporary Mute or Timeout – If behavior persists, limit the user's ability to send messages for a period.

3. Kick from the Server – For repeated offenses or serious violations, temporarily remove the user.

4. Permanent Ban – If a user is a persistent problem or engages in severe misconduct, banning may be necessary.

4. Conflict Resolution and Handling Disputes

Even in the best communities, conflicts will arise. Knowing how to de-escalate tensions and resolve disputes effectively is key to maintaining harmony.

Steps for Conflict Resolution

1. Stay Neutral and Listen to Both Sides – Avoid taking sides immediately. Gather information from all parties involved.

2. Move Private Discussions to DMs – Some disputes are best handled privately to prevent public escalation.

3. Encourage Open Dialogue – Allow members to express their concerns, but set limits to keep discussions constructive.

4. Enforce Rules Fairly – Apply rules consistently without favoritism.

5. Use a Dedicated Conflict Resolution Channel – Create a private channel for moderation staff to discuss and handle disputes.

Encouraging Positive Interactions

- Reward good behavior by recognizing helpful members.

- Organize community events to strengthen relationships.

- Provide feedback mechanisms where members can share their thoughts on the server's moderation.

5. Encouraging Engagement and Community Growth

A safe community is also an active and engaging one. Encouraging participation prevents toxicity and fosters a positive atmosphere.

Ideas for Keeping the Community Engaged

✅ Host Regular Events – Gaming nights, Q&A sessions, art showcases, or book discussions.
✅ Create Interactive Roles – Let members choose roles based on interests.
✅ Run Contests and Giveaways – Reward active members with perks or small prizes.
✅ Use Polls and Surveys – Get feedback from the community on events and improvements.

By keeping members engaged, you reduce the likelihood of negativity and rule-breaking, leading to a healthier and more vibrant community.

Conclusion

Building a safe and inclusive Discord server requires clear guidelines, strong moderation, inclusivity efforts, and positive engagement strategies. By fostering a respectful and welcoming atmosphere, you create a community where members feel comfortable expressing themselves without fear of harassment or discrimination.

Maintaining server safety is an ongoing process that involves:

✓ Constantly updating and reinforcing rules.

✓ Training moderators to handle conflicts effectively.

✓ Using moderation bots to ensure a fair environment.

✓ Encouraging diversity, respect, and active participation.

In the next section, we will explore how to troubleshoot common Discord issues, including connection problems, bot errors, and ways to contact Discord support when needed.

7.3 Troubleshooting Common Issues

7.3.1 Fixing Connection and Audio Problems

Discord is a powerful communication tool, but like any online platform, users may occasionally encounter connection and audio issues that impact their experience. These problems can be frustrating, especially if you're in the middle of an important meeting, gaming session, or study group. Fortunately, most Discord connection and audio issues can be resolved with some basic troubleshooting steps.

In this section, we will explore the most common connection and audio problems in Discord and how to fix them effectively.

1. Common Connection Issues and How to Fix Them

Discord Won't Connect or Stuck on Connecting Screen

If Discord gets stuck on "Connecting..." or won't load properly, the issue is often related to network problems, server outages, or firewall settings. Try these troubleshooting steps:

Step 1: Check Discord's Server Status

Before troubleshooting your own connection, ensure that Discord's servers are not down.

- Visit Discord's status page to check for any ongoing outages.
- If there is a server outage, you may need to wait for Discord to resolve it.

Step 2: Restart Discord and Your Device

- Close Discord completely by using Task Manager (Windows) or Force Quit (Mac).
- Restart your computer or mobile device and relaunch Discord.

Step 3: Check Your Internet Connection

- Restart your router and modem.

- Switch from Wi-Fi to Ethernet if possible, as wired connections are more stable.

- Run a speed test at speedtest.net to check your internet connection.

Step 4: Disable VPN or Proxy

- VPNs and proxy servers can interfere with Discord's connection. Try disabling them temporarily.

- If you need a VPN for work or security, consider using a different VPN server.

Step 5: Allow Discord Through Firewall and Antivirus

- Go to Windows Defender Firewall (or your antivirus settings).

- Ensure Discord.exe is allowed through both public and private networks.

- Temporarily disable your antivirus to see if it is blocking Discord.

Step 6: Change DNS Settings

If Discord still won't connect, try using Google's DNS (8.8.8.8, 8.8.4.4) or Cloudflare's DNS (1.1.1.1):

- On Windows, go to Network Settings > Change Adapter Options > Right-click your connection > Select Properties > Click IPv4 > Use the custom DNS.

- On Mac, go to System Preferences > Network > Advanced > DNS and enter the new DNS addresses.

1.2 High Ping and Lagging in Voice Calls

If you experience lag, robotic voices, or delayed messages in Discord voice channels, this is usually due to high ping or network congestion.

Step 1: Check Your Internet Speed

- Use Speedtest.net to check if you have low upload/download speeds or high ping.

- If your internet is slow, try restarting your router or reducing network usage (pause downloads, stop video streaming).

Step 2: Switch to a Closer Server Region

- If you're in a voice channel, click Edit Channel > Server Region and select a region closer to you.

- If you don't have permission to do this, ask a server admin to change the voice region.

Step 3: Close Background Applications

- Heavy applications like Steam, Netflix, and large file downloads can cause lag in Discord.

- Close unnecessary apps using Task Manager (Ctrl + Shift + Esc) in Windows or Activity Monitor in macOS.

Step 4: Disable QoS (Quality of Service) in Discord

- Go to User Settings > Voice & Video.

- Scroll down and disable "Enable Quality of Service High Packet Priority."

2. Common Audio Issues and How to Fix Them

No Sound from Discord (Mic and Speakers Not Working)

If you can't hear anything in Discord or your microphone isn't working, follow these steps:

Step 1: Check Your Output and Input Devices

- Go to User Settings > Voice & Video.

- Under Input Device, select the correct microphone.

- Under Output Device, select the correct headphones or speakers.

Step 2: Increase Volume in Discord

- Make sure the volume slider is not set to 0.

- Right-click a user in a voice channel and increase their individual volume if they are too quiet.

Step 3: Check System Volume and Sound Settings

- On Windows, right-click the speaker icon in the taskbar > Select Sounds > Playback Devices and set your preferred device as default.

- On Mac, go to System Preferences > Sound > Output/Input and select the correct device.

Step 4: Restart Your Audio Driver

- On Windows, open Device Manager, go to Audio Inputs and Outputs, right-click your device, and select Disable, then Enable it again.

Microphone Not Working (Other People Can't Hear You)

If your microphone isn't picking up sound, try the following:

Step 1: Grant Microphone Permissions

- On Windows, go to Settings > Privacy > Microphone, and allow apps to access your microphone.

- On Mac, go to System Preferences > Security & Privacy > Microphone, and enable access for Discord.

Step 2: Reset Voice Settings in Discord

- Go to User Settings > Voice & Video.

- Scroll down and click "Reset Voice Settings."

Step 3: Check "Input Sensitivity" Settings

- Under User Settings > Voice & Video, disable "Automatically Determine Input Sensitivity" and adjust the slider manually.

Step 4: Test Push-to-Talk Mode

- If your microphone isn't working in Voice Activity mode, switch to Push-to-Talk and see if it works.

3. Advanced Fixes and Additional Help

Updating Discord and Your Audio Drivers

- Ensure Discord is updated by restarting the app.

- On Windows, update your audio drivers in Device Manager > Sound, Video, and Game Controllers.

- On Mac, update to the latest macOS version.

Reinstalling Discord

- If all else fails, uninstall Discord and reinstall it from discord.com.

Contacting Discord Support

If none of the above fixes work, you can contact Discord Support at support.discord.com.

Conclusion

Connection and audio issues in Discord can be frustrating, but most of them can be easily fixed with the right troubleshooting steps. Whether it's fixing lag, improving microphone performance, or resolving no-sound issues, following these solutions will ensure you have the best experience on Discord.

Next Section: 7.3.2 Resolving Bot and Permission Errors

In the next section, we'll explore common bot-related issues, troubleshooting bot commands, and fixing permission problems in Discord servers.

7.3.2 Resolving Bot and Permission Errors

Discord bots are an essential part of many servers, helping to automate tasks, moderate chats, and add fun and functionality to communities. However, users and server administrators often encounter issues with bots, particularly related to permissions. This section will guide you through the most common bot-related errors and permission issues, along with their solutions.

Understanding Discord Bots and Permissions

Before diving into troubleshooting, it's important to understand how bots function in Discord and how permissions work.

What Are Discord Bots?

Discord bots are automated programs that can perform a variety of tasks within a server, such as:

- Moderation (banning/kicking users, filtering messages).

- Music playback (streaming music into voice channels).

- Information retrieval (weather updates, cryptocurrency prices, etc.).

- Role management (automatically assigning roles based on user actions).

Bots interact with servers based on the permissions granted to them, which are controlled by roles. If a bot doesn't have the correct permissions, it won't function as expected.

Understanding Discord Permissions

Discord permissions define what users and bots can do within a server. Permissions are split into:

- User permissions – What individual users can do (e.g., send messages, mute members).

- Role permissions – What members in a specific role can do.

- Channel permissions – Custom permissions for specific channels.

- Bot permissions – Special permissions required for bots to function properly.

If a bot isn't working as expected, there's a high chance it's due to permission issues.

Common Bot Issues and How to Fix Them

1. Bot Not Responding to Commands

Possible Causes:

- The bot is offline or not running.

- The bot lacks the necessary permissions.

- The bot's command prefix is incorrect.

- A bot-related API or service is down.

How to Fix It:

1. **Check if the Bot is Online**

   o Go to your **Server Members List** (Server Settings > Members) and look for the bot's status.

   o If the bot is **offline**, visit the bot's website or hosting platform to ensure it's running.

2. **Verify the Bot's Permissions**

   o Navigate to Server Settings > Roles > [Bot's Role].

   o Ensure the bot has the necessary permissions to send messages, manage roles, and access channels.

3. **Check the Bot's Command Prefix**

   o Some bots use !, ?, or . as their prefix (e.g., !help).

   o Use the default prefix or check the bot's documentation for customization options.

4. **Restart the Bot**

   o If you're hosting a custom bot, restart it through your server or hosting provider.

5. **Check for API Issues**

   o If the bot relies on an external API (e.g., a music bot streaming from YouTube), verify if the service is experiencing outages.

2. Bot Not Assigning or Managing Roles Properly

Possible Causes:

- The bot doesn't have the Manage Roles permission.
- The bot's role is lower than the role it's trying to assign.
- Role hierarchy prevents the bot from making changes.

How to Fix It:

1. **Enable "Manage Roles" Permission**
   - Go to Server Settings > Roles > [Bot's Role].
   - Ensure that Manage Roles is toggled on.

2. **Check the Bot's Role Position**
   - Go to Server Settings > Roles.
   - Drag the bot's role **above** the roles it needs to assign.

3. **Ensure Users Don't Have Conflicting Roles**
   - If a user has multiple roles, make sure no role conflicts with the bot's ability to assign them a new one.

3. Bot Cannot Access Certain Channels

Possible Causes:

- The bot lacks Read Messages or Send Messages permissions in specific channels.
- The bot is blocked from seeing certain channels.

How to Fix It:

1. **Check Channel-Specific Permissions**

- o   Go to Channel Settings > Permissions.

- o   Ensure the bot has both Read Messages and Send Messages enabled.

2. **Move the Bot to the Correct Role**

- o   Assign the bot a higher-ranked role with broader permissions.

3. **Check if the Bot is Muted or Blocked**

- o   Sometimes bots are accidentally muted by users or restricted by administrators.

4. Bot Not Playing Music or Audio Issues

Possible Causes:

- The bot lacks Connect or Speak permissions in voice channels.

- The music source (e.g., YouTube) has blocked the bot.

- The bot is already in use in another voice channel.

How to Fix It:

1. **Ensure the Bot Has Voice Channel Permissions**

- o   Go to Server Settings > Roles > [Bot's Role] and enable Connect and Speak.

2. **Restart the Bot**

- o   Disconnect the bot and invite it back.

3. **Check if the Bot is Already Playing in Another Channel**

- o   Some bots can only play music in one voice channel at a time.

4. **Use an Alternative Music Bot**

- o   If YouTube or other services have blocked the bot, consider alternatives like Hydra, Mee6, or Rythm.

Advanced Troubleshooting: Debugging Custom Bots

If you're running your own bot, issues may arise due to coding errors, API rate limits, or hosting problems.

1. Check for Errors in the Bot's Logs

- If you're hosting your bot on a server, check the logs (console.log in JavaScript, for example).

- Look for error messages related to missing permissions or API failures.

2. Verify API Tokens and Intents

- Discord bots require Intents to access server data.

- Go to the Discord Developer Portal and check if the necessary intents (GUILD_MESSAGES, MESSAGE_CONTENT, etc.) are enabled.

3. Restart the Bot and Server

- If the bot runs on a hosting service (e.g., Heroku, AWS, or a private server), restart it to resolve temporary issues.

Conclusion

Bot and permission errors are common in Discord but are usually easy to fix. By ensuring your bot has the right permissions, adjusting role hierarchy, and troubleshooting technical issues, you can keep your server running smoothly. If you're using custom bots, always monitor logs and API access to prevent downtime.

By following these troubleshooting steps, you can ensure your Discord bots function properly, improving automation, moderation, and overall user experience.

In the next section, we will cover **"7.3.3 Contacting Discord Support,"** which explains how to get direct assistance from Discord's support team for more complex issues.

7.3.3 Contacting Discord Support

Despite its user-friendly design and robust infrastructure, Discord users may occasionally encounter issues that require assistance beyond basic troubleshooting. Whether it's a technical glitch, an account security concern, or a policy-related question, reaching out to Discord Support can help resolve these problems efficiently.

In this section, we'll explore when to contact Discord Support, the different support channels available, how to submit a request, and alternative ways to get assistance.

1. When Should You Contact Discord Support?

Before contacting Discord Support, it's important to determine whether your issue requires direct intervention from Discord's team. Below are some common scenarios in which reaching out to support is necessary:

1.1 Account and Security Issues

- Compromised or hacked account – If you suspect someone has accessed your account without permission, and you're unable to recover it.

- Locked or disabled account – If Discord has disabled your account due to a ToS violation or security reasons, and you need clarification or appeal options.

- Two-Factor Authentication (2FA) issues – If you lost access to your 2FA codes and can't log in.

1.2 Billing and Nitro Subscription Problems

- Failed payments – If you're charged incorrectly for Discord Nitro or server boosts.

- Subscription cancellation issues – If you're unable to cancel or manage your Nitro subscription.

- Refund requests – If you need a refund for an accidental purchase.

1.3 Technical Issues

- Login errors – If you're experiencing repeated login failures despite using the correct credentials.

- Server crashes or missing channels – If you suddenly lose access to a server or channels without explanation.

- Voice, video, or connection issues – If basic troubleshooting doesn't fix persistent audio, video, or connectivity problems.

1.4 Reporting Violations and Abuse

- Harassment or abuse – If you're being harassed, doxxed, or targeted by malicious users on Discord.

- Scams and phishing attempts – If someone tries to steal your credentials or scam users via Discord.

- Server policy violations – If a Discord server is violating Discord's Terms of Service (e.g., promoting illegal activities).

If your issue falls into one of these categories, it's a good idea to contact Discord Support directly. Otherwise, you might be able to resolve your problem through self-help resources or community support (explored later in this chapter).

2. How to Contact Discord Support

Discord provides multiple ways for users to seek support, depending on the nature of the issue. Below are the primary methods to get assistance:

2.1 Submitting a Support Ticket

The most direct way to contact Discord Support is by submitting a support ticket through their official website. Here's how:

Step 1: Visit the Discord Support Page

1. Open your browser and go to https://support.discord.com.

2. Click on "Submit a request" in the top right corner.

Step 2: Select the Relevant Category

Discord provides different request types, including:

- Help & Support – General technical issues and troubleshooting.

- Trust & Safety – Reporting harassment, abuse, or violations.

- Billing – Subscription, payment, or refund inquiries.

- Bug Reports – Reporting a software bug or glitch.

Select the category that best fits your issue to ensure your request is handled by the right team.

Step 3: Fill Out the Ticket Form

When submitting a ticket, you'll need to provide:

- Your email address (make sure it's one you actively use).

- A detailed description of the issue (including any error messages).

- Screenshots or attachments (if applicable).

- Your Discord username and tag (e.g., User#1234).

Once you've completed the form, click "Submit" and wait for a response.

2.2 Using Discord's Twitter Support

If you need real-time updates on outages or urgent issues, Discord has an official Twitter support account:

- @discord support – Posts updates on major service disruptions and quick responses to user concerns.

You can tweet at them or check their latest posts to see if others are experiencing similar issues.

2.3 Reaching Out via the Discord Help Center

The Discord Help Center provides a comprehensive knowledge base with guides on common issues. Before submitting a ticket, it's worth searching for solutions in the FAQs and troubleshooting articles.

2.4 Joining the Discord Community Server

Discord has an official community server where users can discuss issues and get help from experienced members:

- https://discord.gg/discord-feedback – A server where you can ask general questions, report minor bugs, or suggest new features.

3. Tips for a Faster Response from Discord Support

To speed up the support process, consider the following best practices when submitting a ticket:

Provide Clear and Concise Information

- Describe the issue accurately and in detail.
- Include error messages, timestamps, and steps to reproduce the problem.

Attach Screenshots or Logs

Visual evidence helps Discord's team quickly identify the issue. If possible, attach:

- Screenshots of error messages or unusual behavior.
- Video recordings (for voice and video issues).
- Audit logs (if dealing with server administration problems).

Be Patient and Check Your Email Regularly

Discord Support typically responds within 24-72 hours, but complex issues may take longer. Check your email spam folder to ensure you don't miss their reply.

Follow Up if Necessary

If you don't receive a response within a few days, consider:

- Replying to your support ticket email to request an update.
- Checking Discord's official Twitter account for service updates.

4. Alternative Ways to Find Solutions Without Contacting Support

If you want a faster resolution, try these self-help methods before submitting a ticket:

Searching the Discord Knowledge Base

Visit support.discord.com and use the search bar to find guides related to your issue.

Checking Discord Status Page

If you're experiencing connectivity issues, check https://status.discord.com for real-time updates on server outages.

Asking the Community

Many Discord-related questions are already answered on:

- Reddit (r/discordapp) – Community-driven discussions on common problems.
- Discord Feedback Server – The official server for reporting bugs and discussing new features.

Conclusion

Discord Support is a reliable resource for resolving technical, security, and policy-related issues. By understanding when to contact support, how to submit a ticket effectively, and alternative troubleshooting methods, you can resolve most problems quickly and efficiently.

If you ever find yourself stuck, remember that Discord has a strong community and detailed help resources that can often provide solutions faster than direct support.

Next Section: Chapter 8 – Mastering Discord for Different Use Cases

In the next chapter, we will explore how to **use Discord for work, education, and community-building**, with best practices for maximizing productivity and engagement.

CHAPTER VIII
Mastering Discord for Different Use Cases

8.1 Using Discord for Work and Productivity

8.1.1 Creating a Professional Workspace

Discord, originally designed for gamers, has evolved into a versatile communication tool that businesses, freelancers, and remote teams can leverage for work and productivity. With its powerful voice, video, and text chat features, file-sharing capabilities, and customizable permissions, Discord can function as a virtual office where teams collaborate seamlessly.

In this section, we'll cover how to create a professional workspace on Discord, including setting up a dedicated server, organizing channels efficiently, customizing roles and permissions, and integrating useful bots and third-party tools to enhance productivity.

1. Setting Up a Dedicated Discord Server for Work

The first step in using Discord for work is creating a dedicated server for your team or business. Unlike casual servers that might host a mix of gaming and social discussions, a professional Discord workspace should be structured for efficiency, organization, and security.

Step 1: Creating Your Server

1. Open Discord on your desktop or mobile device.
2. Click on the "+" (Add a Server) button on the left-hand sidebar.

3. Select "Create My Own", then choose "For a club or community" (this option is better for businesses than personal servers).

4. Enter a professional server name (e.g., "Acme Corp Team Workspace").

5. Upload a logo or branding image for easy recognition.

6. Click "Create", and your server is now ready!

Step 2: Setting Up Essential Channels

To keep your workspace organized, structure your server with clear channels and categories. Here's a recommended setup:

Category: General Communication

- **#announcements** → For important updates and company-wide messages.
- **#general-chat** → A casual chatroom for team discussions.
- **#feedback-and-suggestions** → A space where employees can share improvement ideas.

Category: Work and Collaboration

- **#team-meetings** → A text channel for scheduling and organizing meetings.
- **#task-assignments** → For delegating work and tracking progress.
- **#project-updates** → A space for teams to share weekly or daily updates.

Category: Departments and Teams

- **#marketing** → For marketing team discussions.
- **#development** → For software engineers and developers.
- **#customer-support** → A dedicated channel for handling customer inquiries.

Category: Voice Channels

- 🔊 **Team Calls** → For general team voice discussions.
- 🔊 **Client Meetings** → A private room for client calls and presentations.
- 🔊 **Break Room** → A casual space for employees to relax and chat.

By structuring your Discord server with clear categories, organized channels, and specific purposes for each space, your team can navigate efficiently and avoid unnecessary clutter.

2. Customizing Roles and Permissions for a Professional Environment

In a professional setting, server security and role-based permissions are crucial for maintaining order and protecting sensitive data. Discord allows administrators to create custom roles with different levels of access.

Step 1: Defining Roles

Navigate to Server Settings → Roles, then create the following essential roles:

1.   Admin → Full control over the server (usually the manager or team lead).

2.   Team Member → Standard role for employees with access to work-related channels.

3.   Guest/Client → Limited access to specific channels (for external collaborators).

4.   Moderator → Users who help enforce rules and maintain order.

5.   Bot → Used for bots that automate tasks (explained later).

Step 2: Setting Permissions

For each role, adjust permissions carefully. For example:

- Admins can create, delete, and manage channels.

- Team Members can send messages but cannot modify server settings.

- Guests/Clients can only see designated channels to avoid access to internal discussions.

By customizing permissions, you ensure team members have access to relevant information while keeping the server secure and professional.

3. Integrating Bots and Third-Party Tools for Productivity

One of Discord's greatest strengths is its ability to integrate bots and third-party applications to streamline workflows and automate tasks. Here are some of the most useful tools for productivity:

Recommended Discord Bots for Work

1. Trello Bot – Syncs Trello project boards to track tasks directly in Discord.

2. Asana Bot – Integrates with Asana for project management updates.

3. Zapier – Automates workflows by connecting Discord to external services.

4. Google Calendar Bot – Sends reminders and upcoming meeting alerts.

5. MEE6 – Automates moderation and can send scheduled announcements.

How to Add a Bot to Your Discord Server

1. Visit a bot website (e.g., top.gg).

2. Select the bot you want and click "Invite".

3. Choose your work server and grant necessary permissions.

4. Configure bot settings based on your needs.

These bots help reduce manual work, ensuring that your team remains organized and focused.

---

4. Best Practices for Running a Professional Discord Server

To maintain a productive and professional workspace on Discord, follow these best practices:

Establish Clear Communication Guidelines

- Define acceptable behavior and set guidelines for professional conduct.

- Pin important messages in relevant channels to ensure visibility.

- Encourage organized discussions instead of chaotic message spamming.

Schedule and Automate Team Meetings

- Use Google Calendar Bot to schedule regular team meetings.

- Record important discussions via Craig Bot (a voice recording bot).

- Assign meeting moderators to keep discussions focused and efficient.

Keep Notifications Under Control

- Encourage team members to customize their notification settings to reduce distractions.

- Use @mentions sparingly to avoid overwhelming members.

- Set up slow mode in general channels to prevent message spamming.

Regularly Update Roles and Permissions

- Remove inactive members to keep the workspace organized and secure.

- Adjust access for employees based on job responsibilities.

- Perform monthly audits of roles and permissions.

Conclusion

Setting up a professional workspace on Discord goes beyond just creating a server—it requires organization, role management, effective integrations, and strong communication practices. When structured properly, Discord can serve as a powerful alternative to Slack, Microsoft Teams, or Zoom, offering a cost-effective, user-friendly, and flexible platform for businesses and remote teams.

In the next section, we will explore "Managing Team Collaboration on Discord", where we discuss task delegation, team coordination, and project tracking using Discord's features.

8.1.2 Managing Team Collaboration on Discord

In today's digital landscape, remote work and virtual collaboration have become increasingly common. While traditional tools like Slack, Microsoft Teams, and Zoom dominate the professional workspace, Discord has emerged as a viable alternative for team communication and collaboration. Originally designed for gamers, Discord's real-time voice, text, and video capabilities make it a powerful tool for teams, whether they are working on projects, managing a business, or organizing events.

This section will explore how teams can effectively use Discord to collaborate, manage tasks, and stay organized in a professional setting.

1. Why Use Discord for Team Collaboration?

Discord offers several advantages for workplace collaboration:

✅ Real-time Communication – Instant voice and text chat for quick decision-making.
✅ Customizable Server Structure – Channels, roles, and permissions help streamline workflows.
✅ Integration with Productivity Tools – Connects with Trello, Google Drive, Notion, GitHub, and more.
✅ Free and Accessible – No need for expensive enterprise software.
✅ Cross-Platform Compatibility – Works on PC, Mac, Linux, iOS, and Android, ensuring seamless communication.

Unlike traditional corporate tools, Discord allows teams to communicate in a more casual yet efficient way, reducing email overload and improving engagement.

2. Setting Up an Organized Team Server

A well-structured server is key to effective team collaboration. Here's how to set up a Discord workspace for your team:

2.1 Structuring Your Server for Productivity

When setting up your team's Discord server, consider organizing it into categories and channels that reflect your team's workflow.

💼 **Categories & Channels Example**

- ◆ **GENERAL ADMIN**

    - 🔊 **#announcements** – Important company-wide updates.

    - 📌 **#rules-and-guidelines** – Server etiquette and policies.

    - 🎉 **#introductions** – New members introduce themselves.

- ◆ **TEAM COMMUNICATION**

  - o 💬 **#general-chat** – Casual team discussions.

  - o ◻◻ **#voice-meetings** – For voice/video meetings.

  - o 🔔 **#daily-standups** – Quick team updates.

- ◆ **PROJECT MANAGEMENT**

  - o 💼 **#project-A** – Discussions and updates for a specific project.

  - o ✅ **#task-progress** – Tracking ongoing tasks.

  - o ◻◻ **#tech-support** – IT-related issues.

- ◆ **RESOURCE SHARING**

  - o 📎 **#important-links** – Google Drive, Notion, etc.

  - o 📖 **#learning-resources** – Articles, tutorials, or guides.

Each **team or department** can have its own section to keep discussions organized and reduce clutter.

2.2 Setting Up User Roles and Permissions

Proper role management ensures smooth operations and security. Here's how to configure roles:

☐ **Admin** – Full control over the server, settings, and permissions.
⬤ **Managers** – Can create channels, manage messages, and moderate discussions.
☐ **Team Leads** – Can assign tasks and manage project-specific channels.
☐ **Team Members** – Can send messages, join voice calls, and collaborate.
○ **Guests/Clients** – Limited permissions to access only relevant channels.

To set up roles:

1. Go to Server Settings → Roles

2. Create New Roles and assign permissions accordingly.

3. Assign Users to Roles under the "Members" tab.

This helps maintain privacy, security, and efficiency by ensuring that only the right people can access specific channels.

3. Effective Communication Strategies on Discord

3.1 Setting Up Meeting and Voice Channels

One of Discord's biggest advantages is seamless voice and video communication. Here's how to optimize it for team meetings:

✎ Voice Channels for Meetings

- Create permanent meeting rooms (e.g., #weekly-sync).
- Use Push-to-Talk for better audio control.
- Enable Noise Suppression to reduce background noise.

🎥 Video Calls & Screen Sharing

- Click "Go Live" to share your screen.
- Use Discord's built-in whiteboard bots for brainstorming.
- Record meetings using third-party tools like Craig Bot.

3.2 Utilizing Text Communication Effectively

- ◆ Use Threaded Conversations – Helps keep discussions organized.
- ◆ Utilize Pinned Messages – Save key decisions for quick access.
- ◆ Set Channel Topics – Indicate the purpose of each channel.
- ◆ Use Mentions Wisely – Avoid excessive @everyone or @here notifications.

Encouraging clear and concise communication prevents information overload and keeps discussions productive.

4. Integrating Productivity Tools with Discord

4.1 Bots and Integrations for Productivity

Discord supports various bots and third-party integrations that enhance workflow:

🚀 Task Management Bots

- ✅ **Trello Bot** – Manage project tasks within Discord.
- 🗒 **Todoist Bot** – Assign and track tasks in real-time.
- 🎯 **Asana Integration** – Syncs tasks and deadlines.

🔊 Notification & Alerts

- 🖼 **Zapier** – Automate notifications from external tools.
- 🔔 **GitHub Bot** – Receive instant updates on code changes.
- 📅 **Google Calendar Bot** – Set reminders for meetings.

📄 File Sharing & Documentation

- 📁 **Google Drive Bot** – Quick access to shared files.
- 🗒 **Notion Integration** – Centralized team documentation.

By integrating these tools, Discord transforms into an **all-in-one productivity hub** for your team.

---

5. Best Practices for Managing a Productive Team on Discord

Setting Clear Guidelines and Expectations

To maintain a professional environment:
✓☐ Establish guidelines for communication etiquette.
✓☐ Set expectations for response times and availability.
✓☐ Use dedicated channels for project discussions to reduce clutter.

Encouraging Team Engagement

- Host weekly check-ins in the #daily-standups channel.
- Use reaction-based polls to make decisions quickly.
- Organize virtual team-building activities like trivia nights.

Keeping Your Discord Server Secure

- Enable Two-Factor Authentication (2FA) for all admins.

- Limit invite permissions to prevent unauthorized access.

- Use moderation bots like MEE6 to filter spam and enforce rules.

A secure and well-managed Discord workspace leads to efficient collaboration and improved team productivity.

Conclusion

Discord is more than just a chat app—it's a powerful collaboration tool that can help teams work smarter, not harder. By structuring your server efficiently, leveraging voice and video communication, integrating productivity tools, and maintaining a professional environment, your team can maximize productivity while fostering engagement.

In the next section, we will explore how Discord can be used for education and study groups, helping students and teachers collaborate effectively.

8.1.3 Best Practices for Business Servers

Discord has evolved beyond gaming communities to become a powerful tool for businesses and professional teams. With its customizable servers, real-time communication, and seamless integrations, businesses can use Discord to foster collaboration, manage projects, and enhance productivity. However, to make the most of Discord as a business tool, it is essential to establish structured workflows, enforce security measures, and implement best practices that promote professionalism and efficiency.

In this section, we'll explore the best practices for setting up, managing, and optimizing a business server on Discord.

1. Structuring Your Business Server for Efficiency

The foundation of an effective business server lies in its structure. A well-organized server ensures smooth communication, easy navigation, and clear access to resources. Here's how you can achieve that:

1.1 Organizing Channels and Categories

A business Discord server should have dedicated channels for different topics and teams. Using categories to group related channels improves organization.

Recommended Channel Categories and Channels:

✓ General Administration

- **#announcements** – Official company updates and important notices.

- **#rules-and-guidelines** – Policies for communication and server etiquette.

- **#support-desk** – A place for employees to request technical or administrative help.

✓ Team Collaboration

- **#general-chat** – Casual discussions and team bonding.

- **#project-updates** – Status updates for ongoing projects.

- **#task-assignments** – Tracking tasks and delegating work.

✓ Department-Specific Channels

- **#marketing-team** – Discussion on marketing strategies and campaigns.

- **#development-team** – Software development discussions and debugging.

- **#sales-and-customer-support** – Handling client interactions and leads.

✓ Meeting & Voice Channels

- 🔊 **Daily Stand-Ups** – Short team meetings for daily updates.

- ⬜ **Brainstorming Sessions** – Spaces for creative discussions.

- ⬤ **Client Meetings** – Private channels for client discussions.

By **segmenting communication into categories and channels**, employees can quickly find relevant discussions without cluttering the workspace.

---

2. Setting Up Roles and Permissions for Security & Access Control

To maintain professionalism and prevent misuse, it is crucial to set up roles and permissions correctly. This ensures that employees have access only to the necessary channels and that sensitive information remains protected.

2.1 Creating User Roles

A well-structured role system differentiates permissions between executives, managers, employees, and guests.

Example Role Hierarchy:

◆ Admin (Full Control) – Business owners, IT managers, or HR personnel who manage server settings and policies.
◆ Managers (Moderators) – Department leads who oversee team-specific channels.
◆ Employees – Regular staff with access to company-wide channels.
◆ Clients & External Partners – Limited access to project-specific channels.
◆ Bot Role – A dedicated role for bots to automate tasks and moderate discussions.

2.2 Configuring Permissions

Assigning permissions strategically prevents unnecessary modifications and security risks.

✓ **Best Practices for Role Permissions:**

- Restrict admin rights – Only trusted personnel should modify server settings.

- Disable '@everyone' ping – Prevents excessive tagging and spam.

- Limit sensitive channel access – Financial, HR, or legal discussions should be private.

- Use read-only channels – Prevents unnecessary messages in announcement channels.

By structuring roles and permissions effectively, businesses protect confidential information, reduce distractions, and maintain order.

3. Using Bots and Automation for Productivity

Bots can automate tasks, improve efficiency, and enhance engagement within a business server. Here are a few use cases for bots in professional environments:

Recommended Bots for Business Servers

✓ MEE6 – Automates announcements, moderates messages, and assigns roles based on user activity.

✓ TrelloBot – Syncs with Trello for project management updates.

✓ Google Calendar Bot – Notifies members of upcoming meetings and deadlines.

✓ Zapier – Automates workflows by connecting Discord with external apps like Slack, Google Drive, and Asana.

✓ PollBot – Conducts quick polls for decision-making.

By integrating bots, businesses reduce manual tasks, streamline workflows, and improve productivity.

4. Implementing Communication Guidelines for Professionalism

Unlike casual gaming servers, business servers must uphold **professional etiquette**. To ensure smooth communication, establish clear guidelines.

Best Practices for Business Communication on Discord

✓ Use Professional Language – Avoid slang, excessive emojis, or memes in formal channels.

✓ Keep Messages Concise – Use bullet points, summaries, or threads for long discussions.

✓ Tag Responsibly – Avoid overusing @mentions to prevent unnecessary notifications.

✓ Schedule Messages – Use bots or Discord's scheduling features for timed announcements.

By setting clear communication standards, employees stay focused and maintain professionalism within the server.

5. Managing Meetings and Video Conferences on Discord

Discord's voice and video capabilities make it a great alternative to Zoom or Microsoft Teams for virtual meetings and presentations.

Tips for Hosting Effective Meetings on Discord

✓ Use Stage Channels – Ideal for hosting webinars, company-wide meetings, or Q&A sessions.

✅ Mute When Not Speaking – Reduces background noise during discussions.

✅ Share Screens Efficiently – Optimize screen sharing by selecting specific windows instead of the entire screen.

✅ Record Meetings (If Necessary) – Use third-party bots or software for recording important discussions.

With these meeting strategies, businesses can enhance remote collaboration while maintaining productivity.

6. Encouraging Employee Engagement and Team Bonding

Discord isn't just for work—it can also help boost team morale and strengthen company culture.

Ideas for Fostering a Positive Workplace on Discord

🎊 Virtual Coffee Breaks – Casual voice chats where employees can relax and socialize.

🎮 Game Nights & Trivia – Use Discord's built-in activities for team-building events.

🏆 Recognition Channels – Celebrate employee achievements in a #kudos-and-recognition channel.

🔊 Feedback Sessions – Allow employees to voice concerns or suggestions in structured discussion threads.

By incorporating team-building initiatives, businesses create a more engaging and supportive work environment.

7. Keeping Your Business Server Secure and Up-to-Date

Cybersecurity is crucial when using Discord for business purposes. Follow these best practices to protect your server:

Essential Security Measures

🔐 Enable Two-Factor Authentication (2FA) – Prevents unauthorized logins.
🚫 Disable Dangerous Permissions – Restrict 'Manage Server' and 'Administrator' permissions.
☐ Use Verified Bots Only – Avoid potential security risks from unknown bots.
📜 Monitor Server Logs – Track activity logs to identify suspicious behavior.

By prioritizing security and regular updates, businesses protect sensitive data and maintain a safe online workspace.

Conclusion

Discord offers a powerful, flexible, and cost-effective platform for businesses looking to enhance collaboration and productivity. By structuring servers effectively, enforcing security measures, integrating useful bots, and maintaining professional communication, companies can transform Discord into a highly efficient business tool.

As businesses continue to embrace remote work and digital collaboration, Discord is likely to play an even greater role in modern workplace environments.

Next Section: 8.2 Discord for Education and Study Groups

In the next section, we'll explore **how teachers, students, and tutors can use Discord for educational purposes**, from virtual classrooms to study groups.

8.2 Discord for Education and Study Groups

8.2.1 Setting Up a Classroom Server

Discord is not just for gaming communities—it has become an essential tool for education and virtual learning. Many teachers, students, and tutors use Discord to create interactive, collaborative classroom environments that enhance engagement and facilitate communication.

In this section, we will cover how to set up a Discord classroom server, configure essential settings, and implement best practices to ensure a safe and productive learning environment.

Step 1: Creating a Classroom Server

To begin using Discord for educational purposes, you need to create a dedicated server for your classroom or study group. Follow these steps:

1.1 Open Discord and Start a New Server

1. Open Discord on your desktop or mobile device.

2. Click the "+" (Add a Server) button on the left sidebar.

3. Select "Create My Own" to start a new server from scratch.

4. Choose "For a club or community" if you are setting up a larger study group or classroom.

1.2 Name Your Server and Add an Icon

- Choose a clear and professional name, such as "Biology 101 - Study Group" or "Mr. Johnson's Math Class".

- Upload a server icon (e.g., a school logo or subject-related image) to make your server easily recognizable.

- Click "Create" to finalize your server.

1.3 Set Up Basic Server Settings

Before inviting students, configure key settings to ensure a well-organized and secure environment:

- Go to Server Settings > Overview and set an appropriate region for low-latency voice chat.

- Enable "Explicit Content Filter" to keep discussions appropriate.

- Customize the server invite link (e.g., "discord.gg/biology101") to make it easy for students to join.

Step 2: Organizing Channels for Effective Learning

A well-structured server includes **text and voice channels** to facilitate different types of interactions.

2.1 Creating Essential Text Channels

Navigate to Server Settings > Channels and create channels based on subject areas and classroom needs.

Channel Name	Purpose
#announcements	For important updates, deadlines, and assignments.
#general-discussion	For casual student interactions and general inquiries.
#homework-help	For students to ask and answer questions related to assignments.
#resources	A place for sharing class notes, slides, and educational links.
#project-collaboration	For team-based assignments and study groups.

2.2 Setting Up Voice Channels

Voice and video interactions help enhance engagement in online learning. Here are some suggested voice channels:

Channel Name	Purpose
✏ Lecture Hall	For live classes and teacher-led discussions.
📚 Study Room 1	For small-group study sessions.
💬 Office Hours	For 1-on-1 discussions between students and teachers.

💡 **Tip:** Enable Push-to-Talk in voice settings to minimize background noise.

Step 3: Setting Up Roles and Permissions

To maintain order in a classroom server, you should assign roles to students, teachers, and moderators.

Creating User Roles

Navigate to Server Settings > Roles and set up distinct roles:

Role Name	Permissions
Teacher/Admin	Full control over the server (manage channels, kick users, assign roles).
Moderator	Help enforce rules (mute disruptive students, manage text channels).
Student	Participate in discussions, access learning resources.

Assigning Permissions

Adjust permissions for each role:

- Teachers/Admins: Can create/manage channels, assign roles, and mute/deafen students.

- Moderators: Can delete inappropriate messages and moderate discussions.

- Students: Can send messages, join voice calls, and access study resources.

Tip: Use the @everyone role for basic permissions and restrict it from sending messages in the #announcements channel.

Step 4: Managing Student Engagement

Encouraging Participation

A Discord classroom should promote collaboration and active learning. Consider these strategies:

- Host weekly Q&A sessions in #homework-help.

- Use polls and quizzes in #general-discussion (e.g., "What topic should we review next?").

- Assign team projects where students collaborate in private channels.

Using Bots for Classroom Automation

Discord bots can **enhance productivity** and make learning more interactive:

Bot Name	Function
MEE6	Automates moderation and sends assignment reminders.
PollBot	Creates polls for student feedback.
Kahoot Bot	Integrates with Kahoot quizzes for interactive learning.

Setting Up Assignments and Notifications

Use scheduled messages in #announcements to post homework deadlines and exam reminders.

Step 5: Ensuring Safety and Moderation

Enforcing Community Guidelines

Set clear **rules for respectful communication**, such as:
✓ Be respectful to classmates.

✓ Stay on-topic in study-related channels.

✗ No spamming or off-topic discussions in learning areas.

Moderation Tools

Use auto-moderation bots (like Dyno or MEE6) to:

- Filter inappropriate language.

- Warn students who violate rules.

- Automatically delete spam messages.

Managing Student Privacy

- Restrict access to voice channels unless a teacher is present.

- Enable Safe Direct Messaging in Privacy Settings to protect students from harmful DMs.

- Encourage students to enable Two-Factor Authentication (2FA) for account security.

Step 6: Hosting Live Lessons and Events

Conducting Virtual Lectures

- Use screen sharing for presentations.

- Allow students to raise hands (via emoji reactions) to ask questions.

- Record lectures using external tools for students who miss class.

Hosting Study Groups and Review Sessions

- Organize peer-led study groups in breakout voice channels.

- Use the #project-collaboration channel for team-based learning activities.

Inviting Guest Speakers

- Create a temporary guest role for invited speakers.

- Use Discord's Stage Channels for structured Q&A sessions.

Conclusion

Setting up a Discord classroom server transforms online education into an interactive and engaging experience. With well-structured channels, role-based permissions, moderation tools, and student engagement strategies, educators can create an effective virtual learning environment.

In the next section **(8.2.2 Using Discord for Online Tutoring)**, we will explore how private tutors can use Discord to conduct one-on-one lessons, share resources, and manage tutoring sessions efficiently.

8.2.2 Using Discord for Online Tutoring

Online tutoring has become an essential part of modern education, providing students with access to academic support regardless of their location. Discord, originally designed for gamers, has evolved into a powerful tool for education and tutoring due to its voice and video communication capabilities, screen-sharing features, file-sharing options, and customizable server settings.

This section will guide you through the benefits, setup process, essential features, best practices, and challenges of using Discord for online tutoring.

1. Why Use Discord for Online Tutoring?

Discord offers several advantages over traditional tutoring platforms like Zoom, Skype, or Google Meet:

1.1 Free and Accessible

Unlike some tutoring platforms that require a paid subscription, Discord is free and allows tutors and students to communicate without time restrictions. The platform is available on Windows, macOS, Linux, iOS, and Android, making it easy to access from anywhere.

1.2 Versatile Communication Tools

Discord provides multiple ways to interact with students, including:

- Text channels for written discussions, Q&A, and resource sharing.

- Voice channels for real-time explanations.

- Video calls and screen sharing for interactive lessons and demonstrations.

1.3 Customizable Server Environment

Tutors can organize their server with different channels, assign roles to students, and set up automated bots to help with announcements, scheduling, and even quizzes.

1.4 Community Engagement and Collaboration

Students can use Discord not only for one-on-one tutoring but also for group study sessions, peer-to-peer learning, and academic discussions.

2. Setting Up a Discord Server for Tutoring

To effectively use Discord for online tutoring, you need to set up a well-structured server. Here's how:

2.1 Creating Your Server

1. Open Discord and click on the "+" icon on the left sidebar.

2. Select "Create My Own" and choose For a club or community or For me and my friends depending on your tutoring needs.

3. Name your server (e.g., "Math Tutoring Hub") and choose an icon.

4. Click Create to finalize your server setup.

2.2 Organizing Channels

Create different channels to separate lesson materials, discussions, and Q&A sessions:

- **#announcements** – For posting schedules, updates, and important notices.

- **#lesson-materials** – A dedicated channel for PDFs, videos, and other resources.

- **#homework-help** – Students can ask questions and get quick answers.
- **#general-discussion** – For casual academic conversations and peer interactions.
- □□ **Voice Channels** – For live tutoring sessions and discussions.

2.3 Setting Up Roles and Permissions

To maintain order and prevent disruptions, assign roles:

- Tutor – Full access to manage channels and moderate discussions.
- Student – Can join lessons, ask questions, and participate in discussions.
- Guest/Lurker – Limited access (for potential students or observers).

Set permissions to restrict students from spamming, muting others, or modifying server settings.

2.4 Using Bots to Enhance Tutoring

Bots can automate tasks and make tutoring more efficient. Some useful bots include:

- **MEE6** – Automates announcements, moderates chats, and assigns roles.
- **Carl-bot** – Allows tutors to create self-assignable roles and reaction-based notifications.
- **Poll Bot** – Useful for quizzes and gathering feedback.
- **Tatsu** – Encourages participation through a point-based reward system.

3. Conducting an Effective Online Tutoring Session on Discord

Once your server is set up, follow these best practices to ensure smooth tutoring sessions.

Scheduling Sessions and Notifications

- Use a Google Calendar integration or a scheduling bot to set up regular tutoring sessions.
- Post reminders in the #announcements channel to keep students informed.

- Pin important messages so students can easily find key information.

Teaching Methods on Discord

Different subjects require different teaching techniques. Below are some effective methods based on subject type.

Text-Based Tutoring

For subjects that require written explanations, such as language learning, coding, or history, text-based tutoring works well.

- Use formatted text (bold, italics, code blocks) to highlight key concepts.
- Share links to educational resources, e-books, and research papers.
- Use emojis and reactions to gauge student understanding.

Voice and Video Lessons

For subjects like mathematics, science, or music, voice/video explanations are crucial.

- Use screen sharing to demonstrate problem-solving techniques.
- Enable a virtual whiteboard (e.g., Jamboard, Miro, or AwwApp) for real-time drawing and explanations.
- Record sessions (with permission) for students to revisit later.

Collaborative Learning and Group Discussions

Encourage peer-to-peer interaction by organizing:

- Breakout discussions in different voice channels.
- Group projects where students collaborate on shared documents.
- Interactive Q&A sessions to reinforce learning.

4. Tips for Keeping Students Engaged

Gamification and Rewards

Use Discord's built-in features to motivate students:

- Award students roles and badges for completing assignments.
- Set up a leaderboard system using Tatsu bot to encourage participation.
- Host weekly challenges and quizzes with small rewards.

Encouraging Participation

To prevent students from being passive learners:

- Ask open-ended questions.
- Use polls and reaction-based voting to collect opinions.
- Encourage students to summarize lessons in their own words.

Providing Personalized Feedback

- Use direct messages for one-on-one feedback.
- Create private study rooms for students who need extra help.
- Use screen recording to provide detailed feedback on assignments.

5. Challenges of Using Discord for Tutoring and How to Overcome Them

Distractions and Off-Topic Conversations

- Set clear rules about appropriate discussions in each channel.
- Use moderation bots to filter out unrelated content.
- Assign trusted students as moderators to help maintain discipline.

Privacy and Security Concerns

- Encourage students to use pseudonyms instead of real names.
- Adjust privacy settings to prevent unsolicited friend requests.
- Enable Two-Factor Authentication (2FA) for added security.

Technical Issues

- Have a backup platform (e.g., Google Meet or Zoom) in case Discord experiences downtime.

- Provide troubleshooting guides for common connectivity and audio problems.

- Keep recorded sessions available for students who miss a live class.

Conclusion

Discord has proven to be an effective and versatile tool for online tutoring, offering flexibility, accessibility, and powerful communication features. By properly structuring a server, using the right teaching methods, and keeping students engaged, tutors can create an interactive and productive learning environment.

With the right strategies, Discord can rival dedicated tutoring platforms and serve as a cost-effective alternative for both tutors and students.

Next Section: 8.2.3 Managing Study Sessions with Voice and Text
In the next section, we'll explore how to organize and manage **study sessions**, encourage group collaboration, and utilize Discord's features to maximize learning efficiency.

8.2.3 Managing Study Sessions with Voice and Text

Discord is a powerful tool for organizing and managing study sessions, whether for small student groups, online tutoring, or large academic communities. The platform's combination of text channels, voice channels, video calls, file sharing, and integrations with third-party tools makes it an excellent choice for collaborative learning.

In this section, we will explore how to effectively manage study sessions using Discord's voice and text features, ensuring a structured, productive, and engaging learning experience.

1. Setting Up an Effective Study Environment on Discord

Before diving into study session management, it's essential to create a well-organized server where students can easily find resources, join discussions, and participate in study activities.

Structuring Your Study Server

A well-structured server enhances organization and accessibility. Here's how you can set up an effective server for study groups:

Organizing Text Channels for Different Study Needs

- **#announcements** – For important updates, exam reminders, and schedule changes.

- **#general-chat** – A casual space for students to interact and discuss topics outside study sessions.

- **#study-questions** – A dedicated channel where students can ask and answer academic questions.

- **#resources** – A repository for lecture notes, PDF materials, recorded sessions, and useful links.

- **#assignments-and-deadlines** – A channel to track due dates and homework discussions.

- **#break-room** – A place for socializing and mental breaks to keep engagement high.

Setting Up Voice Channels for Live Discussions

- 🔊 **Study Lounge** – A casual place for students to discuss topics informally.

- 🔊 **Focus Room** – A quiet space for deep work or silent study sessions.

- 🔊 **Group Study Sessions** – For scheduled or ongoing study discussions.

- 🔊 **Tutoring Sessions** – For one-on-one or small group tutoring with dedicated tutors.

Using **categories** in Discord to separate these channels makes it easier for students to navigate the server and find relevant discussions.

2. Managing Study Sessions with Text Features

Text channels play a crucial role in asynchronous study sessions, allowing students to interact and share knowledge even when they are not available for voice or video chats.

2.1 Encouraging Active Participation in Text-Based Study Sessions

To make text-based study sessions productive, use the following strategies:

Encourage Question-and-Answer Discussions

- Use a dedicated #study-questions channel where students can post queries.

- Pin frequently asked questions to help new members.

- Encourage students to answer each other's questions, fostering peer-to-peer learning.

Utilize Bots for Study Assistance

Bots can enhance study sessions by automating tasks such as:

- Polls and quizzes – Use bots like QuizBot to conduct quick revision quizzes.

- Flashcards – Use CramBot to help students review topics.

- Timers and Pomodoro Technique – Use bots like StudyLion to manage study time effectively.

Using Markdown for Organized Notes

Discord supports Markdown formatting, which allows users to:

- Bold and *italicize* important points.

- Use bullet points and numbering for structured notes.

- Create block quotes for citing sources.

- Format code blocks (inline code) for programming-related discussions.

2.2 Hosting Asynchronous Study Threads

For long-term discussions, use threads to keep topics organized:

- Students can create threads under specific questions, preventing clutter in the main channel.

- Teachers or moderators can mark solutions to help others quickly find answers.

- Threads help keep discussions focused on individual topics without overwhelming the main chat.

3. Managing Study Sessions with Voice and Video

Real-time voice and video sessions provide **better engagement, instant feedback, and interactive discussions** compared to text-based study.

3.1 Planning and Scheduling Study Sessions

A well-planned study session maximizes effectiveness. Consider the following when organizing live sessions:

- Set a clear agenda – Define what will be covered in each session.

- Choose a convenient time – Use Discord's built-in Event Scheduling feature to plan sessions.

- Encourage preparation – Share materials before the session to maximize participation.

Using a bot like Apollo can help schedule sessions by allowing members to RSVP and get reminders.

3.2 Running Effective Voice and Video Study Sessions

When running study sessions via voice or video, consider these best practices:

Using Screen Sharing for Interactive Learning

- Present slides – Ideal for discussing key concepts and explaining difficult topics.

- Solve problems in real time – Share a whiteboard app like Miro or Google Jamboard for brainstorming.

- Demonstrate code or software usage – Share live coding sessions for programming subjects.

Utilizing Discord's Noise Suppression for Better Audio Clarity

- Enable Krisp Noise Suppression to filter background noise.

- Mute participants when not speaking to avoid audio distractions.

- Encourage using headphones to minimize echo.

Using Breakout Voice Channels for Group Activities

Discord allows you to create multiple voice channels for small group discussions. Assign students to different rooms based on topics to encourage collaborative learning.

4. Keeping Study Sessions Engaging and Productive

4.1 Gamifying the Study Experience

Motivation can be a challenge for students. Use Discord's gamification features to make learning fun:

- Leveling System – Use bots like MEE6 or Arcane to reward active participation with XP points.

- Leaderboards – Recognize top contributors to encourage knowledge sharing.

- Virtual Study Challenges – Organize events like "30-Day Study Streaks" with rewards.

4.2 Encouraging Accountability and Focus

- Use the Pomodoro Technique – Set 25-minute study blocks followed by short breaks.

- Daily check-ins – Have students share their study goals in a dedicated channel.

- Accountability partners – Pair students to keep each other on track.

4.3 Recording and Archiving Study Sessions

- Use Discord's Go Live feature to record lectures and explanations.

- Save key discussions in the #resources channel for later review.

- Summarize key points and pin important messages in relevant channels.

Conclusion

Discord offers a versatile and interactive platform for managing study sessions, whether through text-based discussions or real-time voice and video collaboration. By setting up a well-structured server, using bots and integrations, and encouraging active participation, you can create an engaging and effective learning environment.

As you implement these strategies, remember that consistency and organization are key to maximizing the benefits of using Discord for education. The more structured and engaging your sessions are, the more successful your study group will be.

Next Section: 8.3 Growing Your Discord Community

In the next section, we'll explore how to expand your Discord community, attract new members, and foster long-term engagement.

8.3 Growing Your Discord Community

8.3.1 Promoting Your Server and Gaining Members

Building a thriving Discord community requires more than just creating a server—it takes active promotion, strategic engagement, and effective outreach to attract and retain members. Whether you're managing a gaming hub, a professional networking group, or a fan community, knowing how to effectively promote your server can make the difference between an inactive group and a lively, engaged community.

This section will explore best practices for promoting your Discord server and attracting new members, covering various organic and paid strategies, platform integrations, and community-building techniques.

1. Laying the Foundation for Growth

Before promoting your server, you need to ensure that it is ready to welcome new members. A well-structured, visually appealing, and engaging server is more likely to retain users who join through promotions.

1.1 Optimizing Your Server for New Members

a) Creating a Clear and Engaging Server Description

Your server's description should clearly communicate its purpose and what members can expect. This is often the first impression potential members get, so make it compelling.

- Use concise, engaging language to describe your community.
- Highlight key features: What makes your server unique?
- Include relevant keywords to improve discoverability in Discord's server search.

b) Organizing Your Channels and Roles

A cluttered or confusing server layout can deter new members. Keep your channels structured and organized:

- Use categories to group related channels (e.g., Announcements, General Chat, Voice Channels).

- Set up clear permissions to manage roles and access levels.

- Create a welcome channel with rules, guidelines, and an introduction to your server.

c) Designing an Attractive Server Icon and Banner

Visual branding plays a significant role in attracting new members. Use a professional and eye-catching server icon and banner that reflect your community's theme.

d) Enabling Community Features

If you want to expand your reach, consider enabling Discord's Community Features under Server Settings. This unlocks:

- Server Discovery (for eligible servers)

- Announcement channels for cross-server posting

- Welcome screen customization to guide new members

2. Organic Promotion Strategies

Organic promotion relies on free methods to attract members through networking, content marketing, and social engagement.

2.1 Leveraging Social Media

Social media is a powerful tool for growing your Discord server. Consider promoting your server on:

- Twitter/X – Share updates, post memes, and engage with followers using trending hashtags.

- Reddit – Participate in relevant subreddits and share your server where allowed (e.g., r/discordservers).

- Facebook Groups – Post in communities related to your server's niche.

- Instagram & TikTok – Create visual content (e.g., reels, memes, short clips) to attract interest.

Pro Tip: Share exclusive content or perks for Discord members to encourage sign-ups (e.g., "Join our Discord for exclusive giveaways and events!").

2.2 Promoting in Other Discord Communities

Engage in relevant Discord servers and connect with members who might be interested in your community.

- Find partnership opportunities – Team up with similar servers for cross-promotions.

- Use self-promotion channels – Many servers allow users to share their own Discord links.

- Be active in discussions – Building relationships in other communities can lead to organic growth.

2.3 Creating Shareable Content

Make your server more appealing by sharing high-value content that people want to be part of.

- Create engaging posts (memes, infographics, event announcements) with a call to action.

- Make YouTube videos explaining what your server offers.

- Write blog posts about your community's niche and include your server link.

Example: A gaming server could create "Top 10 Strategies for Winning in [Game Name]" with a Discord invite for more discussions.

2.4 Utilizing Invite Rewards and Referral Programs

Encourage existing members to invite their friends:

- Host referral contests (e.g., "Invite 5 friends and win a special role or Discord Nitro!").

- Offer exclusive channels or perks for members who bring in new users.

- Use invite tracking bots to monitor referrals.

3. Listing Your Server on Discord Directories

3.1 Submitting to Public Server Listings

Several third-party websites allow you to list your Discord server for free:

- Disboard (https://disboard.org/) – One of the most popular server directories.
- Top.gg (https://top.gg/servers/) – Lists both bots and servers.
- Discord.me – A user-friendly directory with many categories.
- Discord Server List (https://discordserverlist.com/) – Another growing directory.

Tip: Regularly bump your server on Disboard to keep it visible on the front page.

3.2 Optimizing Your Server Listing

When submitting your server to directories:

- Use relevant keywords in the title and description.
- Select the right categories and tags for better discoverability.
- Encourage upvotes and engagement to stay ranked higher.

4. Paid Promotion Strategies

If you have a budget, paid promotion can accelerate server growth through targeted advertising.

Running Discord Ads on Social Media

Platforms like Facebook, Instagram, Twitter, and Reddit allow you to run ads to attract new members.

- Target audiences based on interests related to your Discord.
- Use eye-catching images and compelling ad copy with a call to action.

Partnering with Influencers

Collaborate with YouTubers, Twitch streamers, or TikTok influencers in your niche.

- Sponsor shoutouts to promote your Discord server.

- Host joint events or giveaways to drive traffic.

- Feature guest appearances to attract their audience to your server.

Boosting Posts in Online Communities

Some platforms (e.g., Reddit, Facebook) allow paid post boosting to increase visibility.

- Promote engaging posts related to your Discord.

- Target specific communities that align with your server's niche.

5. Retaining and Engaging Members

Attracting members is only half the battle—keeping them engaged is crucial for long-term growth.

Hosting Events and Giveaways

Regular server events and competitions encourage participation and retention:

- Trivia nights, gaming tournaments, Q&A sessions

- Discord-exclusive giveaways (Nitro, gift cards, merchandise)

- Live streams and community spotlights

Assigning Active Moderators

A well-moderated server fosters a positive and welcoming environment.

- Appoint trusted moderators to enforce rules and engage with members.

- Use automated bots to handle spam and moderation tasks.

Encouraging User-Generated Content

Let members contribute by:

- Creating custom emotes and stickers.

- Sharing fan art, memes, or guides.

- Suggesting new channels or features to improve the server.

Conclusion

Growing a successful Discord community requires strategic promotion, active engagement, and consistent community management. By using a mix of organic marketing, social media outreach, directory listings, partnerships, and paid promotions, you can attract and retain a loyal member base.

Next Section: 8.3.2 Encouraging Engagement with Events and Giveaways Now that you know how to attract new members, let's explore how to **keep them engaged** with fun activities and interactive events.

8.3.2 Encouraging Engagement with Events and Giveaways

Building a thriving Discord community requires more than just attracting new members— it's about keeping them engaged, active, and invested in the server. One of the best ways to foster engagement is by organizing events and giveaways, which provide members with exciting reasons to participate and interact.

In this section, we'll explore different types of events, how to plan and execute them effectively, and how giveaways can incentivize participation and grow your community.

1. Why Events and Giveaways Matter in a Discord Community

The Role of Events in Community Engagement

Events are a powerful tool for keeping a Discord server lively and interactive. When executed well, they:

- Encourage members to participate regularly rather than being passive observers.

- Help members form connections with one another, strengthening the community.

- Provide a sense of belonging by making members feel valued.

- Increase server retention rates, ensuring that people stay engaged over time.

A well-structured event calendar can turn a Discord server into a dynamic, fun, and engaging space, giving members a reason to return.

The Impact of Giveaways on Engagement

Giveaways are a great way to reward active members, attract new users, and boost engagement. By offering prizes, you can:

- Encourage members to participate in discussions and events.

- Create excitement and anticipation, making the server feel more active.

- Incentivize behaviors that benefit the community, such as sharing content, inviting friends, or contributing ideas.

However, giveaways should be strategic and meaningful rather than excessive or random, ensuring that they enhance community engagement rather than attracting only short-term participants.

2. Types of Discord Events to Encourage Engagement

2.1 Voice Chat Events

Live voice chat events help members interact in real-time, making the server feel more personal and connected.

Game Nights

For gaming communities, hosting weekly or monthly game nights is an excellent way to engage members. These can include:

- Casual multiplayer games (e.g., Among Us, Jackbox Party Pack, Fortnite).

- Competitive tournaments with prizes for winners.

- Discord-integrated games, like PokéMeow or IdleRPG bots.

Karaoke and Music Sessions

Using Discord's voice channels and music bots, you can organize:

- Karaoke nights, where members take turns singing.

- Listening parties, where members enjoy music together.

Q&A Sessions and AMAs (Ask Me Anything)

If your server has an expert, content creator, or industry professional, hosting Q&A sessions or AMA events allows members to interact with them directly.

2.2 Text-Based Community Challenges

For servers with active text channels, written challenges can encourage creativity and participation.

Art and Design Contests

Members can submit digital art, graphic designs, or drawings based on a theme. Winners could receive Nitro subscriptions or custom Discord roles.

Writing and Storytelling Events

Servers focused on literature or creative writing can hold flash fiction challenges, poetry slams, or collaborative storytelling contests.

Meme and Caption Contests

Casual and fun, meme or caption contests encourage members to create humorous content related to the community's theme.

2.3 Server-Wide Activities

These activities involve the entire server, fostering interaction among all members.

Trivia Nights and Quizzes

Using bots like TriviaBot, you can create themed quizzes on various topics (e.g., gaming, movies, general knowledge).

2.3.2 Virtual Watch Parties

With Discord's screen-sharing feature, servers can host movie nights or anime screenings.

2.3.3 Roleplaying and Interactive Stories

For fandom-based or fantasy-themed communities, members can engage in ongoing roleplay adventures, contributing to an evolving storyline.

3. Running a Successful Giveaway on Discord

Choosing the Right Prizes

The prize you offer should align with your community's interests. Some popular giveaway items include:

- Discord Nitro (highly desirable for boosting Discord experience).
- Gift cards (Amazon, Steam, PlayStation, Xbox).
- Game codes or in-game items (for gaming servers).
- Merchandise or custom-designed avatars.

Avoid offering generic cash prizes, as they may attract users who have no real interest in the community.

Setting Up a Giveaway

To host a successful giveaway, follow these key steps:

Choose a Giveaway Bot

Many Discord bots help automate giveaways, ensuring fairness. Some popular choices are:

- GiveawayBot – Simple and easy-to-use.
- MEE6 – Has giveaway features as part of its premium plan.
- Dyno – A multi-purpose bot with giveaway tools.

Define Entry Rules and Conditions

Ensure the giveaway encourages engagement rather than just passive participation. Common entry conditions include:

- Reacting to a giveaway post with an emoji (e.g., 🎉).

- Posting a message in a specific channel.

- Inviting a certain number of friends to the server.

- Participating in an event (e.g., trivia night or meme contest).

Promote the Giveaway

Announce the giveaway in the server's announcements channel and encourage members to share it. If possible, pin the giveaway post so it's easy to find.

Ensure Fairness and Transparency

Use a bot's random selection feature to pick a winner fairly. After the giveaway ends, publicly announce the winner and deliver the prize quickly to maintain trust.

4. Best Practices for Hosting Events and Giveaways

Creating a Community Calendar

To keep engagement consistent, create a monthly event schedule that includes:

- Regular game nights.

- Weekly trivia contests.

- Monthly art or meme competitions.

This helps members anticipate and prepare for upcoming activities.

Involving Moderators and Event Organizers

Having a dedicated event planning team ensures smooth execution. Moderators or selected volunteers can:

- Manage event logistics.

- Keep track of contest entries.

- Enforce giveaway rules.

Avoiding Common Pitfalls

Some common mistakes to avoid include:

- Overdoing giveaways, which can attract users who only join for free prizes.

- Neglecting fairness, leading to complaints or distrust.

- Failing to deliver promised rewards—always ensure winners receive their prizes.

Conclusion

Hosting events and giveaways is one of the best ways to create an active and engaged Discord community. Whether through game nights, contests, trivia, or roleplaying, interactive activities bring people together and make the server a fun place to be. Meanwhile, giveaways can boost participation and reward loyal members, but they must be thoughtfully planned and fairly executed to avoid attracting short-term users.

By implementing these strategies, you can build a vibrant Discord server that keeps members engaged for the long term.

Next Section: 8.3.3 Maintaining an Active and Healthy Community

In the next section, we'll discuss **how to maintain long-term engagement** by fostering a positive, inclusive, and well-moderated community.

8.3.3 Maintaining an Active and Healthy Community

Creating a Discord community is only the first step—keeping it active, engaging, and positive requires consistent effort. A thriving server is one where members feel valued, engaged, and safe while participating in meaningful discussions and activities. In this section, we will explore strategies for maintaining an active and healthy community, covering areas such as member engagement, content moderation, event planning, and community culture.

1. Encouraging Engagement and Participation

Welcoming New Members

The first impression matters! New members should feel welcomed and guided when they join. Here are a few ways to create a friendly onboarding experience:

- Automated Welcome Messages: Use bots like Mee6, Dyno, or Carl-bot to send automatic welcome messages in a dedicated #welcome channel.

- Introduce Key Channels: Provide a server guide or pinned messages to explain important channels and rules.

- Assign a Welcome Role: Create a role (e.g., "Newcomer") with limited permissions that unlocks more features once they engage in the server.

- Encourage Introductions: Have an #introductions channel where new members can share something about themselves.

Fostering Conversations

An active server thrives on consistent discussions. Here are ways to spark engagement:

- Daily/Weekly Prompts: Post discussion topics, polls, or challenges (e.g., "What's your favorite game this week?").

- Question of the Day: Encourage members to share opinions on a fun or thought-provoking topic.

- Use @Mentions Sparingly: Pinging members can boost engagement but overuse can annoy them.

- Encourage User-Generated Content: Let members share memes, artwork, projects, or recommendations in dedicated channels.

Creating Engaging Roles and Rewards

People enjoy recognition and progression in a community. Implement role-based incentives to encourage activity:

- Activity-Based Roles: Assign special roles based on participation (e.g., "Veteran," "Active Member," "Top Contributor").

- Leaderboard and XP Systems: Use bots like Mee6 or Arcane to track and reward engagement.

- Exclusive Channels for Active Members: Unlock private lounges for engaged users to build a sense of exclusivity.

2. Managing Community Culture and Rules

Establishing and Enforcing Server Rules

Clear rules set expectations and prevent toxic behavior. Here's how to implement effective guidelines:

- Create a #rules Channel: List server rules clearly, including expectations on language, spam, and behavior.

- Use Reaction Roles for Agreement: Require members to react with an emoji to acknowledge the rules before accessing the server.

- Warn Before Banning: Use a three-strike system (warn > mute > ban) for rule violations.

Common Rules to Include:
✓ Respect all members (no harassment, hate speech, or bullying).
✓ No spam or excessive self-promotion.
✓ Keep content relevant to the channel.
✓ No NSFW content unless the server allows and tags it properly.

Moderation Tools and Best Practices

A well-moderated server prevents drama and ensures a safe space. Here's how to manage moderation effectively:

- Use Bots for Auto-Moderation: Bots like Dyno, Carl-bot, and Automod can filter spam, mute trolls, and detect banned words.

- Assign Trusted Moderators: Create a staff team to monitor discussions, resolve conflicts, and assist users.

- Have an Appeal System: If bans or mutes happen, allow users to request an appeal in a private channel or Google Form.

Handling Conflicts and Toxic Behavior

Even the best communities face disagreements. Handling conflicts professionally is crucial. Here's how:

1. Stay Neutral: Moderators should not take sides but instead mediate discussions.

2. Use Private Chats for Disputes: Move heated conversations to DMs or a private moderation channel.

3. Issue Clear Warnings: Let the involved members know which rule was violated and what action will be taken.

4. Kick/Ban as a Last Resort: Only ban users who continuously disrupt the community after multiple warnings.

3. Hosting Events and Community Activities

Organizing Regular Events

Events keep members excited and engaged. Here are some ideas:

- Game Nights: Host Minecraft, Among Us, or Jackbox sessions.

- Movie or Anime Watch Parties: Use Discord's screen-sharing feature to stream together.

- Trivia Contests: Use a bot like TriviaBot to run fun quizzes.

- Art or Writing Contests: Encourage members to showcase their creativity.

- Q&A Sessions with Special Guests: Invite streamers, influencers, or industry experts.

Scheduling and Promoting Events

To maximize participation, promote events effectively:

- Create an Announcement Channel: Post event details with a clear date, time, and how to join.

- Use Discord's Event Feature: Allows users to RSVP and receive reminders.

- @Mention Interested Users: Tag specific roles (e.g., @Gamers for game nights, @Artists for art contests).

- Offer Small Rewards: Recognize winners with special roles, Discord Nitro gifts, or custom emojis.

Running Giveaways and Incentives

Giveaways attract members and boost engagement:

- Discord Nitro Giveaways: Offer Nitro to active contributors or as a special event prize.

- Custom Role Rewards: Let winners create a unique role name and color.

- Exclusive Server Perks: Give access to private voice channels or premium content.

Recommended Giveaway Bots:

- GiveawayBot

- Carl-bot

- Mee6

4. Monitoring Server Growth and Making Improvements

Tracking Engagement Metrics

Monitor server activity using built-in tools and bots:

- Server Insights (For Partnered Servers): Provides engagement stats.

- Stat Tracking Bots: Use ServerStats or Statbot to track user activity.

- Monitor Voice and Text Activity: See which channels are most popular.

Gathering Feedback from Members

Regular feedback helps improve the community. Use:

- Polls and Surveys: Ask members what they like/dislike about the server.

- Suggestion Channels: Let users submit ideas for new channels, events, or rules.

- Periodic AMA Sessions: Have moderators answer questions about server decisions.

Adapting and Evolving Your Server

A successful community evolves over time. Keep things fresh by:

- Introducing New Features: Experiment with new channels, bots, or themes.

- Archiving Inactive Channels: Remove clutter by hiding unused channels.

- Adjusting Server Structure: If the community grows, reorganize categories for better navigation.

Conclusion

Maintaining an active and healthy Discord community is a continuous process. By fostering engagement, enforcing clear rules, hosting exciting events, and listening to feedback, you can create a vibrant and welcoming space for your members.

In the next section, we will explore best practices for using Discord in different professional and educational settings to maximize its potential.

Conclusion

Resources for Further Learning

As you reach the end of *The Complete Discord Guide: From Setup to Advanced Features*, you now have a solid foundation in using Discord effectively. Whether you're using it for gaming, business, education, or community building, Discord offers a wealth of features to explore. However, mastering Discord is an ongoing process, as the platform continuously evolves with new updates, integrations, and security enhancements.

To stay updated and continue improving your skills, it's essential to engage with the right resources. This section will provide you with some of the best resources for further learning, troubleshooting, and staying connected with the Discord community.

1. Official Discord Resources

1.1 Discord's Official Website

🔗 https://discord.com
The first place to look for any official information about Discord is their official website. This site provides:

- Latest updates and announcements

- Access to Discord's features and pricing plans

- Security and privacy policies

It's a great starting point for learning about the latest developments on the platform.

1.2 Discord Support and Help Center

🔗 https://support.discord.com

If you ever run into technical issues or have questions about using Discord, the Discord Support and Help Center should be your first stop. It includes:

- Step-by-step guides on setting up and managing servers
- Troubleshooting solutions for common technical problems
- Explanations of Discord's policies and safety features

1.3 Discord Blog

🔗 https://discord.com/blog

The official Discord blog is an excellent resource for staying up to date with new features, announcements, and insights from the Discord team. Topics include:

- New feature rollouts
- Community success stories
- Best practices for managing servers

By following the blog, you can ensure you're always using the latest features to enhance your Discord experience.

1.4 Discord's YouTube Channel

🔗 https://www.youtube.com/c/Discord

For those who prefer video tutorials, Discord's official YouTube channel offers:

- Visual walkthroughs of new features
- Tips and tricks for optimizing your Discord experience
- Explanations of security updates and policies

Subscribing to this channel ensures you never miss important updates.

2. Community-Driven Learning Resources

2.1 Discord Subreddit (r/discordapp)

∞ https://www.reddit.com/r/discordapp

Reddit hosts an active community of Discord users, where you can:

- Ask questions and get real-time help

- Find tips on server management and bot integration

- Stay informed about the latest Discord trends and issues

This subreddit is a great place to learn from experienced users and participate in discussions about Discord's development.

2.2 Discord Unofficial Wiki

∞ https://discord.fandom.com/wiki/Discord_Wiki

The Discord Fandom Wiki is a community-maintained resource that contains:

- Detailed explanations of Discord's features

- Guides on setting up bots, permissions, and integrations

- Troubleshooting steps for common errors

Since it's updated by the community, you can often find in-depth answers to advanced Discord topics here.

2.3 YouTube Tutorials by Expert Creators

Apart from Discord's official YouTube channel, many experienced users and tech influencers create high-quality Discord tutorials. Some of the best channels include:

- Senpai Gaming – Focuses on how streamers can optimize Discord.

- TechHut – Covers advanced Discord server management and bot usage.

- LTT (Linus Tech Tips) – Occasionally features Discord-related content in broader tech discussions.

Searching "Discord tutorials" on YouTube will help you find step-by-step guides suited to your needs.

3. Learning Discord Bots and Automation

3.1 Official Discord Developer Portal

🔗 https://discord.com/developers

If you're interested in creating your own bots, the Discord Developer Portal is the best place to start. It provides:

- API documentation for bot development

- Step-by-step guides for integrating Discord with other platforms

- Resources for managing OAuth2 authentication and webhooks

3.2 Top Websites for Discord Bot Development

If you want to dive deeper into coding custom bots, these websites offer excellent learning resources:

- GitHub Repositories – Explore open-source Discord bots to learn from real-world examples.

- Discord.js Guide (https://discordjs.guide) – A fantastic resource for JavaScript-based Discord bot development.

- Python Discord Bot Development (https://realpython.com/how-to-make-a-discord-bot-python/) – A beginner-friendly tutorial on using Python to build bots.

By learning to code your own Discord bots, you can customize and automate your server like a pro.

4. Staying Updated with Discord's Latest Features

4.1 Follow Discord on Social Media

To stay in the loop with breaking updates and announcements, follow Discord on:

- Twitter/X (https://twitter.com/discord) – For real-time updates on new features and security alerts.

- Facebook (https://www.facebook.com/discord) – For community stories and updates.

- Instagram (https://www.instagram.com/discord) – For lighter, fun content related to Discord culture.

4.2 Join Official and Unofficial Discord Servers

There are many servers dedicated to Discord support and learning, including:

- Discord Testers (https://discord.gg/discord-testers) – A place to test new features and provide feedback.

- Discord Developers Server (https://discord.gg/discord-developers) – A hub for bot developers and server admins.

- Discord Resources Hub (https://discord.gg/resources) – A community-driven knowledge base with expert tips.

Final Thoughts

Discord is an incredibly versatile platform with endless possibilities. Whether you're using it for gaming, business, education, or content creation, the key to success is staying informed and continuously learning.

By leveraging the official resources, community discussions, and hands-on experimentation, you'll become a Discord expert in no time. Keep exploring, engage with the community, and make the most of everything Discord has to offer!

🚀 *Now go out there and build, communicate, and connect like never before!*

Acknowledgments

First and foremost, **thank you** for picking up *The Complete Discord Guide: From Setup to Advanced Features.* Whether you're a first-time user or someone looking to master the platform's advanced capabilities, I appreciate your trust in this guide as a valuable resource.

Writing this book has been an incredible journey, and knowing that it has reached readers like you makes it all the more meaningful. Discord is a powerful tool that connects people across the globe, and I hope this book has helped you navigate and utilize it effectively—whether for gaming, business, education, or simply staying in touch with friends and communities.

I want to express my gratitude to the **Discord community**—a diverse, passionate, and ever-evolving group that constantly pushes the platform to new heights. Your creativity, feedback, and enthusiasm shape the way Discord continues to grow. To the countless Discord server administrators, moderators, bot developers, and content creators who contribute to making Discord an engaging and inclusive space—thank you for your dedication and innovation.

A special thanks to the **Discord team** for continuously improving the platform and providing users with new and exciting features. Their commitment to building a robust and secure communication space has made it easier for people worldwide to connect and collaborate.

Finally, to **you, the reader**—thank you for investing your time in learning more about Discord. I hope this book has empowered you to make the most of its features and has inspired you to explore new possibilities within the platform. Your support and curiosity mean the world, and I truly appreciate you allowing this book to be part of your learning journey.

If you've found this guide helpful, I would love to hear your feedback! Feel free to share your thoughts, recommend the book to others, or even reach out with any questions or suggestions for future editions.

Once again, **thank you**, and happy Discord-ing! 🚀

www.ingramcontent.com/pod-product-compliance
Lightning Source LLC
LaVergne TN
LVHW081329050326
832903LV00024B/1085